Clive Barker's
Short Stories

Clive Barker's Short Stories

Imagination as Metaphor in the Books of Blood and Other Works

Gary Hoppenstand

Foreword by Clive Barker

McFarland & Company, Inc., Publishers
Jefferson, North Carolina, and London

For Ray B. Browne with gratitude

The present work is a reprint of the library bound edition of Clive Barker's Short Stories: Imagination as Metaphor in the Books of Blood *and Other Works, first published in 1994 by McFarland.*

LIBRARY OF CONGRESS CATALOGUING-IN-PUBLICATION DATA

Hoppenstand, Gary.
  Clive Barker's short stories : imagination as metaphor in the Books of blood and other works / Gary Hoppenstand.
    p.   cm.
  Includes bibliographical references and index.

  ISBN 978-0-7864-9355-5
  softcover : acid free paper ∞

  1. Barker, Clive, 1952–   —Criticism and interpretation. Horror tales, English—History and criticism.   3. Short story.   I. Title.
PR6052.A6475Z68 2014
823'.914—dc20   94-8010

BRITISH LIBRARY CATALOGUING DATA ARE AVAILABLE

© 1994 Gary Hoppenstand; foreword © Clive Barker. All rights reserved

No part of this book may be reproduced or transmitted in any form or by any means, electronic or mechanical, including photocopying or recording, or by any information storage and retrieval system, without permission in writing from the publisher.

Cover image © 2014 iStockphoto/Perseomed

Manufactured in the United States of America

McFarland & Company, Inc., Publishers
  Box 611, Jefferson, North Carolina 28640
    www.mcfarlandpub.com

ACKNOWLEDGMENTS

As with any book-length study of this nature, it is impossible to attempt the project without the much needed contributions of others. Several very talented people helped me with this book, and I would like to gratefully recognize their efforts. First, I would like to thank four eminent scholars of popular culture studies — professors Doug Noverr, Dean Rehberger, Garyn Roberts, and Kay Rout from the Department of American Thought and Language at Michigan State University — for generously taking time out of their hectic schedules in order to assist me with the rough draft of this book. I would like to thank as well Professor Joseleyne Slade, chairperson of the Department of American Thought and Language, and Dr. John Eadie, dean of the College of Arts and Letters at M.S.U., for their ongoing support of my research activities. In addition, Mark West, the manager of the Curious Comic Shop, was most helpful locating for me the many Clive Barker interviews published in both popular and obscure magazines over the past several years, while the owner of the Curious Book Shop, Ray Walsh, provided me with that obscure horror fiction book when I needed it. Also, without the understanding of my wife Becky, this book would never have been written. And for their aid in the preparation of the manuscript, I would like to offer a big "thank you" to Kristine Blakeslee, Jacque Shoppell, Brett Berry, and Karen Helton. Finally, I would like to express my deepest appreciation to Clive Barker himself, for his indulgence in answering my sometimes foolish questions, for his endless generosity, and for his remarkable kindness.

CONTENTS

ACKNOWLEDGMENTS		v
FOREWORD	Regarding *Imagination as Metaphor* by Clive Barker	1
INTRODUCTION	Exiting Banality: A Personal Journey	3
ONE	Text and Subtext: Clive Barker and the State of Horror	9
TWO	Highways of the Dead: *Clive Barker's Books of Blood, Volume One*	45
THREE	New Murders, Ancient Evils: *Clive Barker's Books of Blood, Volume Two*	65
FOUR	Confessions of a Dark Fancy: *Clive Barker's Books of Blood, Volume Three*	83
FIVE	Sexual and Political Puzzles: *Clive Barker's Books of Blood, Volume Four*	101
SIX	Mother's Fine Children: *Clive Barker's Books of Blood, Volume Five*	127
SEVEN	Twilight and Other Illusions: *Clive Barker's Books of Blood, Volume Six*	151
EIGHT	Embracing Imagination: Uncollected Short Fiction and Final Comments	171
WORKS CITED		211
SELECTED BIBLIOGRAPHY		213
INDEX		217

FOREWORD

Regarding *Imagination as Metaphor*
by Clive Barker

This author prays daily for three things. A story to tell (preferably something to keep him profitably engaged for a healthy span of time); an audience who will come to find the tale when it is told; and informed, enthusiastic analysts (critical, and in my case, probably psychological too) who will seek the impulses that move beneath the surface of the narratives, and remark cogently upon them.

The desire for the first two is self-explanatory; the desire for the latter is in need, perhaps, of some illumination. I know several authors who are repulsed by the notion of their work becoming fodder for academic study. They protest, perhaps too much, that they have no desire to be scrutinized by professors, or put on university reading lists. It would surely stifle their creativity if they read so much as a word of theory about their tales, they claim, by inducing a crippling self-consciousness.

I consider such protestations tosh. Any story worth the telling is a maze of hidden meanings—some of them most certainly concealed from the author—and while I have railed against the kind of pseudo-detached, criticism-as-an-exact-science approach which is still practiced in some quarters (this is an age when physics itself is giving up claim to exactitude and detachment), I find *good* criticism often rearouses my appetite for the work in question.

Of course, while the learned are content to study *A Midsummer Night's Dream, Beowulf,* or *Sir Gawain and the Green Knight*—each of which, it scarcely need be remarked, is a work of visionary fantasy—they all too often neglect the magical and miraculous elements which have helped these masterworks endure. There is a kind of academic sleight-of-mind which keeps populist fiction from being a legitimate source of interest until the author is dead, and the bones of the author's intent can be fought over without fear of his of her opinion spoiling the debate. A variation on that trick takes the fright out of Poe, the sex out of Whitman, the Devil out of Melville. In short, it seeks to tame.

But the *fantastique*, perhaps more than any other genre, defies domestication. It is imagination in action; an account — at its best — of how the mind transforms reality; makes it metaphor, makes it myth; uses it to harrow and heal. The critic who tackles contemporary *fantastique* is therefore a welcome sight, because the field is a difficult one. A fresh vocabulary has to be forged — the old definitions are laughably stale, as witness several recent essays on the so-called *weird tale* — and a plethora of late twentieth century concerns must be folded into the mix: the influence of cinema upon the reader's expectations; the decay of the Christian belief system which underpins so much of this work; the significance of feminist thinking on *fantastique* writing; and so on and so forth.

All of this is by way of introduction to the work of Gary Hoppenstand, whose study of my early short fiction you hold in your hand. It would be out of place for me to speak of it in detail (the spectacle of the Writer turned Analyst in order to analyze his Analyst's Writings would be more appropriate in Wonderland, I suspect) but I would like to here thank Gary for his insights, his empathy, his enthusiasm and perhaps most of all, his commitment to working in this troubled territory. He has been both tactful and gracious in his enquiries, while never failing to pursue a question until he is satisfied, which is right and proper. He has also alerted me to a new, and welcome, wave of critical works by writers who, like himself, are interested in studying the influence and significance of the cultural artifacts with which we live: the books, television shows, movies, comic books and theme parks that are daily shaping our imaginative lives. There may be grim news in such analyses (I suspect the minds presently being formed by MTV and Hollywood's blander blandishments will be difficult to rouse from lethargy) but we will surely be better prepared for the struggle ahead if we know how the land lies. It falls to authors and critics alike to better understand the way our culture is shaped, and it pleases me mightily to be the subject of a study that will, I trust, be a contribution to that understanding.

I leave you, then, in the hands of my analyst, in the hope that once he has told you a thing or two about my dream-life, you'll come back to the dreams themselves with your appetite stronger than ever, and your strokes in that dream-sea more certain for his instruction.

— *Los Angeles, Spring 1994*

INTRODUCTION

Exiting Banality:
A Personal Journey

One important precept to be found in Clive Barker's fiction is that miraculous imagination can be discovered in the most commonplace of settings.

My introduction to Clive Barker's imagination began simply enough, and without much fanfare. In April of 1986, I made my annual pilgrimage to the national Popular Culture Association convention. I enjoy attending the massive PCA conferences because they allow me to visit with colleagues from my graduate school days and to catch up on the latest scholarly developments in the burgeoning field of popular culture studies. Because my teaching schedule rarely permits me the opportunity to travel, I look forward to attending academic conferences; they are my excuse to visit some of the most vital (and not so vital) cities in this country.

I always make it a point of honor to visit the major bookstores in each of the cities where the current convention is being held. Atlanta was the PCA meeting site in 1986, and I quickly learned that it's one of the great bookstore cities of the Southeast. In retrospect, one particular establishment—its name I can't now remember—that specialized in the sale of used books became for me a momentous place, a special place; it was where I first encountered Clive Barker. Not the man, of course, but his fiction.

When I initially entered this nameless, yet oh so important, bookstore, there was nothing to distinguish it from hundreds of other used bookstores just like it in cities across the country. Numerous tables were scattered helter-skelter about the place, and sprawled across their tops were decaying pyramids of garishly illustrated paperback books, their spines cracked, their well-thumbed pages yellowing, their covers bent at the edges and soiled. In this corner, beneath a handmade cardboard sign illustrated with crayon roses, were the romances. In that corner, beneath a paper dagger dripping with blood, were the mysteries, and elsewhere in random order under their identifying icons were the repositories of other popular genres: westerns, science fiction, how-to books, celebrity biographies, self-help books—and the horror section.

I made a straight dash to that last section. Horror fiction has always been one of my favorite reads, for a number of reasons. Some of the best novels being written today (and some of the worst) are horror novels. Certainly, a number of the more successful horror novelists—authors like Stephen King, Dean R. Koontz, and Anne Rice—write well-crafted books, and their success on national best-seller lists is an indication not only of their abilities as entertaining writers, but also of the mass market popularity of the horror story. However, in this bookstore the horror section was virtually hidden in the back of the place, and it was mislabeled as "occult fiction," with two bulbous eyes suspended between mesmerizing concentric circles that hung above the area, virtually out of sight of all but the most dedicated of horror fiction afficionados.

The person who organized this area either was embarrassed about the material, thinking it perhaps little better than the pornography sold behind the counter, or else she or he was unsure exactly what constituted a horror novel, since pseudo-scientific books dealing with "Big Foot" and UFO sightings were crammed in between the garishly illustrated TOR horror paperbacks and the novels of Robert R. McCammon and Peter Straub. Perhaps the ultra-conservative South took a dim view of stories highlighting gross violence. After all, horror fiction is politically and socially charged in a subversive sort of way, and can be embarrassing to those who don't fully understand it.

As I sifted through the store's horror section, attempting to separate the dross from the gold, I was approached by a person who appeared to be the manager of the store. He was rather short in stature, round in form, and sported a well-trimmed beard. His clothing indicated that he had spent a great deal of money on them. They were clothes that no mere minimum wage clerk could afford to buy. He asked if he could help me find anything, and I replied that I was looking for something new and unusual in the genre.

He gave me a slight smile and suggested that if I was *really* looking for something uncommon, then he had a special room downstairs where he kept his "collectable" books, and that I should follow him. I could think of no valid reason not to follow him to the store's inner sanctum, and thus told him to lead on. As we proceeded through a rusty-hinged steel door and down a flight of uneven wooden steps thickly caked with dust, I asked my guide if he was the store's manager. He said that he wasn't the manager, but the owner. He also said that he enjoyed reading and collecting horror fiction. He told me that few of his customers were interested in his horror section. Nearly all of his readers wanted romances or mysteries, but not horror novels, and thus his most favored of areas was generally ignored, and this seemed to bother him.

When we reached the bottom of the steps, we turned left into a dingy, ill-lit corridor. The first door we came to displayed a massive double bolt lock, and as he fished out his ponderous key ring from his pants pocket to unlock the door, the owner stated that whenever he saw someone looking through the horror books — and if he thought the customer a sincere connoisseur of the horror tale (how he could tell this about anyone even now baffles me; do we who enjoy the well-wrought tale of terror have a secretive crimson gleam to our eye, an extra dribble of spittle on our lower lip?) — then he would invite that individual, as he had done me, to peruse his special collection. Intrigued by his enthusiasm, I wondered what awaited beyond the proverbial locked door.

The store's owner finally located the proper key, opened the door and thus revealed the stygian blackness within. Resorting to memory, he slapped his hand against a wall inside the absolute darkness, flicked a switch, and a dingy yellow light somewhat less brilliant than the light in the corridor dimly illuminated the room. As I stepped through the entrance, I was briefly overpowered by the musty, unventilated smell of old books.

It was a small, square room. A quick glance revealed unfinished wooden bookshelves lining the walls. A single dim light bulb hung overhead in the middle of the ceiling; a cracking concrete floor, with a rusty drain set in the center, lay underneath. My guide escorted me to the wall to the immediate left as we entered, and directed my attention to the center shelves. Located there were the usual collection of Arkham House titles, Donald Grant limited editions, and several Gnome Press anthologies: in other words, there was nothing shown to me that I hadn't seen in a dozen other bookstores that specialized in rare fantasy and science-fiction editions.

I think he quickly recognized my growing indifference. He muttered several barely recognizable comments like "This won't do" and "You probably already have this one" as he shuffled his fingers across the colorful spines of books. Finally, he proclaimed "Ah-ha," which startled me a bit, then he yanked out three slender hardcover books. He offered them to me, and in a challenging tone announced his bet. "There's no way you've heard of this author," he stated. "I just got these in from my contact in London, and my contact assures me that in a couple of years this guy is going to be on top, as big as Straub, as big as King, even." At the time I thought that if this room was wired, it would sound like a drug deal was being made. For years I've entertained the suspicion that book collectors are akin to drug addicts, but this particular situation seemed to me especially ludicrous. I was in a dark, damp room in a nameless bookstore in a foreign town with a total stranger offering me a promise that I sincerely doubted could ever be achieved by such an unknown quantity. It's the type of scene one would expect to see in a television detective show, not in the dull life of an academic in search of a simple good read. I took the three volumes, collectively titled *Clive Barker's Books of Blood*, determined to be unimpressed.

Indeed, my host was right: I had never heard of Clive Barker. But I certainly was startled by what I saw in the dust-jacket illustrations of the three books. The cover of *Volume Three* had Marilyn Monroe illustrated in her classic pose with her skirt billowing up around her thighs, yet nestled underneath that skirt are a row of jagged teeth, which draws the eyes upward to the monstrous eyes lurking behind the image of the famous Hollywood star, the tableau framed by miniature skulls, a shadowy Nosferatu, and a grinning, eyeless Mickey Mouse. The picture was shocking, yet beautiful in a grotesque way. *Volume Two* featured the profile of a beautiful woman. Her hair, which is streaming back from her classic features, is intertwined by writhing, grotesque figures. A small skull dangles by its hair from the woman's earlobe. A devastated, post-apocalyptic landscape recedes into the background. Overall, the images were again beautiful, but ugly. The cover illustration of *Volume One* was the most detailed with bizarre and wonderful figures. A handsome young man, partially naked, is surrounded by characters from one's worst nightmares, and most bizarre dreams.

I turned *Volume One* on its spine. The British publisher named Weidenfeld & Nicolson I had never heard of. "This Clive Barker fella who wrote the stories also illustrated the cover," my anonymous host informed me. He no doubt noted my growing interest in the three books. I opened the cover of *Volume One*; inside, on the title page, I was greeted with the quote, "Everybody is a book of blood; Wherever we're opened, we're red." It was a pun, and a rather humorous one given the context that it preceded a horror anthology.

We were suddenly interrupted by one of the owner's employees. He requested his boss's assistance with one of the store's cash registers, which apparently decided to chew up a roll of receipt tape. My host excused himself, but before he left he invited me to take my time looking through the Barker books. And as he disappeared down the corridor and back up the stairs, he, like General Douglas MacArthur, proclaimed that he would soon return. Well, I decided, if he was going to give me the time, then I was going to read the first story in *Volume One*. It was simply (and repetitively) titled "The Book of Blood," and it was only eleven pages long. The quality of this story would help me determine if the three books were worth owning.

I began reading. Often one hears the expression, "the reader was transported to another world by the narrative power of the story." I had generally thought this cliché to be just another one of those hyperbolic comments that one sees printed on paperback covers to help sell the books. Yet, when reading "The Book of Blood," I truly lost track of time. It must have been at least fifteen minutes since the store's owner had left me, and I had just finished reading the last sentence when he returned, both startling me and returning me to the world of the commonplace. He asked me what I thought of the books, and to postpone him a bit while I collected my thoughts, I inquired about the price of the three volumes. He quoted me an ungodly figure, and I paid it.

Returning to the convention site, I had some time to deliberate about Mr. Barker and his *Books of Blood*. The introductory story reminded me of Ray Bradbury and *The Illustrated Man* (1951), but even Bradbury's anthology was a mere single volume, and I didn't know then that Clive Barker had also written three more *Books of Blood*, in addition to the first three. I told myself that what I had encountered was an "event," a phenomenon that had no comparative analogy in the horror genre. Here, I had just purchased a complex, interconnected anthology of unique and highly imaginative short fiction. And as I read the remainder of the stories in the *Books of Blood* over the next few weeks, I was convinced of a simple truth: that Clive Barker would indeed have a great impact upon the realm of fiction, not only in the province of the horror story where he rivals such giants as Stephen King and Anne Rice, but also in the greater world of fantasy itself, where he has distinguished himself as one of the most innovative and entertaining authors around.

The simple truth that I first suspected back in 1986 has now come to fruition. Today, Clive Barker is a literary sensation, having demonstrated an expertise in a number of different and demanding entertainment forms. Since he initially caught my eye, over the past several years I have witnessed not only his mastery of the short story, but also his mastery of the short novel, the epic novel, film directing and producing, and screenwriting. As I investigated further into Barker's artistic history, I learned of his success as a playwright and illustrator. This young man, in the span of less than a decade, has successfully crammed into his brief life four or five different careers, an amazing feat worthy of "Ripley's Believe It or Not." Barker's achievements are indeed unmatched by his peers.

Ultimately, two things happened to me that day in Atlanta. The first is that I began to map out this book that you are now holding in your hand. I immediately recognized that Clive Barker's writings, and the horror genre as a whole, deserved some sort of scholarly recognition. And I haven't been the only one harboring these thoughts. It's been my pleasure to note that over the past several years there has been a grudging acceptance of the horror genre by literary critics and academics, and a number of fine studies have been recently published. I've also witnessed the explosion of critical debate that the writings of Stephen King have generated. My feelings about the voluminous attention paid to King are mixed; though I appreciate King's significant contributions to the genre, he's not the only important talent. Other authors, like Clive Barker, are as deserving of serious analysis.

Clive Barker is just now beginning to receive this serious analysis. Recently, Underwood-Miller has published a massive collection of material by and about Clive Barker, entitled *Clive Barker's Shadows in Eden*. In addition, media critic James Van Hise has published several short stories about Barker, and Eclipse Books has just released a slickly-produced "scrapbook" entitled *Pandemonium*, which celebrates Barker's contributions to film and fiction.

However, despite the growing recognition paid to Clive Barker, to my knowledge there has yet to be written a detailed and lengthy examination of Barker's writings.

This book is intended to be a cross between a reader's guide and a literary analysis. My focus, as stated in the book's title, is Clive Barker's short fiction. With my critique of Barker's short stories, I have decided not to provide detailed plot synopses, unless a specific review of the narrative is important to the discussion of the author's thematic issues. This study is thus meant to be a supplement for those readers already familiar with Clive Barker's writings. It is also meant to be an argument for Barker's artistic legitimacy, both within the confines of the horror genre, and within the larger encircling sphere of contemporary literature. I begin my argument on a personal note in this introduction (since all literary journeys are of a personal nature in the beginning; fiction first has to catch us emotionally before it can speak to us intellectually), and from personal observation, I then progress to a more abstract analysis of Barker's work. The first chapter offers an extensively documented overview of Clive Barker's place in the horror genre. It briefly surveys his life and considers his artistic philosophy. The remainder of this study's chapters analyze, in detail, the stories in each volume of the *Books of Blood*, while the final chapter investigates Barker's tales not collected in the *Books of Blood*. The final chapter also provides a general summary of the major themes evident in Barker's short fiction. Though I have attempted to be thorough, there yet remains a considerable portion of Clive Barker's work that requires additional critical discussion, such as his novels, his plays, his illustrations, and his films. Perhaps this is a future project awaiting my, or someone else's, attention.

The second thing that happened to me in Atlanta the day I discovered Clive Barker is, upon reflection, somewhat ironic, for I learned an important lesson, a lesson frequently taught in Clive Barker's writings, that in the midst of banality there resides wondrous imagination. The way I happened upon Clive Barker is the way he happens upon his work. To achieve imagination, one must recognize and understand the fetters of imagination. Barker's short fiction does just that for us; it shows us the fetters that otherwise bind us as we lead our pedestrian lives. The path to miracles, however, is not without its price. There is a warning stated at the conclusion of the framing story, "The Book of Blood," that says, "It's best to be prepared for the worst, after all, and wise to learn to walk before breath runs out." Clive Barker aptly demonstrates in his short fiction that miracles can be comprised of both beauty *and* horror. Our tour through imagination—Barker's imagination—may be frightening or grotesque or amusing, or all three, but the trip is certainly worth the effort. Exiting banality is what Clive Barker is all about.

CHAPTER ONE

Text and Subtext: Clive Barker and the State of Horror

Clive Barker and the Literate Horror Story

Occasionally the remark is made that Clive Barker is the British equivalent of Stephen King. Of course, now that Barker is a resident of the United States, this comment is not wholly correct, but the basic premise is a valid one. Both King and Barker are best-selling authors who base their work in the field of imaginative fiction, specifically fantasy of the darker variety. Both King and Barker have become easily identifiable with their work. They are each celebrities of a sort, and the mere mention of their names on a book's cover is a guarantee of sales and of mass reader satisfaction. King has been intimately involved with Hollywood, writing and directing films, and Barker, as well, has been a moviemaker, involved in writing and directing for the silver screen. King and Barker have legions of fans who worship their work, and both can command the media's close attention when they publish a new book or release a new movie.

However, subtle distinctions do exist between these two giants of the horror genre, distinctions that are perhaps culturally based, and that reveal themselves to be significantly profound when more fully investigated. Back in March of 1989, I visited London at the invitation of Clive Barker to view the filming of the movie *Nightbreed*, which Barker had written and was directing. When I dropped in a number of London's finer bookstores, I noticed that Clive Barker's books were prominently displayed. Barker's short novel *Cabal* was being promoted, and it was featured everywhere, in window displays and table displays and paperback bins. A few of Stephen King's titles were generally available as well, but for the most part, King's books were shelved with the rest of the science fiction or horror selections. They were not given any special attention with regard to promotion or display. I asked several of the clerks who worked in these bookstores how the Stephen King sales were doing, and almost unanimously I was told that King did all right, but the horror writer who really was "hot" at the moment was Clive Barker.

In the United States, this situation is somewhat reversed. Stephen King dominates the national best-seller lists, frequently holding the number one spot in both hardcover and paperback sales at the same time. Stephen King monopolizes the promotional schemes at the local Waldenbooks and B. Dalton retail outlets. Clive Barker, though certainly more visible than most other horror writers, is nonetheless less prominent than King. Barker's books tend to be in the general fiction section, or if the store is a Waldenbooks, in the horror fiction area. They are not offered as displays in window fronts. Clive Barker's recent epic fantasy novel, *Imajica*, barely crept its way onto the national best-seller lists, then crept back down again.

Though I don't have any hard sales figures in front of me, I think it's fairly safe to say that King does better in the United States than Barker, and Barker does better than King in England. If this premise *is* true, then looking at the reasons behind such a difference may be useful. Despite their many commercial similarities, what are the unique qualities that distinguish the two authors?

The answer to this question came to me, in part, during a recent telephone conversation with Clive Barker. We were discussing the publication of *Imajica*, and I complimented him on the depth and complexity of his novel, to which he replied that he in fact did spend a great deal of time and effort on the writing of *Imajica*, and this made him admire the near superhuman productivity of Stephen King. I answered that I, too, was in awe of King's long list of books that were published in a relatively short period of time. However, I said that I noticed a number of stylistic problems in King's work, areas that looked as if they were hurriedly written, whole chapters that appeared superfluous, narrative structures that seemed in dire need of an editor's hand. Barker replied that he thought that these "weaknesses" in King's work actually were strengths, that they created in King's fiction a sense of immediacy, an intimacy, that drew his readers closer to him. In retrospect, Barker was exactly right in his observation: King *is* a "conversational" writer, a writer people feel comfortable being with.

And this brings us to the first of three significant differences between Clive Barker and Stephen King — differences that reveal not only the aesthetic breadth of the horror genre, but that also raise the question of what exactly a horror story accomplishes for its audience. Stephen King is a less literary author than Clive Barker. This statement is not necessarily meant to be a criticism of King (some highly literary writers are awful novelists), but it is meant to identify precisely within what narrative traditions King and Barker are operating. King is primarily a storyteller. His talent descends from the prehistoric oral raconteur who chanted tribal myths and legends around the communal campfire. King's essential goal is to tell a good story. If some literary style happens to accompany the story, then that's serendipitous; having style is not crucial to the story being told, however. A number of other best-selling authors are like King in that they are fundamentally storytellers, mega-successful writers like Louis L'Amour, Barbara Cartland, and Danielle Steel. Though any of these authors may be attacked on artistic grounds, their skill at entertaining a mass audience cannot be denied. Their prose is simple, compelling to read, lacking refinement, yet direct in its appeal. They show us that the storyteller is less concerned with elaborating the cloth of his or her tale, and more concerned with the basic weave of the fabric itself. The storyteller is politically conservative. The story is not meant to challenge the *status quo* but to justify it. The storyteller is socially orthodox. Strict morality is defended, and violation of that morality is condemned. In other words, the storyteller is not out to change society, but to defend it. The storyteller is a cultural gate-keeper.

Though King writes horror stories, the underlying messages of those stories are not all that revolutionary. Morality is at issue in nearly all of his fiction. For example, the evils of child abuse are highlighted in *The Shining* (1977), as well as in *Carrie* (1974) and *It* (1987). Community standards of virtue are at issue in *'Salem's Lot* (1975) and *Needful Things* (1991), while "The Mist" (1980), *Christine* (1983), and *The Stand* (1978, 1990) challenge the role of "ungodly" technology in today's society. Most of King's work is politically conservative, safe, non-challenging and thus non-threatening to traditional standards of basic morality. And this is a primary reason why he is so popular in the United States. Historically, King's fiction became popular in this country during a period when the U.S. was gradually moving right of center politically, and even though King himself exhibits the trappings of the 1960s counter-culture adolescent rebel, his work reveals itself to be something that even a staunch conservative wouldn't be offended reading.

Clive Barker, on the other hand, is a more literary author than King. Unlike Stephen King, Barker is concerned about the "art" of writing. Though he is aware of the importance of entertainment, Barker doesn't sacrifice style and substance for the sake of that entertainment. Both King and Barker are mindful of their literary heritage. King's non-fiction study of contemporary horror mass media, entitled *Danse Macabre* (1981), stands as one of the finest analyses of the genre. Unfortunately, King doesn't seem to incorporate much of what he knows into his fiction. He duplicates the image of the horror story, but not its heart, as raw and ghastly as that heart may be. Conversely, Clive Barker tends to begin his writing in the traditional formulas of the horror genre, but then as his narratives progress in the telling, he discards the shell of formula, subsequently creating a new type of story in the process, one that may not be easily recognizable but one that certainly has great vitality. In addition, Barker's erudition manifests itself prominently in his stories. The *Books of Blood*, for example, are teeming with allusions to a variety of great authors, such as Dante, Goethe, Poe, Mary Shelley, Kafka, and many others. Barker claims in an interview conducted in the March 1991 issue of *Writer's Digest* that he writes "a kind of fiction which relates to a whole texture of imagery which appears in painting and poetry and mythology and folklore." He continues, "I wanted there to be in *Weaveworld*, for instance, echoes of *Peter Pan*, of the fairy tales of the Brothers Grimm, of the Book of Genesis, of William Blake" (26). In another interview conducted with Nick Vince for *Pandemonium*, Barker states that examples of his favorite literature include *Moby-Dick* (1851), *Peter Pan* (play, 1904; book, 1911), the poetry of W.B. Yeats, and the work of Gerard Manley Hopkins (10–12), thus illustrating the quality, versatility, and diversity of his interests.

Barker doesn't hide his education as King does; he embraces it. The result of Barker's versatile use of literary allusion is that the reader can take from Barker several different things. If the reader desires simple entertainment (and there's nothing wrong with that), then simple entertainment can be found. A number of Clive Barker's short stories in the *Books of Blood* are real hair-raisers and are quite compelling to read. If, however, the reader desires something more than entertainment, then Barker offers complexity, style, a masterful sense of language and its use, and most importantly, a history, in his writing. Clive Barker places himself within the great traditions of literature, and thus the reader can take from Barker the sense that he does not condescend to us. He respects our intelligence, and though much of what he does can be loosely classified as horror fiction, Barker does not revel in the gratuitous violence of the genre, as do many of his peers. Barker envisions the horror tale as a vehicle for political and social debate, and not as a mere opiate for mindless thrill alone.

The very conventional nature of King's work — which is the second significant difference between Barker and King — makes him a "safe" writer, while the highly inventional texture of Barker's fiction gives that fiction an insurgent quality, a dangerous edge. King may show the trappings of outrageousness in his horror stories, but the best of his efforts often rely too much on the simple technique of *the scare*. King's overriding goal in his horror fiction is to frighten his reader, as he tells us in *Danse Macabre*, and if art and substance don't accomplish this goal, then he reverts to what he terms the "gag reflex of revulsion" level of writing (36–37). Frequently, the result of this technique is that during those crucial, climactic moments in his stories where he could be a powerful writer, he instead depends on mere histrionics. King ultimately does little in his work but entertain, and little in King challenges us to challenge ourselves. When he should turn outward, addressing society as a critic, he regrettably turns only inward to the tormented soul, to the self-centered protagonist. King's characters are the troubled adolescent, the abused spouse, the self-doubting writer. Thus, when King introduces *the scare* to his story, the horror is safely contained within the character. King is a comfortable read; he is an armchair author whose stories should be ideally experienced on a cold and windy evening next to a roaring fireplace. The chills King elicits are of the more pedestrian variety, and they really don't pierce to the soul of what *truly* frightens (and also amazes) us.

The "comfortable" horror tale is a recent innovation. Its inception began in the twentieth century in the pages of pulp magazine fiction, like *Weird Tales*, specifically in the efforts of pulp authors like H.P. Lovecraft. Lovecraft never really scared his audience, but he did give his readers a pleasant shiver, a pleasing diversion or escape, and an interesting speculative concept here and there. Lovecraft's many followers, authors like Robert E. Howard and Clark Ashton Smith, did much the same thing in their horror tales, and they, in turn, influenced subsequent generations of the genre's authors. The comfortable branch of the horror story also seeks entertainment as its central purpose, and King comes from this tradition. Some of his early short stories like "Jerusalem's Lot" (1978) are directly imitative of Lovecraft.

But the true artistic heritage of the horror genre, a heritage founded well before Lovecraft in the origins of the novel itself in both Europe and America, is one of political and social insurrection. From Horace Walpole's *The Castle of Otranto* (1764/1765), the first Gothic novel, to Matthew Lewis's *The Monk* (1796), to Mary Shelley's *Frankenstein* (1818), to Robert Louis Stevenson's *The Strange Case of Dr. Jekyll and Mr. Hyde* (1886), the Gothic tale fundamentally critiques the human condition. These novels (and many others like them) probe sensitive sexual mores, investigate the role and function of social taboos, and most importantly, they loudly proclaim that there is a dark side to the human spirit, that evil is as much a part of our condition as is good, and that the triumph of good over evil, if it occurs at all, is an arduous thing. The Gothic tale is antiestablishment. It attacks institutional authority, and the basis for that authority. It reveals the capriciousness of law and announces that there is a higher power than even God, which for lack of a better word can be called "Fate," that punishes moral transgressions and that shows us that the only constant in life is death: the ultimate revolt against order and the orderly. The Gothic tale challenges everything we take for granted. It is despised by the literary critic because it subverts the conventional realism of the novel. It is equally despised by the scholar because of its common, "penny dreadful" origins. The Gothic tale, when done well, makes the reader nervous. It definitely is not a safe story. And Clive Barker's fiction follows this particular tradition.

For example, survey the collection of short stories in the *Books of Blood* and you will notice that Clive Barker attacks a variety of institutions—including religion, the police, politics, heaven and hell, and the government—in essence questioning institutional order itself. In his article entitled "Outlaws" published in the anthology, *Splatterpunks: Extreme Horror* (1990), Paul M. Sammon writes, "In a broader sense splat [as a sub-category of the horror genre] can also be seen as yet another example of anarchy erupting through (and because of) a period of social repression, specifically, the vicious conservatism of Ronald Reagan and Margaret Thatcher" (291). Sammon goes on to say that Barker became popular about the same time that Thatcher became powerful, and that Barker's work, as an example of "splatterpunk" writing, is a fictive backlash against the "vicious" conservative political state.

Clive Barker discovers satire in the most commonplace of social agencies. He wakes us from our lethargic condition and alerts us to that which controls us, and to that which ultimately feeds upon us. At times, Barker's point is humorous or horrifying (or both simultaneously), and Barker's message, if not pretty at moments, is profound. When Clive Barker turns inward with his writing to develop a particular character or to provide background to a particular setting, he never loses sight of his purpose: an outward examination of life and death and the deeper meaning of each. He discards easy, rational explanations, showing these to be superficial or, even worse, hypocritical. He nurtures philosophical complexity of thought and action. "Right" and "wrong" are relative concepts, and are intricately blended in his characters. For Clive Barker, even the most horrible villain can be pathetic, and the most handsome of protagonists can be vile. This quality of moral ambiguity is also derived, in part, from the Gothic story, where the Gothic author elicits sympathy for the most offensive of heroes, as with Matthew Lewis's debauched monk, Ambrosio, from the novel, *The Monk*.

Even though Clive Barker's fiction is dangerous and comes to us from that dangerous, dark Gothic past, his bottom-line message to his readers is not so dark. In fact, it's quite optimistic, and this philosophical quality illustrates the third significant difference between Clive Barker and Stephen King. It's an undeniable fact that King is a talented writer. The colossal sales figures of his books provide ample proof of his ability to entertain a mass audience. Stephen King does satisfy on a superficial level; he, indeed, gives his many readers what they want. But despite King's talent for writing "mere" entertainment (and there is absolutely nothing wrong with this ability in and of itself, of amusement for amusement's sake), there exists no soul to companion that powerful entertainment. King fails to provide a unifying vision to his work. There appears to be no artistic motivation to his fiction other than diversion, or perhaps some type of auto-catharsis. A variety of messages underscore his novels and short stories; unfortunately, none of these messages is significant enough to anchor any sort of philosophical worldview.

Clive Barker's work, conversely, makes a point. From his earliest literary endeavors in experimental theater to his elegant short fiction to his epic fantasy novels, Barker has established, and has constantly maintained, a unified, artistic vision. He has written in a variety of styles, from humorous to horrific, and in a number of genres, from satire to mystery, and yet he weaves a constant, subtle thread from story to story. Barker revels in metaphor. He delights in the well-turned phrase, the nicely stated philosophy, the profound articulation of the human condition. He identifies the many layers of life's (and death's) meaning in humanity's struggle for survival, for an identity, and he underscores his writing with a complexity that is simple, and a simplicity that is complex. Clive Barker has commonly been cited (mainly by hasty critics and uninformed readers) as a master of the horror story. This certainly might be an accurate statement if Barker wrote only horror fiction. But he does not. Instead, he writes allegory. He writes fables. His fiction is simile and metaphor detailing the layers beneath the surface. Barker says of his relationship to the horror genre,

> The most interesting work in any genre, however, is surely going on at the perimeters, where definitions blur. This is nowhere more evident than in the group of books collectively stamped horror. Here there are brilliantly constructed thrillers (try Thomas Harris's *Silence of the Lambs*); there are baroque romances (Anne Rice has put the blood back into bodice ripping); there are subtle, psychological pieces (our own Ramsey Campbell has long been a master of that particular form). All of the above could be categorized as horror fiction, but in approach, purpose and style they are utterly different from one another.
>
> Asked to define my own place in this parade of dark fictions I'd ask to be filed where some dyslexic clerk might slip me, somewhere between Baum and Burroughs (William, not Edgar Rice); by which I mean that the kind of fiction I write is often a fiction of invented worlds (even when it's set on earth; or perhaps *especially* then): the traveller's tale as written by a man just back from Hell by way of Oz and 42nd Street ["FT Forum 4"].

The trappings of horror sometimes swirl in and out of Barker's stories. His "books" *are* written in blood after all, but blood is the symbol of life as well as death, and Barker is aware of this duality. In fact, I think it's safer to claim that Barker writes more of comedy than of horror. Many of his tales, even the grisly ones, often end happily. A number of instances throughout the *Books of Blood*, for example, illustrate how love triumphs in the end. Or if love doesn't triumph, if lovers aren't united when all else fails, then knowledge is gained of the delicate relationship between life and death, between the world of living and the world of death. Knowledge *is* power, Barker might tell us.

Clive Barker fully understands that the various aspects of the human condition (or inhuman condition, if you will)—such as knowledge, love, imagination, and fear—in his writing reflect deeper, more profound, more fundamental concerns. In an article entitled "The Tragical History of Dr. Faustus," Barker states, "It is not that the old stories are necessarily the *best* stories; rather that the old stories are the *only* stories. There are no new tales, only new ways to tell" (11). Barker pays homage to archetype in his fiction. He inks his pen in the life force of the essential story. He escorts his reader through concepts fundamental to our species—and our survival. And this makes Barker not only a unique and important horror writer, but a unique and important writer, period. Though innovation in his *Books of Blood* is readily apparent, Barker's tales of death and life are connected to our most distant memories, our darkest fears and our brightest hopes. For Barker and his short fiction, what is new is actually quite ancient. And this quality—the ability to blend or fuse the old with the new—discloses the tremendous might behind his artistic punch, the efficacy that supports the telling of tales that we already know, but haven't heard before.

Clive Barker and the Ideology of Horror Fiction

In the slender book *Supernatural Horror in Literature* (1945)—which, along with Stephen King's *Danse Macabre*, is perhaps the best study of the horror genre written by a prominent author of horror fiction—H.P. Lovecraft sees an elitist function in the horror story. Lovecraft claims,

> The appeal of the spectrally macabre is generally narrow because it demands from the reader a certain degree of imagination and a capacity for detachment from everyday life. Relatively few are free enough from the spell of the daily routine to respond to rappings from outside, and tales of ordinary feelings and events, or of common sentimental distortions of such feelings and events, will always take first place in the taste of the majority; rightly, perhaps, since of course these ordinary matters make up the greater part of human experience. [12.13]

Of course, Lovecraft himself fantasized about the role of his literary art, and even about his life, as being a cut above the common experience. His work is ripe with paranoid reflections of ethnicity and social class; his horror fiction often mirrors an inner dread of outer social forces. Lovecraft is horror fiction's version of Sir Arthur Conan Doyle. Conan Doyle was condemned during his prolific writing career for paying heed to the popular, to the desires of the common herd. He wanted to write historical romances; instead, he was brought back to his immensely successful Sherlock Holmes stories time and again by financial necessity. Conan Doyle entertained a love/hate relationship with his Holmes character. Writing detective stories brought him fame and money, but he wanted artistic fulfillment, a feeling that his fiction was a step beyond the mundane drivel that appeared in the serial fiction magazines of his day. Lovecraft, too, experienced mixed feelings concerning his work in the horror genre. He wrote not for money (as he lived in perpetual poverty during most of his adult life), but for an artistic sense, a sense that he felt distinguished him from the lowly masses he so despised. Yet from the accounts of those who knew Lovecraft personally, he was a charming and gracious man, an unflappably generous editor, and a selfless writer who always took time to encourage his aspiring fellow writers. He was a seeming contradiction.

But Lovecraft's literary generosities were a product of the man's view of his relationship to his art and to those who admired his art. Lovecraft loved those who loved him, as a land baron loves his loyal peasants, as a nobleman loves his serfs. Lovecraft's dealings with his life and friends are closely akin to his philosophical perception of horror fiction. What he wrote wasn't pulp; what he wrote was artifice. Despite Lovecraft's many other "on target" observations in his *Supernatural Horror in Literature*, when he claims an elitist reading of the genre, he is only half right. The horror tale *is* elitist when it serves as a vehicle of social criticism, but when horror fiction strives to entertain as well as criticize, then it denies the limited accessibility that Lovecraft so advocates. The successful horror tale both entertains and challenges. It is both accessible to a mass audience and limited in its appeal. The reason for this seeming contradiction is because, unlike Lovecraft's claim that the "rappings from outside" appeal to a relative few, the tale of supernatural terror is fundamentally reflective of humanity's basic fear of its own mortality. One must by necessity add the individual's trepidation of death and dying to Lovecraft's short list of one's "daily routine." Horror fiction is thus merely a highly stylized and symbolically sublimated response to a basic fact of life that is frightening in its finality, yet fascinating because of its unknown landscape. In other words, horror fiction is both scary and alluring because death is both scary and alluring. Clive Barker fully understands this underlying paradox of the genre, and his *Books of Blood* frequently utilize images that are grotesque *and* beautiful.

In his study entitled *The Philosophy of Horror: or, Paradoxes of the Heart*, Noël Carroll defines the genre, in part, by stating, "'Horror,' as a category of ordinary language, is a serviceable concept through which we communicate and receive information" (13). Carroll goes on to muddy up things by proposing an elaborate, yet silly, distinction between "horror" and "art-horror," providing the latter with syntactically cumbersome limitations. Carroll got it right the first time: horror is a mode of communication, a method of symbolically expressing a number of elements associated with mortality. In his *Books of Blood*, Clive Barker establishes as the central metaphor of the six-volume anthology a powerful textual metaphor. The anthology's opening story, "The Book of Blood," makes that crucial connection between horror and communication, between text and subtext. Simon McNeal is transformed by the dead into a living textbook of horror stories. McNeal's very body serves as Barker's philosophical touchstone for all of his short fiction (and even his novels); McNeal is a fictive character who literally embodies dark fiction. His tragedy is that he forfeits his identity, mean and self-centered though it may be, for the sake of miracle. And Barker intends this miracle to operate as a message, to serve as communication.

Joseph Grixti is more correct in his understanding of the social-psychological function of the horror story. He writes in *Terrors of Uncertainty: The Cultural Contexts of Horror Fiction* that "fictional horrors as social and cultural products... are of significance because they form part of the symbolic structures which we use to make sense of and ascribe meaning to our existence" (xii). For all of its often criticized lack of "artistic" merit, or its lack of sophistication, fundamentally, the horror story is one of *the* most important types of fiction (and, no doubt, types of film, too) supporting that structure that we call reality. Because it is so artless, because it is basic in what it does (*the scare*), and in what it reflects (our collective, cultural nightmares), the horror story is the most essential of essential narratives. Clive Barker understands this basic, fundamental quality of the horror story and provides in a number of short stories a bloodcurdling wallop of shock and suspense, such as that specifically seen in "The Midnight Meat Train" and "Rawhead Rex." Barker ably demonstrates in these and his other stories that he comprehends exactly what frightens us, both at a social level and at a personal level. In fact, as illustrated in "The Midnight Meat Train," what happens outside of the subway train (i.e. the authority behind the train's existence) is actually more scary than the gruesome acts that occur within the subway.

Barker is well aware of how frightening a dysfunctional social system can be, perhaps even more frightening than a threat against personal safety. Hence, when Barker so effectively attacks those social support institutions that should supposedly provide some measure of security at a larger level, organizations like the police and the church, he has most effectively touched a chilly (and chilling) finger on our rapidly beating pulse. Nothing shakes us up so much as an assault upon those things which shore up our notions of reality. Nothing scares us quite so much as knowing that we really don't know the world we live in.

Yet Clive Barker not only can strike us between the eyes in his fiction with a rather ugly two-by-four, displaying exactly how artless he can be if he so wishes, but he can also dazzle us with narrative subtleties, with deft character descriptions, with nuance and style and metaphor—in other words, with his art. And this ability, the ability to make art out of horror, is what distinguishes him from his best-selling peers like Stephen King. Like Barker, Louis S. Gross views the "art" of horror fiction as a type of pedagogy. What Gross claims about the Gothic novel in his book, *Redefining the American Gothic: From* Wieland *to* Day of the Dead, equally applies to what Clive Barker does in his short fiction,

> Gothic fiction is first and foremost, literature where fear is the motivating and sustaining emotion. This fear is shared by the characters within the story and the reader. The Gothic thus examines the causes, qualities, and results of terror on both mind and body. It does so in a process of epistemological inquiry, and because it is concerned with the acquisition and internalizing of kinds of knowledge, the Gothic finds an

appropriate vehicle in the quest narrative or, more specifically, the *Erziehungsroman* or narrative of education [1].

Certainly, all of Barker's novels involve some element of the quest narrative. In Barker's epic fantasy adventure, *Imajica*, for example, the quest as essential story frames the entire narrative. But Gross sees the quest story as something more than physical adventure: he also views it as a quest for meaning, for knowledge, and ultimately for comprehension.

A number of Barker's stories in the *Books of Blood* utilize this thematic quest of the soul, for a soul. Many of the journeys in these tales are internal, and the horror that is revealed is as often psychological in nature as it is supernatural. For example, in the short story "Dread," Barker's sociopathic character named Quaid desires to know more information about the emotion of human fear. During the process of his education, as he tortures and terrorizes others in the name of "research," however, the tables are turned on Quaid, and he becomes the one terrorized. The final irony in the story is that Quaid does, in fact, learn a great deal about fear, but this knowledge is bought at a terrible personal price. The foundation of Barker's art is the basic understanding that the best horror story challenges us to look at ourselves, to peer into our emotional identity, to rummage around a bit and examine what frightening or wonderful things that we discover there.

James B. Twitchell establishes a psychological connection between art and the horror story. In his study *Dreadful Pleasures: An Anatomy of Modern Horror*, Twitchell says of his methodological approach,

> I hope to show that horror sequences are really formulaic rituals coded with precise social information needed by the adolescent audience. Like fairy tales that prepare the child for the anxieties of separation, modern horror myths prepare the teenager for the anxieties of reproduction. They are fantastic, ludicrous, crude, and important distortions of real life situations, not in the service of repression (though they certainly have that temporary effect), but of instruction [7].

Unfortunately, Twitchell shouldn't limit the impact of horror fiction to the adolescent; it influences the adult as much as the teenager. Authors like Stephen King and Clive Barker are successful because they appeal to a wide audience, crossing both age and gender boundaries rather effectively. Where Twitchell really hits the target in the above comment is when he notes the distinction between the idea that horror is repressive and the idea that horror is instructive. Much of what Clive Barker does in his writing favors instruction over repression. That is not to say that Barker doesn't include a strong measure of eroticism in his fiction. He uses sex perhaps better than any of his peers, accurately portraying the powerful sexual nature of the individual specifically, and humanity in general. His novel *Imajica*, for instance, is as erotic as it is adventurous.

Those critics who perceive the horror story as a repressed expression of sexuality fail to understand that the tale of horror is most effective when sex is at issue. Barker's "Rawhead Rex" derives much of *the scare* from the various sexually charged scenes in the story. The threat of rape, of animalistic oral consumption, and of the conflict between male and female fetishism make the story a frightening examination of the conflict between the feminine and masculine sides of our natures, literally between life (as woman) and death (as man). If we agree with Twitchell's idea that adolescents harbor "anxieties" about sex, then we should also concede to the fact that adults might also experience similar anxieties. *The scare* in horror fiction, as Barker knows, is heightened when some form of sexual tension is introduced. Barker neither exploits sex for its own sake in his work, which thus transforms sex into a form of pornography, nor does he ignore its existence, as Stephen King tends to do in many of his novels. In a recent interview conducted in a magazine entitled *Marvel Age*, Barker briefly remarked about King's failure to recognize the potential function of sex in the tale of terror by stating that "the erotic-horror link is almost non-existent in his [King's] work" (13). Indeed, Stephen King might be called the "boy scout" of horror novelists because he so excludes sex from much of his writing—though several of King's most recent efforts, like the film *Sleepwalkers* (1992), and the novel *Gerald's Game* (1992), deal with explicit sex. Unlike King, however, Barker frequently incorporates sex as a reflection of love, as a fundamental element of salvation, and as a metaphoric expression of life. A more detailed analysis of Barker's use of sex as an important thematic device will follow in the final section of this chapter.

In his various treatments of fictional protagonists, Clive Barker has his characters embody not only a wide range of sexual experiences (e.g. the protagonists of "In the Hills, the Cities," and "Human Remains" are homosexual), but also a wide range of non-stereotypic gender roles (e.g. note the tremendous power wielded by Jacqueline Ess in "Jacqueline Ess: Her Will and Testament," a power that is quite atypical of what is generally granted to women in horror fiction). Barker possesses an ideological position regarding sex and gender; he jokingly says that he kills everyone in his stories without concern for race, sex, or religion. Dismissing Barker's levity, his comment illustrates how sensitive he is to the complexity of human sexuality. He writes about the topic as he writes about politics or religion. He demonstrates in his fiction his awareness of the many subtle distinctions that are to be found in any human endeavor. Margaret L. Carter in her book *Specter or Delusion?: The Supernatural in Gothic Fiction* ultimately sees the writer of the Gothic story as a critic of culture, as someone who uses Gothic fiction as a device to challenge the author's own worldview, as well as society's worldview (123). Though Carter is focusing her claim upon the Gothic author's use of the supernatural in his or her fiction (and Barker, himself, employs the supernatural in this same way), a similar notion can be applied to Clive Barker's utilization of sex as thematic device in his short fiction. Barker is fundamentally a critic of his society in the *Books of Blood*, and sex is but one more implement by which he can lay open for our scrutiny our own intricate natures.

Not all critics are as willing to concede to the horror genre's potential for complexity. Walter Kendrick, in *The Thrill of Fear: 250 Years of Scary Entertainment*, seems to dispute a psycho-sexual interpretation of the horror story, as well as a mythic interpretation. He says in the introduction to his book that,

> Instead of adopting the standard family tree of scariness, I've explored how fear blends into other feelings and cohabits with them. Instead of forcing run-of-the-mill work to yield up deeper, richer, more stable meanings, I've tried to read culture's throwaways on their own terms — not as unconscious folklore, unwitting criticism of gender roles, unsuspected assaults on the status quo, or any of the other blind ingenuities with which critics of popular culture try to credit them. I've gone in search not of meanings but of feelings... [xxvi].

And then after saying this, Kendrick goes on for the next 260 plus pages looking for meaning in the horror genre, discovering significance in the genre's use of sexuality, and reviewing this so-called "run-of-the-mill work" (i.e. horror classics) to death. Kendrick is one of those scholars who appear to be embarrassed dealing with the horror story. He loudly proclaims how terrible the stuff is, and then condescends to it by showing us how he can slum about in the muck. Most everything that Kendrick attacks in his overly apologetic analysis of the horror story can be easily found in Barker's work. Yet Barker doesn't apologize to anyone for what he does. Instead, he uses the horror story as a narrative vehicle best able to communicate his artistic interpretations of life and death. Barker recognizes in horror the thing that media critic Les Daniels calls in his book, *Living in Fear: A History of Horror in the Mass Media*, "an authentic attraction." In the same passage, Daniels goes on to say, "A fondness for fabricated fright is almost a universal human characteristic, although there are those who reject it, either because they find expressions of this impulse too terrifying or because they consider the whole genre crude and degrading" (1). Barker, and Barker's many readers, know that the horror genre is not degrading, that it is instead a viable, vibrant literature, a literature that extols imagination over pedestrianism, versatility over formula. Of course, that is not to say that horror fiction is not without its bad novels, its bad authors, its formula. All fiction, though, is susceptible to artistic weakness. Perhaps because of Walter Kendrick and other critics like him, the horror story suffers from an image problem. Perhaps because it deals with various social taboos in an openhanded fashion, horror fiction may be difficult for so-called serious authors or scholars to take seriously, difficult to give the recognition it deserves.

This returns us to Lovecraft and his elitist viewing of the horror genre.

Unlike either Lovecraft, on the one hand, or Kendrick, on the other, Clive Barker defies an overly simplistic reading of the genre. His fiction ranges from high art to high camp with deceptive ease. He is *not* ashamed of the medium in which he works; he advocates the horror story as an ideal means of both entertainment and instruction. Barker manipulates the tale of horror as a sculptor does clay. He forms it to meet a personal vision, as well as a larger, grander vision of humanity and the human condition. He crafts it, shaping it either as satire or love story or erotic fantasy. John G. Cawelti's rather simple explanation of the genre's function is probably the best suited to Clive Barker. Cawelti says in his important study of popular formulas, *Adventure, Mystery, and Romance: Formula Stories as Art and Popular Culture*, that the horror story suggests to its reader that "the unknowable can be known and related to in some meaningful fashion" (49). Clive Barker in his *Books of Blood* indeed attempts to discover meaning in the "unknowable." He seeks to critique the way we think and the things we do and the institutions we establish *via* imagination. Barker thinks that the horror story is a fundamental way in which he can accomplish his artistic objectives.

In her scholarly examination of horror fiction, *The Tale of Terror: A Study of the Gothic Romance*, Edith Birkhead states that other "[horror fiction authors] with more insidious art, will set themselves to devise stories which evoke subtler refinements of fear...It may well be that this track will lead us into unexplored labyrinths of terror" (228). The following two sections will briefly review Clive Barker's life and will outline Barker's discussion of horror's "subtler refinements." The intent is to allow the author the opportunity to describe himself and what he does in his own words. After all, who better than Clive Barker can tell us about the subtext of his own imagination?

A Sketch of Clive Barker's Life and His Art

Clive Barker's startling rise in popularity has been as sudden as it has been dramatic. On several occasions when discussing his great success in both publishing and film making, Barker has commented informally to me that the whole thing makes him somewhat uneasy. Just over a decade ago, Barker was living on public assistance in England, unsure of his future, his artistic ambitions, and his next meal.

Contrast this past situation with the cover of the March 1991 issue of *Writer's Digest* which in large typeface proclaims: "Terror-Master Clive Barker's Rules for Writing Million Dollar Fiction." Indeed, Clive Barker has made it. He is one of but a handful of professional authors who can command "million dollar" payments for his fiction. His commercial success in writing and directing films is equally impressive. Barker is that rare cinematic bird — the movie auteur — who has near total artistic control over his motion pictures. A film like *Nightbreed*, for example, because it defies the traditional conventions of the typical monster movie, would have never been made if it weren't for someone like Clive Barker, a person who could take artistic chances and get away with them in an otherwise imaginatively retarded medium.

Yet Barker remains modest about his good fortune. "Success makes me nervous," Barker tells his interviewer Douglas E. Winter. Barker continues by saying,

> I mean it's great, smashing. But it makes me nervous. I didn't have any huge ambition for the books [*Books of Blood*]. I did them because I wanted to do them. And it's a little confounding to have the response that they've had. I've been working in the theater for a long time, and doing illustrations, laboring without a great deal of cash. Suddenly to have things blossom in front of me — it's knocked my equilibrium a little bit. It's made me think much more closely about what I want to do [218].

Despite his modest pretensions, Clive Barker is the single most influential talent working in fantasy film and fiction today. He has developed a "cutting edge" entertainment that touches a wide range of mass media and an even wider range of unabashed literary imitators. As Ira Levin influenced the horror genre in the 1960s, and as Stephen King influenced it in the 1970s, Barker has profoundly influenced horror fiction in the 1980s by opening it up to wide-ranging philosophical issues, and by expanding the aesthetic parameters of the genre itself, blurring formulaic distinctions, creating new and unusual literary creations in the process. And did all these amazing things before reaching his fortieth birthday.

Clive Barker was born to Len and Joan Barker on October 5, 1952, in Liverpool, England. He was raised near Penny Lane, the street the Beatles made famous. Barker has always professed a "normal" childhood (Winter 208), though the fact that he even needs to make such a claim is an interesting indication of how we are suspicious of the horror fiction writer. After all, we may ask ourselves, how can someone like Clive Barker write this gory stuff, unless something "weird" happened to him as a child? It is a prejudice that reveals more about the questioner than the subject, but, unfortunately, it is a prejudice that Barker (and Barker's successful peers like Stephen King) have had to tolerate. Barker himself contends that exploring an author's past for a rationale that explains why he or she writes horror fiction reveals only half-truths (Winter 208).

Clive Barker's father worked in "industrial relations," and his mother was a school welfare officer. Clive has a younger brother named Roy, who is married and has children, and who once owned a grocer's shop in North Wales (Jones 10). Roy now markets computer games in Liverpool. Barker says that Roy was educated as a "marine engineer," and that this continued a strong nautical heritage in his family. Barker states in an interview conducted with Michael Brown for *Pandemonium*, "My father [Len] was in the Navy, my grandfather was a ship's cook and so he [Roy] carried on the tradition. My godfather, who's now dead unfortunately, was a sea captain. Many of my father's peers that I knew when I was a kid were related to the sea, to the river" (20). Barker goes on to say that he incorporated his knowledge of the sea into the writing of his novel, *Weaveworld*.

Barker credits, in part, his mother Joan for introducing him to fantasy. She gave him to read *Peter Pan* and *The Wind in the Willows* (what he terms "benign volumes"), but Barker quickly adds that he became acquainted with the "darker stuff," like Poe, on his own (Wiater, *Dark Dreamers* 15—16). Barker tells interviewer Stanley Wiater in *Dark Dreamers: Conversations with the Masters of Horror* that he never envisioned his literary career as being fixated upon dark fantasy or horror fiction, and that he hopes in a larger retrospect of his work 30 or 40 years from now that his horror fiction will be seen as just an element of his overall efforts, and not the single dominant element at that (16).

Barker claims in his discussion with Stanley Wiater that his parents recognized his imagination as a child, but instead of being pleased they were worried. Barker remarks,

> I think they [my parents] had the conventional belief of making sure that I somehow found a purpose in life which would pay the mortgage and allow me to be a sane and productive member of society. So they let me get on with my interests, but they certainly didn't encourage them [16].

Belying his current youthful good looks and his slender build, Barker describes himself as a child as being an "overweight, spectacled youth, bullied by sixth-formers" (Winter 209). He escaped the hassles of his adolescence by becoming immersed in the imaginative world of books and art. Barker comments about this escape into imagination in his interview with Douglas Winter, "It's the whole notion of commanding the world *via* what you created, and retreating toward a world where you knew the ground rules because you just invented them. But it was also a world where I could work through the problems" (209).

In the same Winter interview, Barker says he wrote his first play at age eleven, and that it was produced by his mother for the local Boy Scout group. He subsequently became his school's playwright. "We had the usually dry-as-dust productions of *Macbeth* or whatever, and I thought it was pretty boring. So I decided to write plays about magicians and dragons and mad Nazis—I've been consistent, you see—and they were pretty popular" (210). Barker identifies Edgar Allan Poe as an influence in his creative life, and specifically he mentions "The Masque of the Red Death" (1842) as one of his favorite Poe tales. (Barker employs in several of his *Books of Blood* stories narrative elements from Poe's horror writings, including a sequel to Poe's "The Murders in the Rue

Morgue" (1841) entitled "New Murders in the Rue Morgue" and an updated interpretation of "The Masque of the Red Death" entitled "The Age of Desire.") Barker also states that horror movie posters and horror movies like George Pal's *War of the Worlds* (1953) and Hitchcock's *Psycho* (1960) all had an impact upon his developing imagination. He remembers watching the audience during a screening of *Psycho* and saying to himself that he wanted to entertain people someday in a similar fashion (Winter 210–211).

Although Barker recollects being impressed by a lecture given by horror fiction author Ramsey Campbell entitled "Why Horror?," his interests would take several different directions before returning to the writing of dark fantasy fiction. He attended the University of Liverpool and wanted to study art, but at his parents' insistence that he study something that would be useful to him, he took classes in philosophy and English. He claims not to have been involved very much in school, having instead a more compelling interest in the theater. Barker declares in the Winter interview, "I never took much notice of my courses. I got on with writing plays and making pictures and doing all the other things I had done beforehand" (212).

In 1977, Barker moved to London, where he did some work as an artist, and where he also became involved in London's avant-garde theatrical community, such as the Theater of the Imagination, the Hydra Theater Company, and the Dog Company (Stroby 22). During this period, Barker wrote eleven full-length plays that stretched the parameters of the medium. These plays were (and are) decadent, bizarre, wonderfully imaginative and, at times, frighteningly vivid. Many of the narrative themes that Barker would later employ in his short fiction and novels he first developed in his drama. A number of critics have suggested that Barker's theatrical work is contemporary *grand guignol*, but his plays, though possessing elements of *grand guignol*, are much more sophisticated and much more imaginative than the limiting confines of a single genre (and this is also the case with his fiction). The fanciful richness of his drama is reflected by the titles of his plays, such as *Crazyface* (1982), *Colossus* (1983), and *The Secret Life of Cartoons* (1984), to name just a few.

When asked by interviewers Richard A. Lupoff and Richard Wolinsky about the connection between his work as a film director and his work as a playwright, Barker replied that there is a strong relationship with the two (18). Barker's experience in the theater also had a great impact on his fiction. Dramaturgical elements appear in his writing, such as in his short story "Sex, Death and Starshine," but perhaps even more importantly, aspects involving staging, scene construction, and the portrayal of characters in Barker's short stories and novels reveal a very theatrical mind. Barker, it seems, is always aware of his effect upon his audience. The scenes in his stories are noticeably visual and very much staged as if presented in the theater. His protagonists are quite theatrical as well. They exhibit a certain showmanship that one does not find in Stephen King, for example.

Barker mentions in the Lupoff and Wolinsky interview that one of the problems involved with working in the theater is that sometimes one's efforts are compromised. Barker states,

> Well, *The Secret Life of Cartoons* had a great life on the fringe in England and in Europe and Edinborough, the festival. And then it had a disastrous life on the West End when it became a legitimate production. In part because I lost control of it. With all these movies and all this stuff, maybe I'm coming across as a control freak. But, I genuinely do think that sometimes things get lost. An essence gets lost. Some producers came in, they cast some stars and the thing was lost [18-19].

Barker utilizes this sense of artistic compromise and theatrical prostitution in "Sex, Death and Starshine." In both real life and the fictional interpretation of real life, Clive Barker rebels against over-simplification and its subsequent aesthetic concessions. He claims that when *The Secret Life of Cartoons* moved to the West End, because it cost a great deal of money to produce a play there, the people funding the production had to insure that the play appealed to as wide an audience as possible so that a financial return on its investment could be realized. By cleaning up *The Secret Life of Cartoons*, Barker alleges that they made it a bad play. He says to interviewer Lupoff, "Suddenly, you find that you're losing control of the stuff you really loved. And, a lot of the nice stuff goes and it gets coarsened in a curious kind of way because it gets simplified. Suddenly, it's Vaudeville and it lost it" (Lupoff and Wolinsky 19).

Clive Barker discusses the importance of his involvement with the theater in an interview conducted in the Winter 1987 issue of *American Fantasy* magazine. He contends, "An awful lot of the way that I write, and the reason I am how I am in relation to the work I do has got a lot to do with the fact that I came out of the theater" ("British Invasion" 46). Barker elaborates upon this by saying that the audience has always been of primary importance to him and his work and that audience response is a crucial element of his artistic motivations. He never becomes bored with that "exciting moment," that instant when his audience becomes "enthusiastic" about his efforts ("British Invasion" 46). "I'm...excited to see what the audience is up to, how they respond," Barker proclaims in the *American Fantasy* interview, "And therefore a lot of my attitudes to books and the writing of books and how the books are received is rooted in that theater experience" ("British Invasion" 46).

Barker also helped to produce two early short motion pictures during the period that he was involved in the theater. The first of these films is entitled *Salome,* and it was shot in 8 mm in the cellar of a florist's shop. The second short film, *The Forbidden* (which was not based upon the short story that appeared in the *Books of Blood*), was shot in 16 mm (Atkins 135). There is currently some discussion among several British television producers of releasing these two films on video in England and the United States in the near future.

In essence, then, Barker as playwright developed two significant attitudes that later affected both his writing of horror fiction and his work as screenwriter and director in the cinema. The first of these attitudes is his view of artistic control. Barker is a very controlled author and film director. Structure is of paramount concern to him. The structuring of his plot and his characters' motivations, and his use of metaphor and subtext to advance his philosophical agendas are deliberately crafted in his work. One typically thinks of horror fiction as being wild and out of control, yet Barker has always sublimated the visceral effect of the horror story to a deeper message, a message that echoes issues of the larger human condition. He has tapped the raw energy and power of horror, and *via* his control of narrative form he has directed that power into significant venues of social concern, such issues as the importance of a self-aware life, of imagination in relationship to people's quality of living, and of a tolerant, enlightened outlook about the role of morality. The second of Barker's attitudes that evolved from his theatrical period involves his understanding of the audience's importance to the professional storyteller. Unlike a number of so-called "great" literary giants—like James Joyce, for example, who bragged about his delight in deliberately making his fiction so obscure that only a select few of his readers could truly understand what he was writing—Barker pays close attention to what his audience thinks. He may challenge his readers to decipher the meaning in his well-crafted literary metaphors and in his elaborate use of levels of text and subtext, but he is never far out of sight of his reader's expectations. Barker employs a degree of sophistication in his work, but he understands the fact that if no one wants to read his stories or see his films, then his message is defeated, lost. For Barker, his audience is perhaps his most important artistic concern.

Along with the theater, the art of illustration has played a considerable role in the development of his writing as well. In an interview conducted with Mike Maddox entitled "Clive Barker: On the Beauty of the Beast," Barker says,

> Well, the artwork's very important to me. Very important to me. It always has been. It was the first art practice that I was really involved in. It certainly preceded writing, as it does for most kids who have some artistic bent, as it's a very simple activity at its base. It's something that for me has a very immediate, almost journalistic appeal. The reporting and setting down of sights that the mind's eye has seen, or is actually still *seeing* in the act of drawing. For me it's a very unpretentious activity [25].

Barker states that he works with his drawings without being under the "commercial pressure" of deadlines, and thus his intent with his illustrations is to "make some kind of diary of some inner landscape" (Maddox 25). Barker's interest in illustration helps explain his fascination with motion pictures, and also with his desire to write well-visualized characters in his fiction. Yet of these three mediums—print, film, and illustration—Barker feels that illustration is the most immediate; he tells Mike Maddox,

> Sometimes it [illustration] helps me to develop the way a character looks, the way a monster is, or *sometimes* there are things that can *only* work as drawings, that really have no literary equivalent. That have no cinematic equivalent as well. It remains to be a very simple activity ... I mean, even a book — I handwrite everything — requires transferring into typescript, from typescript into galleys, and from there to a finished book. But a drawing is a drawing is a drawing. Once you have finished it, there it is [25].

Perhaps this powerful visual side to Clive Barker's fiction and movies accounts for the recent explosion in the comic book medium of Barker's work. A number of comic book interpretations of his stories and his films have been published, and Barker now finds that he enjoys an impressive following of people who came to his efforts through these comic book adaptations. His best-selling fantasy novel *Weaveworld* has been issued as a comic book by Epic Comics, and several of his short stories from his *Books of Blood*, including "Revelations" and "Son of Celluloid," have been re-interpreted in comics form and have been published in beautifully packaged productions by Eclipse Books. A major comics title, *Tapping the Vein*, also published lavishly illustrated versions of Barker's short stories, while several comic book series have evolved from characters that Barker first developed in print or in film — such titles as *Clive Barker's Hellraiser, Clive Barker's Nightbreed, Clive Barker's Nightbreed vs. Rawhead Rex*, all distributed by Epic Comics. Recently, Marvel Comics has released a new superhero comic book series, entitled "Razorline," that is based upon concepts developed by Barker. In the September 1989 issue of a British magazine entitled *Speakeasy*, Barker describes in an interview his adolescent background in the comics. When asked if he was at all familiar with the horror comics tradition, Barker replies that he wasn't, and that his introduction to E.C. Comics came through the movies, like the 1972 film *Tales from the Crypt* ("To Hell and Back" 25). Barker says of the relationship between his childhood and comic books, "I plugged into a great period. My first exposure to Marvel [a comic book publisher] was really the classic Kirby/Lee *Fantastic Four*, which now, looking back on it, still looks first rate. I loved that. I'd probably have been 13 or 14, and there was a small sweetshop in Liverpool which traded comics" ("To Hell and Back" 25).

As Barker has had a tremendous impact upon the horror genre in both print and movies, he also currently influences the direction of horror comic books. When his stories are adapted into comic book format, they give that format a more literary quality. His stories also give comics a slick, sophisticated look. His illustrators and story-line adaptors of his work have seemed to have effectively caught his literary stylistic nuances. Interestingly, Barker's relationship with the comics is circular. He alleges in the "To Hell and Back" interview,

> I think the two major narrative impulses which brought me to the way I write were comics and movies, no doubt about that. I mean in terms

of the sensation value. I do love sensation in narrative, I do love the hook and the twist and the sudden eruptions of tone. You can move from high comedy to low comedy and from low comedy to black violence within a panel in a comic, and the best comics do just that, and that's true of movies too [25].

Hence, in part, from the influence of the comics, Barker has been inspired to write his fiction and make his films, and, in return, from these stories and movies new comic books have been adapted and published. His imaginative work has come full circle to that medium that initially helped to spark his creative impulses.

Interviewer Michael Brown asked Clive Barker how he got into writing, to which Barker answered,

> Writing got into me. Writing is one of several creative processes I'm involved in, and I'm not hugely interested in any of them as processes. What I'm interested in, what I'm fixated on, is the process of imagining and using whatever forum is in front of me at the time—whether it be the screen, the stage, the page or the canvas—as a means to explore this internal territory, to make an account of the dream journey. I discovered writing later than I discovered drawing because when you're a kid it's easier to draw than to write [18-19].

Barker says it wasn't until he was eight or nine years old that he began to "grasp the idea of stories"; he could tell stories orally, but it took him a while longer to write them down. Barker claims his primary motivation in starting to write was to influence people. "Everybody likes to do something they could do well," he suggests; "Just as there were people in my class [as an adolescent] who were better mathematicians or better chemists or better sportspersons than I was, storytelling seemed to be the gift I had" (Brown 19).

Barker contends in the W.C. Stroby interview for *Writer's Digest* that rather than beginning his literary career at the novel level first, then working towards the short story, the fact that he began with the short story form first was for him advantageous. "I think one of the best things that happened in my career," Barker tells Stroby, "was that I had the bad sense—in terms of commercial propositions, but good sense, I think, aesthetically—to begin with short fiction" (25). Barker asserts that if he had an agent during this seminal moment in life, then this agent would have advised him against starting with short stories because nobody would buy them (Stroby 25).

But Clive Barker maintains there was a very practical reason, from his particular point-of-view, to begin his professional literary efforts with short fiction,

> In fact, [writing short fiction] was good for me, because I realized you could actually put a lot of material in 30 pages. And if you're going to write 700 pages, they better be full. You better have an idea which is

going to justify that length, justify the audience reading the thing for that long [Stroby 25].

Working with short stories allowed Barker to master his control of ideas. As essentially an "idea" author, Barker was able to get his literary feet wet at a more manageable level before moving on to the greater task of writing a novel. When asked if he would recommend the short story as a place for budding writers of imaginative fiction to start, Barker replies, "It worked for me. It allowed me to clear the decks of ideas which seemed to work for that length, and to start to study the larger scale stuff later on" (Stroby 25).

Clive Barker identifies in an article entitled "FT Forum: Speaking from the Dark" that one of his early influences was Ray Bradbury. He recognized in Bradbury that author's ability to mix "horrors and wonderments" in his short fiction. He claims that Bradbury is "indisputably a master," though in retrospect, Barker feels that some of Bradbury's passages now appear a bit "overwrought." Yet despite this minor aesthetic limitation, Barker recognizes in Bradbury a giant of the genre as he writes, "his [Bradbury's] work has the courage of poetry, which is so often missing in contemporary dark fantasy. Without it, this kind of storytelling can so easily become a heartless catalogue of atrocities, or simply ludicrous" (6). Barker pays tribute to Ray Bradbury in his *Books of Blood* by pastiching Bradbury's notion of the framing story (the idea of the character as living text) from Bradbury's collection *The Illustrated Man*.

Barker also cites as influences upon his writing William Blake ("He had more on his mind than writing a chilling page-turner, but then so, I suspect, do a lot of explorers of the fantastique"), the anthology edited by Kirby McCauley entitled *Dark Forces* ("a book in which every story is unlike the one preceding; perfect proof that a genre which is often perceived as limiting is, in truth, a continent for the roaming"), and the Bible ("one of the greatest of all source books. The one with the most horrors and miracles, the cruelest ironies, the most hideous revenges") (Barker, "FT Forum" 7–8). Barker identifies as the most significant person to have an impact upon his work Jean Cocteau, "My great hero is Jean Cocteau. Cocteau made movies, wrote books, wrote plays, drew drawings.... The fact is, what's remembered most about Cocteau is a *vision*" (Wiater, *Dark Dreamers* 17).

Effectively utilizing his inspiration in reading McCauley's *Dark Forces* anthology ("This was something of a revelation," Barker tells Douglas Winter; "I had been bound by what I thought were the conventions of the genre. Now I thought, 'The options are wide open. Let's see how far we can press this'") (212) and while working on his theatrical career during the day, Clive Barker wrote the first three volumes of the *Books of Blood* at night and on the weekends. It took him only eighteen months to complete these three books, and they were sold to the second publisher—Sphere Books—to which they were submitted. Originally, Barker intended the *Books of Blood* to have been released as a single edition, but Sphere published the anthology in three volumes in 1984. Because of their success, three more volumes were contracted for and were published in 1985. Though it took Barker until between 1985 and 1986 to see the first three *Books of Blood* published in the United States, his reputation preceded him and he was, as Winter says, "something of a legend in American horror fandom, well before the *Books of Blood* were published here" (212).

Barker began writing the *Books of Blood* when he was about twenty-eight or twenty-nine years old. He informs interviewers Richard Lupoff and Richard Wolinsky about this period in his life, "I was writing plays and I was painting. That was what I was doing and then I turned to all this relatively late. I got published, I guess, when I was thirty-one" (12). From the start, Barker had decided to use the *Books of Blood*, in total, as a vehicle to publish a wide variety of tales, from horror to comedy. He originally took this idea to his then theatrical agent, and was told that short stories are difficult to sell. Barker says to Lupoff and Wolinsky, "I only had five of them [stories] at this point. I had written these first five in a state of blissful ignorance. It was actually quite useful because I had gone on and just done it" (12). Barker's agent first took the idea to Gollancz, but they were offended by the subject matter in the stories. "Zombies were involved in sexual acts," Barker tells Lupoff and Wolinsky, referring to the publisher's dislike of the stories, "It was just not cool" (13). His agent then took the stories to Sphere Books, and they loved them, saying that they would publish all that Barker had available. When he informed them that the five tales were all that he had written so far, Sphere asked him for more. "So, I wrote, I guess, another ten," Barker states to Lupoff and Wolinsky, "and they became the first three *Books of Blood*. I was really walking into walls right, left and center. I knew nothing about this stuff. It was just fun" (13).

Barker's editor at Sphere Books who encouraged him with the development of his *Books of Blood* was Barbara Boote. He relates an interesting episode that involved her reaction to one of the stories in the *Books of Blood*, an episode that reveals just how "cutting edge" Barker's work was at the time. Barker alleges that Barbara's support of his efforts was great because she never said "no" to him, except once. She, along with Barker's agent, told him not to publish "In the Hills, the Cities," because of its controversial use of homosexual protagonists. Barker persevered in his decision to include the story in the *Books of Blood*, and later "In the Hills, the Cities" won him the British Fantasy Award. Barker remarks to Lupoff and Wolinsky about his acceptance of the award,

> And she [Barbara Boote] was at the award ceremony, as was my agent who also said that I should never publish this story. That was very gratifying. When I made my little speech having received the award, I actually said, "There are two people in this room, and I'm not going to name

them, who told me I should never publish this story." This, I think, is important that one always remember that however useful agents and editors are and, of course, they are useful, finally your imagination knows best [13].

Considering Barker's recent commercial successes in both writing bestselling novels and in producing/directing motion pictures, it is easy to lose sight of how original, how ground-breaking, Barker's literary endeavors were in the mid-1980s. Not only did he defy tradition in the publishing world by starting his career with the anthology format (considered a terrible mistake in the business of writing for a living), he included in that three-volume anthology a collection of stories that had the potential of offending everybody. Barker, however, made it all work, and the result is a literary achievement unmatched today within or without the genre. His *Books of Blood* fiction became an opportunity for him to praise or criticize people and society. These stories demolished our preconceived notions about the boundaries of the horror genre, and they demonstrated a diversity of ideas and concepts that are dazzling in their inventiveness and originality. But perhaps the single greatest tribute afforded to Barker's *Books of Blood* is how they have influenced other talented authors' writings. From Stephen King to the new "splatterpunk" generation, Barker has become a powerful influence. He has written about otherwise taboo areas, like sexual imagery, and has shown how useful this material can be in delivering a literary narrative. Along with H.P. Lovecraft and Stephen King, Clive Barker has become one of the most important practitioners of the horror tale in the twentieth century. And this reputation is based solely upon his short fiction. He is equally as impressive in his novel writing and movie making.

Volumes *Four* through *Six* of the *Books of Blood* were published in the United States under different titles. They include *The Inhuman Condition* (Poseidon Press, 1986), *In the Flesh* (Poseidon Press, 1986), and *Cabal* (Poseidon Press, 1985, 1988). The American edition of *Cabal* featured the short novel of the same name, published along with the contents of the *Books of Blood, Volume Six*. However, the American edition of this book did not publish the concluding framing story, entitled "The Book of Blood (A Postscript): On Jerusalem Street," the tale that closed Barker's six-volume anthology in its British edition.

Clive Barker says in an interview in the October 1988, issue of *Fangoria* magazine that since the publication of the *Books of Blood*, a great deal has changed for him,

> The first volume of *Books of Blood* was published just over four years ago [from 1988], and since then my life has changed out of all of proportion... The one solid place in the turmoil is the imagination. The one thing I can hold on to is getting up in the morning to do the job of

imagining. It is the most exciting experience I know. That makes it easy to turn down big Hollywood movies for tremendous amounts of money, which is something my agent can't understand [Nutman, "If You Knew" 67].

Barker has recently applied this marvelous sense of imagination to his novel writing. Barker tells his interviewer for *Amazing Heroes* magazine, Mike Maddox, that the transition from short story to novel was an easy one for him. Barker claims that he is an "inclusionist," and because of this trait he enjoys working with the novel since the longer form allows him to include a number of concepts into his writing. Barker states,

> I think it's desire on my part, and I think that popularist art is for the most part inclusionist rather than exclusionist. I wrote in volumes, and viewed them as collections. Into those volumes I put every damn thing that my imagination at that time could whip up. With the novels, the same thing is true. One of the things that the critics are rather unkind about is that very fact. I make or offer no apologies for it. I love the ability a novel provides, to be able to do that [31].

After his initial success with his first *Books of Blood* trio, Clive Barker turned his hand to writing his first novel, *The Damnation Game* (1985). Stephen Jones reports in his article entitled "Clive Barker: Anarchic Prince of Horror" that *The Damnation Game* was given a £32,000 promotion by Sphere Books for its paperback publication in England. Jones also quotes Barker as commenting that *The Damnation Game* is a reworking of the Faust legend (15). Jones cites Barker as saying that he now enjoys working with novels more than short stories because the latter is "a very testing format...one that is difficult to write" (16). Barker's next novel, *Weaveworld* (1987), followed in order of publication his second trio of the *Books of Blood*. *Weaveworld* was the first of Clive Barker's epic fantasy novels. Its 250,000 word narrative recounts the story of a fairy tale world woven into the threads of a magical carpet. It's basically the story of banality's invasion of imagination, and Barker features within the novel's plot a host of major and minor supporting characters, as well as a narrative that examines an apocalyptic confrontation between good (imagination and miracle) and evil (the destructive force of nihilism). Barker continues his interest in apocalyptic imagery (as well as in the subtext lurking behind the surface appearance of reality) in *The Great and Secret Show* (1989). With this novel (as in his others), thematic issues developed earlier in his plays and short fiction are again dealt with (albeit in more detailed fashion). Images from films, books, puzzles, and the theater predominate in *The Great and Secret Show*, and all these images are incorporated as part of the author's philosophical argument about the power of imagination (Hoppenstand 260). *The Great and Secret Show* is the first volume of a projected series of novels that will each feature an investigation into the efficacy of a power that Barker calls "The Art," a power that reveals the source of miracles. But the most ambitious of Barker's novels is *Imajica* (1991). Basically, amidst its complex plot and huge cast of characters, *Imajica* is a feminist examination into the destructive power of a male-dominated society, and like both *Weaveworld* and *The Great and Secret Show*, it emphasizes a setting framed by several different layers of dimensional reality (identified in *Imajica* as the Five Dominions) and by an elaborate discussion of how imagination functions (as metaphor and as magical power). Barker calls his most recent novel, *The Thief of Always: A Fable* (1992), a children's book. It does feature an adolescent protagonist named Harvey Swick, and the bare bones of the novel's plot do allow it a certain measure of accessibility to younger readers, but the Faustian theme of story (similar in some ways to his *The Damnation Game*), as well as the narrative's sense of dark introspection, make it more appropriate for the adult who is young at heart.

Barker says to interviewer Stanley Wiater that the thing he's truly interested in with his novels is the notion of what exists "beyond" us. He tells Wiater,

> You know, writing about the unholy is one way to write about what's sacred. A major slice of me is preoccupied with the transcendental. I have a review here in England for *The Great and Secret Show* titled "The World Beyond: A User's Manual." And I thought, "Well, that's all right!" I like that! I like the idea that this is a fiction which does address, in a very straightforward way, what's going on beyond. In fact, if I wanted to use one phrase to describe the kind of fiction that I'm writing: "These are user's manuals for the world beyond," I wouldn't mind that at all! [Wiater, *Dark Dreamers* 14].

Barker goes on to tell Wiater that he dislikes hearing people attack the word "escapism": "I'm *hugely* preoccupied with the idea of claiming *fantastique* back from the critics and the academics who would dismiss it as being escapist and useless," Barker contends (14). Though his novels possess a thematic unity, Barker likes to perceive them as being distinct from one another,

> I'm always trying very hard to find a new hole to pop out of. New areas to work in. The four novels that I've written have been as different from each other as is possible within the realms of the *fantastique*... What I *don't* want to do is repeat myself. I finished up on the *Books of Blood* feeling that I had discharged my duty to short fiction as best I could. I don't want to go back over old ground. I owe that to my audience, I owe that to myself, to my craft. My craft, as I said before, is my major way of explaining myself *to* myself [Wiater, *Dark Dreamers* 12].

However, despite Barker's statement above that expresses his distaste for repetition, he does connect major themes that run from his plays to his short fiction to his novels and ultimately to his films. What Barker is addressing in this quote is a condemnation of formula, not artistic unity. Throughout his

Books of Blood (and elsewhere in his creative efforts), he deflates formula. Or if he uses it in his stories, he does this in order to turn formula on its ear, to mock its predictability. Clive Barker's novels function as a capstone to his shorter work. They flesh out and expand upon a number of concepts that Barker first investigates in his *Books of Blood* stories. His novels allow him the room to move around with his characters, to explore their inner minds as well as their outer actions. His novels also permit Barker to provide philosophical asides in his writing. They grant him the opportunity (that his short fiction doesn't) of fully discussing with his reader the sophisticated nature of life's meaning, of life's subtext — those things that make the process of living worth the effort, like love and imagination and miracle. So there is unity in Barker's literary diversity, a wholeness to his vision that is most readily obvious in his novels.

Barker has published two short novels, *The Hellbound Heart* (1986) and *Cabal* (1988), both of which have been translated successfully into motion pictures entitled *Hellraiser* and *Nightbreed* respectively. Clive Barker's work in the cinema is as distinguished as is his fiction. To date, Barker has written several screenplays; his credits include writing the screenplays for the films *Underworld* (1985), *Rawhead Rex* (1986), *Hellraiser* (1987), and *Nightbreed* (1990). He has directed two movies, *Hellraiser* and *Nightbreed*, and has produced several films as well, such as *Hellbound: Hellraiser II* (1988) and *Hellraiser III: Hell on Earth* (1992). In addition, Barker produced the film *Candyman* (1992) — written and directed by Bernard Rose — which is based on his story "The Forbidden" from his *Books of Blood, Volume Five*.

Barker was disappointed with how his screenplays for *Underworld* and *Rawhead Rex* were produced, and thus it was a natural extension for him to assume a greater control of his efforts in film. The immediate result was *Hellraiser*. *Hellraiser* is both a story of dark transcendentalism (about a man's quest to find new avenues of pleasure but who instead finds a world of endless torture) and a fairy tale (resplendent with a wicked step-mother). Barker served as the executive producer for the sequel, entitled *Hellbound: Hellraiser II*. Barker says of this sequel,

> I took a hands-off approach to *Hellbound*, because I felt it was Peter Atkins and Tony's [Tony Randel's] movie. It was up to them to do with it what they would. But while watching them, I thought, "I wouldn't mind a slice of this." I wouldn't mind having the opportunity to use full studio facilities, instead of an abandoned house in North London and a small sound stage, which is how I made *Hellraiser*. Watching Tony gave me a focus on the kind of creative control a studio environment can give you, the range of lighting, floating walls, and the ability to physically rearrange things to accommodate the camera. I couldn't do that with *Hellraiser*. The last three years have been a great education, film-wise [Nutman, "Bring" 32].

And thus, the desire to write and direct a studio environment movie led Barker to his work with *Nightbreed*. *Nightbreed* essentially is the story of an epic conflict between nineteenth-century and twentieth-century evil. A mortal protagonist named Boone transforms into an immortal monster, and then acts as a Messiah figure who attempts to protect the sympathetic "Nightbreed" (or ancient, supernatural shape-shifters) from the persecution of the twentieth-century right-wing police state, and of a maniacal serial killer. Barker discusses the making of *Nightbreed*,

> We used some real locations on *Nightbreed*, but not many. Over 80 percent of the film is studio-based. We used five soundstages at Pinewood Studios. Some of those sets are enormous, and we've consequently had some tremendous special effects problems [Nutman, "Bring" 32].

Barker feels that *Nightbreed*, though a bigger budgeted film than *Hellraiser*, is more intimate. He says, "It has a kind of intimacy which I think is a hallmark of what I do on the page, and will remain the hallmark of what I do on celluloid. It's very much a character piece, a real actors' film" (Nutman, "Bring" 32).

Discussing his involvement in the making of motion pictures, Barker states in an interview with Philip Nutman published in the October 1989, issue of *Fangoria* magazine that his directorial debut, *Hellraiser*, was a "showreel," that it was intended to show people in the industry that for a small amount of money he could write and direct a movie, turning that investment into a profit (Nutman, "Bring" 32). *Nightbreed*, for Barker, was quite a leap. He tells Philip Nutman, "'*Nightbreed* now has an $11 million budget. For me, the jump from a $2 million movie [*Hellraiser*] to an $11 million movie is a big one. What we have here is a big, complicated project. The *Star Wars* of horror movies is what we promised, and that is what we're trying..." (Nutman, "Bring" 31). In the two films that Barker wrote and directed, *Hellraiser* and *Nightbreed*, he reversed the traditions of standard horror movie fare. And this presented some trouble for him with *Nightbreed*. Barker suggests to interviewer Stanley Wiater,

> I remember how the studio executives saw the finished film [of *Nightbreed*] and said, "How do we sell this thing—the monsters are the good guys!" [Groans.] The problems started to appear then. But these people have such a low opinion of you and me—the audiences for these kinds of movies—that they are intellectually (and I use the term loosely) condescending to us. That somehow we just *don't care* if a horror film is good or bad; we don't have any critical facilities one way or the other [Wiater, *Dark Visions* 12].

Barker goes on to say that studio executives view horror films as being little better than porno flicks. He claims that studios don't want to take any chances with their investments, so they want to be the second—and not the first — to do something. Barker argues that producers' attitudes about the horror film today reflect the film critics' attitudes about horror film twenty-five years ago; they see it as trash, but commercial trash (Wiater, *Dark Visions* 12). However, Barker views his efforts in film making as being worth the effort, in spite of the industry's many drawbacks. He hopes that in the future, there will be more crossing of genre boundaries in the making of horror movies, that this cross-fertilization (as illustrated in the film *Alien*, which was a cross between the horror and the science-fiction film) will be healthy for the horror genre. Barker dislikes the simple, gut-level, knee-jerk response of many recent horror movies, and thinks that an infusion of new blood (and new ideas) is not only a good thing, but a much needed thing (Wiater, *Dark Visions* 13-14).

Clive Barker makes an important distinction between the book and the movie. Answering Wiater's question about how important it is for Barker to see his books filmed, Barker replies,

> ...if no other movie was ever made of my work, it would not break my heart. The book is the ultimate statement that I can make; it's the most intimate, the most confessional. Movies are fun because you can remake the story. But the book is not the movie, and the movie is not the book. The book is God — in the beginning was the Word, and the Word means the author. I've been driven more crazy by more people directing two movies than I have writing eleven books [15].

Barker's statement is not surprising when considering how important text and textual imagery are to his writings. As mentioned a number of times elsewhere in this study, Clive Barker is a very literary author. He enjoys working with words and producing things with words. His films even are literary. They rely upon the use of metaphor and upon narrative conventions that are perhaps more comfortable in print than they are on the screen. For this reason, Barker's work in the cinema is controversial. His innovations are not only disturbing to the studio heads, but also to many in the film audience. A number of people go to see a film in order to have their expectations met, and when the screenwriter/director plays around with those expectations, it oftentimes makes the audience nervous. Yet Barker continues to persist in making wonderfully imaginative, strikingly innovative movies. Only time will tell if audiences can catch up with Barker's pathfinding artistic vision, or if the movie industry (which is always so intolerant of innovation) will continue to support his work.

Clive Barker and His Literary Agenda

Like many commercially successful authors, Clive Barker has the ability to work hard, to work productively, and to be flexible at the same time. He tells interviewer Philip Nutman, "I find that the more I do, the more I *can* do. It comes down to organization. I set myself a certain word length to write per day when I'm working on a novel" ("If You Knew" 67). Stephen Jones reports that Barker sets for himself a "strict regime" when he writes. Jones says that Barker usually begins his work day (that is, after he has fleshed out his plot and character breakdowns) at 8:00 A.M. and he writes a minimum of 2,000 words each day. He also writes several drafts of each of his stories (16). Barker states, "Writing comes very easily to me...although ideas don't. I have a great many ideas, but I discard a lot of them" (Jones 16).

Barker maintains that, unlike moviemaking (where he interacts with many people), writing for him is a "solitary business." He claims that for the fifteen to eighteen months that it took him to write his novel *Imajica* he had little contact with others (Lackey 11). In his interview with W.C. Stroby, Barker suggests that writing "is still the prime thing...I may take an hour or two off in the middle of the day, but I'll avoid meeting with people or seeing people during the day. I'll avoid business lunches. I'll avoid anything which is going to take me away from the desk for any length of time." (23)

Barker feels that even though he is known as an "idea" author, he is most concerned in his writing with his characters. He mentions to Stroby,

> ...regarding characters, my feeling is this: Get [the reader] to accept one thing, one weirdness, and then the rest of it must follow realistically. I try not to lie about psychology. I don't think I'm mawkish in my writing. I don't think I'm overly sentimental. I try and be emotionally honest within a framework which has one thing askew [23].

Thus, even though Clive Barker deals with fantastic plots and employs a wild sense of imagination in his fiction, he considers himself a realist in character development. He attempts to create a sense of verisimilitude from the character outwards, subsequently engendering from his readers a willing suspension of disbelief through a psychological involvement with these characters.

Barker sees two important things that he must accomplish in his writing if it is to be successful. The first is that the author has to believe in his or her characters, that the author has to get under the skins of the characters and fully understand their motivations and responses to bizarre situations if that author has any hope of convincing the reader to believe in the characters as well. The second thing Barker wants to accomplish is to create "parallel situations," or narrative situations in his fantasy writings that parallel real-life experiences (Stroby 24). Barker asserts, "I don't know anybody who's visited a city of the dead; I don't know anybody who knows a world hidden in a carpet. But I do know of people who have secret lives. So I will look for parallel situations to those of which I'm writing" (Stroby 24).

For Clive Barker, it's important to firmly base his imaginative writings in reality. He claims that settings from both *The Great and Secret Show* and *Weaveworld* actually exist. Barker tells interviewer W.C. Stroby,

> Solid research gives you a great place to move off from. It allows you a springboard, if you like, out into the fantastical. And also sometimes it throws up extraordinary things that you could never have guessed. Going to a prison for a couple of days gave me more insight than I could have imagined [24].

Several of Barker's more intriguing stories feature either a protagonist who comes from a prison background (e.g. Marty Strauss from *The Damnation Game*) or a narrative with a prison setting (e.g. the Pentonville prison from "In the Flesh"), thus reinforcing Barker's argument for the importance of solid research in his writing. Barker says that though it's "wonderful" to draw inspiration from others' work, it's even of greater importance to make sure that your own creativity is rooted more in reality than in the influence of those others. Barker argues that many film makers today fall into this trap; they base their films more upon previous films than they do upon their own original sense of imagination (Stroby 24). Restating the importance of reality in his fantasy, Barker alleges,

> You've got to get drunk and be in danger once in a while. You've got to fall in love, you've got to be hurt—this is an old story but it's exactly true. It's not just about prisons, and it's not just about autopsies. It's about experiencing stuff. It's about writing out of your pain, writing out of your own doubt, writing out of your own anger [Stroby 24].

In essence, then, Clive Barker blends the fantastic with the realistic in order to write fiction that both relates to the human condition and extols the virtues of imagination, of an examined life that recognizes the importance of miracles and the importance of honest emotion. To achieve imagination, Barker suggests to us that knowledge of the street and knowledge of the heart are prerequisites, from both his own artistic viewpoint as well as his reader's. Without the one, the other is a fake; without real life experiences, imaginative magic in fiction is mere fool's gold.

Perhaps the two most controversial aspects of Barker's fiction are his use of violence and sex. Regarding the latter, Barker claims the topic is important to him, though he maintains that the horror genre in general doesn't deal well with the subject. Barker tells Stanley Wiater in the *Dark Dreamers* interview,

> Sex in horror fiction and movies doesn't tend to be the subject of the work as much as it is light relief between the darker goings-on. Or maybe you're just setting up the characters to be murdered in their beds, which again doesn't seem terribly interesting. But sex figures greatly in our sense of ourselves, and in our sense of how we physically appear in the world. Sex affects what our bodies do, how they change, how vulnerable

they are. It affects our sense of personal ambition, and how much we want to achieve in terms of our sexual lives [13-14].

Barker goes on to say that sex also influences our nightmares, and in terms of our response to literature, it influences what we think is scary. He argues that with sex, people relinquish control of themselves, and this matches the similar feeling in horror fiction that produces *the scare*, the feeling that one is not in control, or is losing control. Barker says to Wiater,

> Sexual fever is essentially a place where reason is suspended. One of the things I love about art is you can employ reason and emotions simultaneously. The best fiction pricks the emotions: makes you laugh, cry. Be scared. And at the same time it stimulates the intellect [*Dark Dreamer*, 14].

Barker writes in "An Introduction: The Bare Bones," that sex has all too often been the domain of "the sentimentalist or the pornographer," and has all too infrequently been the domain of the "visionary" (391). For Barker, sex is a transforming act because it sharpens our senses and narrows our focus, thus enhancing our perceptions. Barker claims that, traditionally, horror fiction has involved aspects of "transformation, obsession and perception," and that sex should then be the "perfect stuff" for the genre. Horror fiction, like sex, reminds us that pleasure is lodged within the corrupt, that ecstasy is intermingled with the vulgar (Barker "An Introduction" 391).

Elaborating further upon the relationship between horror fiction and sex, Barker suggests in his interview with Douglas E. Winter, "Sex is about a little madness—how often is horror about madness? Sex is about a little death—how often is horror about death? It's about the body—how often is horror about the body?" (216). Clive Barker seems to perceive sex as something other than thematic device; he also sees it as a form of political statement. In the Winter interview, Barker discusses his dislike of censorship. In particular, he delineates how sexual taboo affects art (214-215). Barker's occasional use of graphic sex (along with his occasional use of graphic violence) is employed primarily to defy social mores, to shock us while at the same time challenging us. Barker wants us to understand that censorship is the true obscenity, and he writes his fiction as a protest against it. If the form of Barker's writing challenges traditional formulas, then the content of his writing also challenges society's level of intolerance.

Returning to the subject of Barker's use of violence in his fiction—which is the other controversial aspect of his writings—Clive Barker explains in the Winter interview,

> Horror fiction without violence doesn't do a great deal for me. I think that death and wounding need to be in the air. You've got to get the reader on this ghost train ride, and there's got to be something vile at the end of it, or else why aren't you on the roller coaster instead? And

> I like to be able to deliver the vileness. There's never going to be any evasion. Whether it be sexual subject matter, whether it be violence, I'm going to show it as best I can [212–213].

Several times in his fiction Barker employs the "ghost train" image (most notably in his novel *The Great and Secret Show*), and it's interesting that Barker draws an indirect comparison between his use of violence in his fiction and a roller coaster ride. An important (though not the crucial) aspect of violence for Barker is the element of thrill, the visceral rush, the roller coaster ride (or more correctly, the ghost train ride) that excites us (for it is a non-threatening thrill). Violence, as Barker uses it in his stories, is a taste of death, a voyeuristic glimpse of the great Mystery, and he intends for it to stimulate, rather than frighten, his audience. Barker says to Winter, "My stories are not written primarily to terrify, but to *excite*. I think of them as adrenaline stories—let's see how bad things can get and still want to go on and read, still want to turn the page to the next story" (217).

Yet despite Barker's sometimes liberal use of violence in his writing, he dislikes his work being labeled as "splatterpunk." Described in part by Paul M. Sammon in his article entitled "Outlaws," splatterpunk as a genre of fiction involves stories that are "inescapably confrontational ... visceral in the extreme, [containing] explicit sex and violence, centered on grotesque set pieces" (275). Several of the more famous (or infamous) literary practitioners of splatterpunk include John Skipp, Craig Spector, and David J. Schow. Barker asserts in an interview conducted by Tim Caldwell that he thinks the splatterpunk distinction to be contrived and artificial, made by those who simply like to argue semantics. He avows that he finds aesthetic moments ("wonderful writing, subtle, intelligent writing") in the so-called splatterpunk canon, as well as "hardcore writing" in the efforts of Charles Grant (a prolific author of horror fiction and a notorious critic of over-use of violence in the genre in general, and of splatterpunk specifically). Barker tells Caldwell,

> I do think that there is a different vision of horror, and this has nothing to do with quiet vs. loud, or splatter punk vs. subtle, it has to do with why we are writing horror in the first place. ... I am writing horror and making horror movies to genuinely disturb people. And I think there is a distinction. I don't think it's a splatter punk-quiet distinction. I think it's a distinction about whether you're making something which genuinely seeks to do something to somebody. Subvert them, throw over their ideas about the status quo, throw over their ideas about sexuality, throw over their ideas about death. ... Or whether, on the other hand, you just want to give people 250 pages of status quo reinforcing moral ideals, good versus evil or that kind of simplistic crap ... I don't want to do that [19].

Barker's rejection of Sammon's (and others') classification of his work as splatterpunk (no doubt engendered, in part, by Barker's reliance upon graphic violence) is because of his general dislike for genre tags as a whole. Throughout the *Books of Blood*, Clive Barker does his best to defy literary traditions, to overturn the horror fiction applecart, to deflate rigid formulas and to mock artistic conventions. Barker objects to over-simplification of his work, and this objection includes his being called a "splatterpunk" author.

Answering a question posed by Stanley Wiater in *Dark Dreamers*, Barker asserts that his early reputation was made on his "extremely visceral stories" like "The Midnight Meat Train" from the *Books of Blood*. But his interest in violence, he argues, is but a small portion of his work. He admits that some of his fiction indulges in the violent (and in *grand guignol*). But he also claims he is "interested in the transcendental and the allegorical, and the fiction of fairy tales" (Wiater, *Dark Dreamers* 15). Clive Barker would rather his stories in the *Books of Blood* be viewed as dangerous instead of gross. He argues that the five tales in his collection *The Inhuman Condition* (*Books of Blood, Volume Four*) are not nearly as gory as those in the first three volumes of the *Books of Blood*. Barker observes,

> And in Book Three, *Human Remains*, which is the story about the hustler who has the doppelgangers, no blood is let in that from beginning to end. *The Yattering and Jack*, no blood is let, or *Son of Celluloid*. When you begin to look at them, I have only three or four notorious stories... ["British Invasion" 48].

Rather than grossing people out, Barker says that his greatest wish is to disturb people. And he adds that the reason why his fiction is so popular is because people want to be disturbed. Barker suggests there is no more use of violence in his writing than what's to be found in the work of Stephen King, Peter Straub, or Ramsey Campbell. "Maybe when the acts of violence do happen," Barker remarks, "I describe them with a little bit more gusto. But that's just a little peccadillo of mine" ("British Invasion" 50).

In addition to his dislike of the splatterpunk tag, Clive Barker also feels a bit uncomfortable with the term *horror fiction*. He argues in the October 1988 issue of *Fangoria* that the basic problem with the genre lies with the publishers. He claims they take the whole of imaginative fiction and then artificially divide it up for their own purposes. He cites as an example of this problem Stephen King's situation. Some of what King writes is science fiction, yet his work is identified as horror fiction and subsequently pigeonholed. Barker adds that some science fiction authors employ strong elements of fantasy in their writing, but they are still labeled as science fiction authors, while some fantasy novels contain powerful horrific elements, but they are still called fantasy. Barker challenges easy genre classification of his work by calling what he writes "imaginative dark fiction." He states, "[My fiction]...is graphic, visceral fiction, by turns also erotic and comical. It is certainly horrific, but also

also fantastical most of the time, so one must be very careful about the terminology" (Nutman, "If You Knew" 28-29).

However, when cornered about the appeal of the horror story (no matter how it is categorized — correctly or incorrectly — by publishers), Clive Barker strongly defends the artistic validity of the genre. He tells Douglas Winter in *Faces of Fear,*

> We populists are made to feel—this is particularly true of horror enthusiasts—that we have to apologize for our taste. How many times have you been at dinner parties where people say, "You *like* that stuff?" I used to go into a whole routine. I'd say, "Look, this stuff has a very good pedigree. Horror is talking about the deepest concerns of the human condition." And I would beat people into submission, not because they agreed with my argument, but because they wanted me to shut up. Finally I thought, "Sod that. I *like* this stuff. If they feel so uptight they can't admit they like a good scare, so be it. That's their problem; it's not mine" [219].

Of course, Barker's defense of horror fiction at a larger level is a defense of popular fiction as a whole. He considers himself to be a "populist," which is an interesting stance when reviewing his sophisticated treatment of the horror story. Clive Barker does not see a distinction between the popular and the elite. He views the entirety of imaginative fiction as belonging to a single spectrum, a spectrum that connects to both the finest and the worst that fiction has to offer. Barker's ability to roam comfortably in both artistic realms, the popular and the elite, is a testimony to his versatility as a writer and a tribute to his sense of aesthetic tolerance.

Instead of thinking in popular versus elitist terms, Barker thinks in a general thematic fashion. For example, in his interview with Stanley Wiater for *Dark Dreamers*, Barker expresses his dislike for "naturalistic fiction." He views "imagination" as a thematic opposite to naturalism, and thus he sees his artistic mission as providing his audience a trip through imagination. Barker suggests, "Were I to write the male menopause novel [his example of naturalistic fiction] — when I reach that age — I would presumably be addressing it to only those people who were actually having a male menopause. Which does not seem to me to be a hugely interesting process" (13). What *does* seem like an "interesting process" to Barker is the Jungian subconscious nature of the horror tale. His thematic stance includes an appreciation of the archetypal power of the genre. Regarding his use of the supernatural in a number of his stories, Barker says,

> I don't believe in ghosts or any of that stuff. I use it as metaphor. I use it as a way to express the deeper things that are going on inside us as human beings. I don't believe in the absolute physical truth of these things; I believe in something much more important. Their absolute psychic truth ["British Invasion" 45].

One argument for H.P. Lovecraft's great success in writing frightening stories is that he never actually believed in the supernatural creatures he wrote about. He could then, with a rationalist's eye, craft tales calculated to make his reader shiver. Clive Barker assumes the same stance, though for a slightly different reason. His rational disbelief in the supernatural allows him a degree of objectivity in his construction of the supernatural as metaphor and horror as literary subtext of the human condition. His artistic agenda is stronger than is his emotional agenda, and he thus perceives the horror story more as a means of philosophical discourse than as over-simplified, gut-level, cheap thrill-for-thrill's-sake fluff.

CHAPTER TWO

Highways of the Dead: *Clive Barker's Books of Blood, Volume One*

"The Book of Blood"

Clive Barker uses "The Book of Blood" as an introductory tale for the similarly titled six-volume collection of stories, the *Books of Blood*. Simon McNeal, the boy who becomes a literal text of the dead, is employed as a framing device much the same way that Ray Bradbury utilizes the "Illustrated Man" carnival freak character to introduce the short stories in *The Illustrated Man* anthology. Thus, the tales in the *Books of Blood* are adventures within adventures, texts within texts. This framing device and Barker's story, which is a narrative extension of this single plot motif, foreshadow the author's interest in the complexity of subtextual symbolism.

In "The Book of Blood," one of the thematic symbols which Barker will use a number of times in his later work is vision. Simon McNeal presents a false picture to those around him. He fools even the experts, like Dr. Mary Florescu, who think he actually communicates with the dead. McNeal's own vision is limited, since he fails to see his doom until it is too late. Only Florescu's vision prevails. As her senses transform to match the entrance of the dead into the mortal sphere, she sees things far beyond the mere physical plane. Ultimately, McNeal's and Florescu's visual contact with each other at the end of the story — the communication established between two lovers by sight alone — functions to dispel the power of the dead.

But vision by itself is meaningless unless the viewer is compelled to use imagination in conjunction with sight. One must understand what one is seeing, and Florescu is successful at accomplishing this leap of cognition, of understanding the "systems within systems" that comprise the nature of existence. Barker's protagonists tend to be transcendentalists. They are not only able to perceive what lurks behind surface appearances, being able to translate the subtext of reality as Florescu translates the hieroglyphics on McNeal's body, they are better able to comprehend the meaning of things. Those not able to use their imagination are destroyed by their limitations. Fuller, for example, is destroyed when he views the landscape of the dead, because his imagination is more confined than Florescu's.

Thus, "The Book of Blood," as a reflection in miniature of the six-volume anthology, is a work of the imagination that values imagination. In Barker's literary universe, the worst sort of evil is reflected in characters who refuse to examine their lives meaningfully. True evil, for the author, is the banality of the commonplace. Barker establishes a multi-layered concept in his work for his readers, where supernatural evil is relative, and perhaps even pitiful or admirable; however, the evil of nightmares is infinitely more valued than the mundane, by virtue of the use of imagination in the creation of those nightmares.

Another theme Barker later uses effectively in his imaginative writings is gambling. Simon McNeal thinks he is playing a game at the beginning of the story, and indeed Barker employs the language of games and gaming throughout "The Book of Blood." But playing games can be dangerous in Barker's fiction. McNeal plays his game, and must pay a horrible price when the game is over.

Clive Barker is able to use sexual themes and imagery efficaciously in his writings, and he is one of the few authors working with the horror genre able to accomplish this feat effectively. For example, in "The Book of Blood" the author describes McNeal's narcissistic fascination with his genitals at the beginning of the story, which reflects his self-centered view of life. Florescu's repressed sexuality is exploited by the dead in order to establish a beachhead at "Number 65, Tollington Place." However, once Florescu comes to grip with her sexual desires, once she establishes her sexual identity, she is able to dismiss the dead's intrusion into her world. By recognizing her love for McNeal she defeats death.

Florescu also serves to foreshadow the frequent use of the strong female protagonist elsewhere in Barker's fiction. Florescu, though fooled by McNeal's tricks initially, nonetheless evolves a powerful identity—as well as a powerful imagination—as the story progresses. She is able to defeat the forces of death, and serves as a symbol for the procreative energy of love.

Which brings us to an important issue in Barker's work. Often, Clive Barker is labeled as a gore monger, as someone who caters to the gross-out in order to achieve cheap shock effects. Barker himself disputes this label. He instead says that a great deal of his fiction ends on an optimistic note. He claims that a good portion of what he writes is comedy of an "all's well that ends well" variety, since at the conclusion of a number of his stories lovers are united, or knowledge is gained, or understanding is achieved. Despite McNeal's torture at the hands of the dead, he is merely being repaid for his guile and vanity. Love, in the shape of Florescu, saves him, ultimately dismissing death, and love will continue to protect and nurture him in the future. Lovers are indeed united at the end of "The Book of Blood," and this union promises forbidden knowledge as Florescu translates McNeal's body/text.

When "The Book of Blood" concludes with McNeal himself transmuted into a literal book of blood, this image serves to highlight the author's own fascination with books and text images. Barker is perhaps the most literary of horror fiction writers working today, and even to label him as a horror fiction writer dismisses the intricacy of his art. He develops intellectual complexity in his writing, and is often fascinated with textual puzzles. For Barker, books are an avenue to the wonders of the imagination. McNeal is a living book. His body will provide tales of wonder and horror for Florescu, and for the reader as well, who will see through Florescu's eyes. Books function, for Barker, as a means of escape *into* reality, as a means to contemplate the examined life, and this is Barker's introductory message. The author's love of books is more exhaustively developed in his epic novel, *Weaveworld*.

Clive Barker leaves the reader with a warning in the final passage of "The Book of Blood." This warning goes, "So read. Read and Learn. It's best to be prepared for the worst, after all, and wise to learn to walk before breath runs out." This is sound advice.

"The Midnight Meat Train"

Along with "Rawhead Rex," Clive Barker calls "The Midnight Meat Train" one of his nastier stories in the *Books of Blood*. Throughout his writing, Barker is able to both dazzle us with the beauty of his language and imaginative concepts and shock us with gross-out horror. "The Midnight Meat Train" certainly qualifies as topnotch gross-out, but aside from the obvious shock value of the story, it is a probing satire of big city life and of social and political hypocrisy.

"The Midnight Meat Train" is first and foremost foremost a rite of passage story, illustrating Leon Kaufman's intellectual growth. Before Kaufman's rite of passage, he is naïve and infantile in his views of New York City. After his initiation into the dark secrets of the city's cannibalistic heritage, which, granted, is a physically violent and deforming ritual, Kaufman is nearer to understanding the truth of things. The individual who undergoes the rite of passage, the process of which demonstrates his worth to society, must also undergo some sort of physical test, a test which proves courage and loyalty. After being granted a revealing look into the "depths" of the city's past, Kaufman is physically branded. His tongue is incised and symbolically consumed, and Kaufman's loyalty is thus proven and insured.

Barker mixes sexual metaphors with violence in narrating Kaufman's descent/ascent to truth. At the beginning of the story, New York City is described by the author in a sexually negative fashion. He invokes an extended comparison between the city and a whore. Barker then interjects violent imagery, the various hideous conditions of the victims of the "Subway Slaughter." Barker's graphic descriptions of vivisection highlight a sensual use of language and image. This paradox of sexual revulsion and attractive violence establishes a sense of unease for the reader, which is later utilized by Barker to frame a political statement.

"The Midnight Meat Train" is not just Kaufman's story; it's Mahogany's as well. Mahogany is an interesting, complex character. On the one hand, he is a brutal serial killer. He thinks of people as slabs of meat awaiting his special preparation. Yet, on the other hand, he is aristocratic. He considers himself as being superior, as being above the "common herd." The irony here, of course, is that he is special. He is a servant of the "City fathers," and his unique work is merely a type of dedicated service to the venerated ancestors of New York. Mahogany is neat and thoroughly efficient in his work, and, from his perspective, these traits are quite admirable. However, Mahogany is not without his moral faults, as his overbearing vanity illustrates.

One of Clive Barker's talents as a writer of imaginative literature is his ability to make that which would otherwise be deplorable into something that is admirable. Mahogany is a killer, yet he is a killer with a purpose who takes pride in his efforts. Barker thus encourages his reader to observe the world from a variety of perspectives. There are no simplistic views of right and wrong. Morality is relative (as it perhaps truly is in today's world). Mahogany is not a totally evil person. He's to be admired for his hard work, and pitied when his age overtakes his abilities. Retirement can be a horrible event in anyone's life, and for Mahogany, his retirement is punctuated with the termination of his very life.

Barker also frequently enjoys establishing contrasts in his fiction. For example, Mahogany is described as wearing conservative business dress. He is someone who would not draw any special attention, and yet this surface appearance masks a brutal killer. The author's use of contrasting opposites is employed on a grander scale to describe the hypocrisy of New York's political establishment. The City fathers, who vow to bring the serial killer to justice are the very ones responsible for those murders. The law is manipulated by the corrupt and decadent, and is used not to protect the masses from evil, but to instead insure that evil has a tasty supper.

The face of evil in "The Midnight Meat Train" is lined with age and dotted with liver spots. Barker inventively employs age as the catalyst of villainy in this story. The City fathers represent two images. The first image is that the frailty of these geriatric monsters is offset by their diabolical need for human flesh. Age is thus shown to be a parasite of life, destroying life to sustain what should rightfully be dead and buried. The City fathers *are* buried underground, but like the vampires of nineteenth-century Gothic fiction, they rise at the most inopportune times to feed on the innocent.

Of course, Kaufman is innocent at the start, but his innocence is stripped from him as he takes his train ride into the bowels of New York City. In Barker's literary world, there is no excuse for innocence. Innocence is a denial of reality, whether that reality is good or bad. Innocence leads to death and destruction, or worse. Kaufman's journey into the dark subway caverns is akin to his outward, cognitive journey. Realization and acceptance of knowledge revitalize him; it, in fact, grants him a spiritual rebirth where his "Palace of Delights" fantasy is replaced with a kind of dedication to social service.

The City fathers suggest a second image. These monsters are the founders and earliest civic leaders of one of the world's great metropolises. The contrast Barker uses here is between corruption and respect. The City fathers, despite their grotesque appearance, are perhaps deserving of veneration and respect. They certainly demand it of their servants. But this respect is tempered by its context. Barker is joking a bit with his reader, as he frequently jokes and puns throughout his work.

One senses that the author does not like the Big Apple. He reacts to the crowded, rude, violent nature of the city as do other non-native New Yorkers: with disgust. His response is both poignant and hilarious. The contemporary, pushy, fractious New Yorker is descended from cannibalistic parentage. The City fathers, Barker implies with his extended joke, are merely more exaggerated versions of the typical New York urbanite. Satire is most effective when the foundation of exaggeration is truth.

Barker also satirizes organized religion in "The Midnight Meat Train," having as the center of Mahogany's (and later Kaufman's) worship, flesh-loving geriatrics. The hypocrisy of religion is frequently attacked by Barker throughout his fiction, and his criticism is perceptive. Barker also lampoons the illusion of social status. The "old blood" of New York, the original "Four Hundred" on the social registry, are a really disgusting group. In Barker's view, revered social status does not necessarily equate with social grace. The image Barker presents here is of an inverted status seeker, a reversed social climber who must descend into the dark, damp earth to achieve the top position of power.

The founding fathers, the bluest of the blue bloods, must necessarily feed on life to preserve life, and this is the form of true monstrosity.

"The Yattering and Jack"

Clive Barker is fond of the archetypal story—what he calls the *essential* story. "The Yattering and Jack" is an essential story, one that involves a narrative dealing with a pact made with the Devil. Barker uses a more involved version of the "pact" tale in his later novel, *The Damnation Game*, where a mortal protagonist makes a bargain with a Lucifer-*esque* analogue, an immortal gambler called Mamoulian. The pact variant in "The Yattering and Jack" does not deal directly with the protagonist sealing a bargain with the powers of Hell, but instead the story recounts the dire aftereffects of a broken contract with the Devil on the pact-maker's child. Thus, this essential tale is not about Faust, but about Faust's son, Jack Polo. The *sins of the father* — or more correctly, the mother — are subsequently visited upon the offspring, and innocent people must contend with evil not of their making.

From the perspective of the medieval, Christian worldview, the Devil is identified as the master of lies. Thus, mortals who make deals with the ultimate deceiver subsequently deserve their fate, because any mortal's misguided attempts to know the unknowable, to exercise power gained from a wicked source, creates disharmony within the mechanistic political structure of Heaven and Earth (i.e. true grace is knowing one's place in the hierarchy of the universe). To cheat the landowner, to cheat the king, to cheat the parish father or the pope, these acts undermine the authority of the medieval power-brokers.

So, deception is condemned and identified with the ultimate Christian symbol of evil — the Devil. Carried over into the nineteenth and twentieth centuries, the pact story in fantasy literature features the forces of evil deceiving and manipulating hapless mortals. However, the pact story is somewhat anachronistic. Since the apocalyptic horrors this century of the two World Wars, the Devil's former handshake shenanigans are quaint, the stuff of comedy. Evil in contemporary horror fiction now requires redefinition in order to be effective, and at the forefront of inventive horror fiction is Clive Barker's work. For example, Barker has changed the parameters of the pact archetype in "The Yattering and Jack." He has made evil more human, and consequently more recognizable. The Devil is no longer presented as stereotyped image, but instead is portrayed by Barker as a multi-faceted creature. The Devil has faults, human faults, and is in fact an extension of mortal fallibility as seen in the minor demon from Hell called the Yattering.

Barker frames the narrative point-of-view in "The Yattering and Jack" equally between Jack J. Polo and the Yattering. This then makes both characters sympathetic. We feel sorry for Jack Polo, forced to deal with a problem that wasn't of his making. We also feel sympathy for the demon, who is forced to succeed with a seemingly impossible task.

In delineating Polo's character, that same character which drives the Yattering insane because of its simplemindedness, Barker is drawing upon fairy tale tradition. The "Jack" persona, in narrative folklore, is the divine fool. Slow in his ability to think or reason and often getting in trouble for his lack of wit, Jack nonetheless overcomes life's obstacles because of personal determination and celestial good fortune. By tale's end, Jack the fool reverses his situation, subsequently being transformed from fool to hero. Polo functions in much the same way, and even sports the traditional name: Jack. Thus, with Polo and the Yattering, Barker constructs an effective narrative vehicle that outlines the comedic confrontation between the hell of mortal banality and the Hell of the Bible.

In fact, even before the farcical, yet deadly, test of wills begins, the author shades the monster from Hell in sympathetic hues. The Yattering's first thoughts, we note, are rhetorical pleas and suicidal considerations. Barker satirizes ritualistic, religious litany by having the Yattering offer a prayer to its masters. And as all too frequently happens in mortal bureaucracies, the Yattering's pleas go unfulfilled. What the author is attacking in this scene is that political system which demands complete personal sacrifice, while offering nothing of real value in return. The demon is told to do or die, in that most trite fashion. Barker shows us that Hell swims in red tape, that the damned afterlife is as bad as our own life, in which even monsters often feel alienated. We pity the Yattering because we have experienced the same frustrations, the same meaningless replies to life's questions.

The Yattering's helpless predicament functions to deflate our preconceptions of good and evil; the demon from Hell is not totally rotten. Because we feel sorry for the Yattering, Barker is able to manipulate our sympathy. Thus, Barker's humanization of evil helps to make this highly abstract quality more understandable. Throughout Christian history, religious dogma has typecast God in his Heaven and Satan in his Hell, and such predictability—though understandable in traditional horror fiction—belies a lack of imagination on the part of the twentieth-century writer. As life becomes more complex today, Barker has shown evil to become more elaborate, less typecast. Barker's skill at constructing fully articulated literary personalities enables him to deflate the predictability of horror formulas. With Clive Barker, anything goes.

And "anything goes" can mean humor as well as horror. Certainly "The Yattering and Jack" is one of the more comical tales in the six-volume *Books of Blood*. At times, the story even contains elements of slapstick (exploding cats and spinning Christmas trees and ambulatory turkey dinners). Verbal comedy is evident as well. Polo utilizes the expression, "*Que será, será,*" in much the same way a stand-up comic uses a catch phrase to unify a performance. The expression is employed a number of times by Polo, juxtaposed with frightening events, though each time uttered, the reader senses greater anxiety on Polo's part. When we last read *Que será, será,* it stands as the Yattering's final *bon mot*.

As in his other work where he criticizes the mundane, day-to-day mind-numbing activities of the modern lifestyle, Barker ridicules unimaginative living in this story by placing a supernatural creature (a creature beyond the natural) in a middle-class environment. Imprisoned in this environment the Yattering shows symptoms of going insane. We see from the Yattering's point-of-view that there are things *worse* than Hell. Game shows, newspaper funnies, waiting for the daily mail, and having nothing better to do with one's time, these are the true parasites of existence the Yattering discovers. The bland, middle-class domestic prison is enough to make even a demon from Hell weep and scream like a spoiled child (and boil the water in Polo's aquarium out of spite, poaching the guppies). It's all wonderful situation comedy. Humor is often had at the expense of someone else's misfortune, and the Yattering serves as a kind of bizarre Charlie Chaplin-like antagonist. But, as in the author's other imaginative work, humor functions as something more than cheap laughs.

The Yattering's brief struggle with Freddy III (Polo's third cat), to a lesser degree, furnishes the story's predominant metaphor, which is the game. In several of Barker's literary efforts, like *The Damnation Game* for example, the game frames the plot. A by-product of game-playing is conflict — conflict being the essential ingredient for nearly all fiction. The specific game played between Jack Polo and his demon is chess. The opening moves of the match were made by his mother. Polo inherits the contest mid-game, and the balance of the conflict focuses on the end-game maneuvering. The Yattering executes a ploy and Polo counters. As the narrative unfolds, the reader learns that the Yattering—being the intellectually inferior creature that it is—underestimates Polo, misinterpreting the protagonist's unbearably prosaic attitude toward supernatural events as mere simple-mindedness. Polo totally fools his opponent, and another game image thus presents itself in the reader's mind: poker. Polo, we understand, is the champion poker player—his poker face providing his most effective stratagem. Poker is after all part con-game, part intestinal fortitude, and Jack Polo, being the better con-artist, defeats his demon, hands down, by the end of the game.

Finally, Barker returns to a favorite theme in "The Yattering and Jack"—love. For the author, love is a very powerful force. It alone, perhaps, can confront and defeat the evils of the world, and Hell. Love for his children enables Polo to defeat a power much greater than himself. As the Yattering involves Polo's two daughters in the battle of wills, taking the game to new heights of competition, victory or defeat is tempered, strengthened, honed by the fire of Jack Polo's familial love. The Yattering perceives this love as a mortal weakness, when, in actuality, it's a tremendous strength.

In a number of his stories, Clive Barker has his protagonists undergo a rite of passage. The results of this passage of the soul are increased knowledge, increased recognition of one's place in the universe, and increased moral fortitude. Polo's rite of passage ultimately involves the sacrifice of his possessions. During his final confrontation with the Yattering, as Polo strikes at the spinning household objects, he destroys his favorite books, his china, his lamps, all those items that tie his life down. The author suggests in Polo's actions during this intense moment in the story that spiritual freedom and spiritual power result from one being liberated of one's possessions. Polo knows that objects are unimportant; those things that *are* important in life include health, security, family happiness. Thus for Polo, the sacrifice of his possessions is worth the effort, is perhaps even demanded. At the conclusion of Polo's rite of passage, he finds the strength necessary to trap and defeat Hell.

And as Barker concludes his story with a joke (the *Que será, será* expression), a comedy ending on a comic note, Jack Polo's casual relationship with his demon and his indifference to the Heavenly consequences of his illicit contact with evil place the protagonist within the existential tradition. The Yattering "juggles theology," attempting to use religion as a weapon against a rather humble, loving father (after all, he doesn't wish for Helen of Troy). Polo dismisses theology, desiring instead some small satisfaction in life (and living) rather than in candy-cane promises of an afterlife. Humanity, not the Devil, is responsible for what is right or wrong in the world.

From Barker's literary perspective, Heaven and Hell are basically interchangeable. They're both part of the same scam, the same hustle, the same bad practical joke. They provide an expression for humanity's misdirected desire for the pretend pot of gold. The reader knows that, for Clive Barker, the transcendental protagonist creates moral strength and assumes responsibility for that strength, that the efficacy in the pot of gold is not pretend power but is instead simple love.

"Pig Blood Blues"

In "Pig Blood Blues," Clive Barker again uses prison imagery, as he did in "The Yattering and Jack." The inmates of this particular "prison" are male adolescents. Barker ironically contrasts the name of the prison with its function. Called Tetherdowne, the detention home's name recalls pastoral images: simple farmers, gently rolling hills, grazing sheep. The official bureaucratic title of Tetherdowne we are told is the "Remand Center for Adolescent Offenders," which differs sharply from the imagined pastoral ideal. This Remand Center is profoundly urban, a prison of walls and fences and bars on windows. The only sheep to be found here, the author implies, are those to be fleeced—or sacrificed. Though Tetherdowne is physically located within a rural setting, residing alongside a farm which plays a significant role in the narrative, the atmosphere of the place is socially claustrophobic. A sense of entrapment surrounds the story's characters. Images of traps, of dark religious rituals, and also of animals and pernicious adolescent "Peter Pan" fantasies of perpetual youth reveal some of the significant metaphors in "Pig Blood Blues."

Neil Redman's feeling of alienation at the beginning of the story is reflective of the delinquent boys' sense of alienation at Tetherdowne. Redman caustically identifies the "Law and Order" mentality, a mentality representing the "general mood of the country," as being mere brutality. Redman himself recognizes this sense of brutality in his own past when he was a policeman. Of course, brutality has several different forms in the story. Dr. Leverthal, for example, is much more than what she first appears to be. The reader later discovers her vicious, animalistic nature. Indeed, throughout his work, Barker attacks the representatives of the indifferent political state. Doctors and policemen and priests who should be working for the well-being of society instead act as the monsters of society, doing much more harm than good.

Typically, the Barker antagonist is masked by false surface appearances, as evident with Dr. Leverthal's character, and the protagonist's ability to successfully probe that surface appearance is crucial to survival. The subtext of Leverthal's personality—the core of her being—is the brute. Her professional, certified demeanor disguises the beast in her nature, and though all the characters in the story to a greater or lesser extent are people masquerading as beasts or beasts masquerading as people, Leverthal is a particularly nasty animal because she pretends to be the healer that she isn't. The promise of a snake-oil remedy, from Barker's perspective, is more vile than evil itself. Leverthal's unpleasant demise at the conclusion of the story aptly fits the severity of her crimes.

In addition to his love of metaphor and subtext, Barker is fond of using jokes and puns in his work. "Pig Blood Blues" is no exception to this. If Barker's characters in this story represent animals of one sort or another, then the featured beast of preference is the pig. The pig functions as the punch-line of the author's extended joke; it is both hero and villain. Redman, the ex-policeman, as he initially converses with Dr. Leverthal, understands that he himself is thought of as the "pig"—a vernacular symbol of the perceived cruel police state. In the boys' eyes, *this* pig is evil. Yet there is another type of pig in the story, a literal creature. This animal, the reader comes to learn, is also more than what it first appears to be. It, too, possesses a subtext of meaning which is dark and evil, yet the boys of Tetherdowne view the queen sow with reverence. From the reader's standpoint, then, the boys' perceptions of good and evil have been switched, turned inside out. The author's joke is not only on the reader, nor only on poor Redman; it is on the boy inmates as well.

Redman's decrepit workshop, full of broken and mishandled tools, no doubt represents the boys' decrepit social condition. Redman is unable to repair either effectively. Though he makes a noble attempt to mend the latter—as he specifically tries to save Thomas Lacey—he is hindered by institutional powers beyond his understanding, and thus he is made impotent. Redman ultimately fails to save the day, paying the price for his failure with his life. He may be accustomed to institutional politics as far as getting money to upgrade the workshop is concerned, but this commonplace experience is with a banal and relatively harmless establishment. When he is confounded by the dark powers of the greater, more nefarious institution called evil, Redman's indoctrination into the workings of this greater institution proves to be deadly.

Barker's protagonist in "Pig Blood Blues" may be fashioned from a heroic mold, but Redman is definitely situated within the ranks of the anti-hero. The author suggests that some things just can't be repaired, no matter how noble one's intentions are. And this notion provides one of the more powerful horror elements of the story. One method of achieving horror in fiction occurs when the protagonist (and the reader who vicariously experiences events through the protagonist) recognizes that his or her actions are unable to avert the malevolent intrusion of the supernatural into the vulnerable, mortal sphere. The protagonist's sense of lack of control over events, like death, presents a frightening scenario—and reflection—of our own uncertainty about life.

When Redman first talks to Thomas Lacey, Lacey says that Redman doesn't know what's really going on. And, ironically, Lacey is right. At this point, Redman is truly in the dark; he can't see through the subtext of events surrounding him. Vision tests his and Lacey's emotional and physical strength. In the animal world, the senses play an important part in survival. Barker uses sense images throughout "Pig Blood Blues." For example, during Lacey's and Redman's struggle with each other—a struggle laced with sexual overtones—a mental war of wills is fought with their eyes, a stare-down if you will. Later, the sense of smell comes into play as the pigsty, smelling of vile fecal matter, becomes the focal point of the narrative. Moral corruption is equated with the stink of physical corruption, and evil smells like it's evil.

Barker also ridicules the organized mind in "Pig Blood Blues." Dr. Leverthal, as the author's symbol of the organized mind, presents an interesting image herself. On the one hand, she serves as that model of banal efficiency mentioned earlier. The doctor is representative of an authority figure who is more interested in naming and categorizing than in understanding reality as it exists in a prison institution. Barker enjoys using the prison setting no doubt because it emphasizes the dehumanization of the human spirit. Leverthal in her capacity assists in this dehumanization process. Too much order is destructive. Too much order denies freedom of thought and, more importantly, freedom of imagination. When the boys of Tetherdowne rebel against the institution, especially at the story's conclusion, they also rebel against the mechanistic, scientific paradigm of the twentieth century. Like his adolescent characters in "Pig Blood Blues," Barker recognizes the great, ambivalent power of the ancient, pagan religions. The boys worship Mystery. They pray to the miracle of imagination, even in its grossest form: the image of the infanticidal pig-mother.

On the other hand, Leverthal's hypocrisy allows Barker to further criticize the indifferent—and consequently harmful—bureaucracy. In addition to the damage Leverthal causes people in her *official* function as doctor, she effects even more havoc as a bureaucrat who betrays the responsibilities of her position. Perhaps Barker is suggesting with this character that social positions of authority are open to corruption, since the human animal is such a corrupting influence. The animal nature in people thrives on the juicy taste of power. In a sense, the humans' animal hungers in the story are a logical extension of the 1980s "Me" generation, the "I got mine; go screw yourself" attitude of the baby-boom yuppie generation. And though the boys at Tetherdowne are not the upwardly mobile brats of the modern corporate structure, they nevertheless sport the same figurative tooth and claw. If the measure of any civilization's worth is judged by how its members support the disenfranchised—those who are mentally ill or poor or who are criminals—then the civilization in "Pig Blood Blues" is a very injurious thing indeed. The only character who is *not* totally self-centered in the story is Redman, who, for example, sacrifices his personal safety for Lacey's sake, though even this sacrificial act may be motivated more by Redman's homosexual libido than by anything else. The author's message is a dark one here. Dangerous jungles, where its inhabitants are forced to live by the "eat or be eaten" axiom, are not necessarily located in Africa or India. Rather, they can exist as easily in a boy's reformatory, or in the feral recesses of the human mind.

Barker's notion of the human mind serving as the medium of "scrawls" and "splashes of graffiti" reinforces his unifying metaphor in the *Books of Blood* of people acting as texts or languages. Of course, Barker is sophisticated in his use of metaphor. Having the traditional gut-level appeal that it does, the horror genre today tends to lack subtle nuances and intricate uses of ideas. Many horror authors feel their job is well-done when they employ violence at the expense of poetry. There can be *both* metaphor and the bludgeon in the contemporary horror tale, as Barker well knows. Thus, his use of the human text image is not heavy-handed and monolithic. It instead assumes a new guise each time it's employed. In "Pig Blood Blues," the human text is emblematic of the graffiti of the mind. The language of this graffiti is unorganized, dangerous, as brutally chaotic as the animal natures of the characters in the story. Graffiti is a powerful language, the language of urban youth, the language of the dispossessed and the despised, the language of the subway and the dim alley wall, the language of an abandoned generation. Graffiti is also the language of revolution and of a destructive nonconformity. Barker's choice of graffiti as being representative of the mental condition of Tetherdowne's inmates is precise. Graffiti also plays an important role in Barker's story, "The Forbidden," where it again functions as a representation of the disaffected urban condition.

The imagery in the scene where Redman first encounters the Kevin Henessey-haunted sow is profoundly sexual. In his fiction Barker possesses the ability to blend and contrast eroticism and the grotesque. Here, the pig—a creature already established in the reader's mind as being slovenly and gross—is beautiful. The sow's beauty contrasts sharply with the sty's fecal-strewn setting and with the monstrous size of the animal herself. Redman, the author implies, is not only impressed with the animal-*ness* of the pig, he is also attracted by her physical beauty. The grotesque is appealing; the unusual is attractive. There is, in addition, a transsexual theme reflected in the pig and Lacey that the reader will discover toward the conclusion of the story. Typically, the sow is not what she initially appears to be, and Barker thus experiments with the type of double transformation, from person to pig and from young male to mature female.

Barker describes the pig as being a "revelation." On the spot, Redman becomes a transcendentalist. Where before he was unable to see the "living truth," now he can recognize sublime beauty in the form of the sow (i.e. the pig's grotesque sexuality). The author describes the animal, from Redman's perspective, as if she were a cat-house monarch. And yet this "seductress" is no cheap date. She literally acts like a queen and is obviously treated as a figure of devotion. The author contrasts images of the senses in Redman's first meeting with the queen sow. Filth surrounds cleanliness. Ugliness contrasts with beauty, albeit sexual beauty. The heat of the setting is pierced by the coolness of the inside of the sow's sty. These images of the senses can lead us to one of the story's thematic concerns. In this particular scene, the mortal world frames a creature of fantasy. The dregs of the mundane encompass imagination. The hidden heart or the masked core disguise the outward appearance of things.

The conversation between Lacey and Redman that occurs on a "carpet of old comic books" provides yet another interesting scene. The "lurid covers of the comics" contrast with Lacey's face, making it look "milkier than ever." Images of the hero, Superman, serve as a foil for the talk about Kevin Henessey. On the one hand, comic books in general function as symbols of adolescence. They are icons of youth, representative of children's ability to believe in fantastic, illogical events and in people who are beyond the normal. In their own primitive way, comics are the literature of the adolescent imagination, and the author uses this as a context for Lacey's explanation of Henessey's supernatural powers. Of course, on the other hand, the flip-side significance of what the comic books' role might be in this pivotal scene in the story lies in the word *comic*. In addition to being the literature of the imagination, comic books can also be funny or mocking. They can attack the conventions of adults or society. From Redman's standpoint, then, he can interpret Lacey's comments as being ludicrous, as being the ravings of a disturbed adolescent mind—as being as silly as a comic book. Often, as in this scene, Barker allows us a multi-layered image which the reader can draw several possible interpretations.

When Dr. Leverthal tells Redman that Henessey thought of himself as "the Nietzschean Superman," as "a breed apart" from the "common herd," as an immortal, reference is thus made to the beast metaphor and to Lacey's comic books — specifically, to the *Superman* comic books. But the most important allusion in Leverthal's discussion, from Barker's point-of-view, is the notion of adolescent immortality. "Pig Blood Blues" is Clive Barker's tribute to J.M. Barrie's *Peter Pan* (play, 1904; novel, 1911). Barrie's play/novel serves as a guide to revealing the subtext of Barker's story. Upon a close examination, the parallels between Barrie's *Peter Pan* and Barker's story are striking. Both works highlight adolescent protagonists who value the power of imagination. Both works feature adult characters who are unable or unwilling to deal with adolescent fantasy, and both works also feature a tribe of "lost boys," lost in both a metaphoric sense and a physical sense from the adult world — in fact, alienated and estranged from the adult world.

Peter Pan is the tyrant "Superboy" of Barrie's story, and a rather nasty little character in Barrie's novel version, who denies the adult world and refuses to grow up, thus protecting his adolescent supernatural powers. "I ran away the day I was born," Peter Pan tells Wendy. "I don't ever want to be a man... I want always to be a little boy and to have fun." Kevin Henessey, the reader learns by the end of the story, is the "Peter Pan" of "Pig Blood Blues"; like Peter, Henessey also refuses to grow up in an adult world, and like Peter, Henessey is an exacting tyrant. Barker's version of the adolescent's desire for eternal youth and power is a darker investigation of the "Peter Pan" fantasy. Clive Barker has transformed an erstwhile snug children's tale into a profoundly disturbing horror story, essentially working with Barrie's basic narrative fabric. Later, in his novel *Weaveworld*, Barker further explores the "Peter Pan" theme, though this time he develops Barrie's concept into an elaborate, novel-length epic fantasy.

The scene later in the story where Redman walks the deserted halls of the Remand Center, alone except for the noise of the television, provides Barker with an opportunity to satirize the television medium itself. The author's scathing attack of the television mentality in this scene highlights the brutal, bestial mindset of the inmates, reinforcing Barker's developing use of his animal metaphor. The satire here is also intended to be much broader in scope. Sex and violence are the only things to elicit a response from the usually docile adolescent television viewers. Otherwise, the author describes the experience as hypnotizing and, by implication, the typical viewer as a mind-numbed zombie hooked on the puerile formulas of standard television fare. Barker again returns to this concept in his novel, *The Great and Secret Show*, with stunning results (the television phantoms are actually granted a type of existence).

As in much his fiction, Barker's protagonists gain some measure of insight into the nature of reality by employing imagination. Redman's imagination permits him an explanation of the mystery of the narrative. Part of that explanation involves acute comprehension. Barker is quite effective at lampooning our social mores. He nudges us—a number of times even jolting us—to examine and evaluate our taken-for-granted beliefs. In the scene where Redman discovers the truth about Henessey, the author shows the reader the brutality of organized religion, as reflected in the Henessey/pig cult of the boys; Barker addresses issues of cannibalism and organized violence found in the accepted Judaic/Christian mindset. He implies that these institutions, though they preach love and compassion, if observed strictly from the standpoint of their rituals, are instead barbaric, pagan, destructive.

By story's end, before he dies, Redman witnesses the miraculous—the transformation of Lacey—but, as anti-hero, all Redman can do is find satisfaction in his captor's (the Lacey/Henessey/sow's) suffering that resulted from the fire in the pigsty. "Pig Blood Blues" is one of the more darkly satirical stories in the *Books of Blood*. Its message transcends the horrific elements of the tale, hence enhancing those elements, and suggests as all good parables should a critical examination of one's life. Barker attacks the faceless institutions that dehumanize people. He also explores the antagonisms between age and youth, between authority and rebellion. Clive Barker frames this investigation in a detailed allusion to J.M. Barrie's *Peter Pan*, though Barker, the master of inventive story-telling, forms this popular children's story around his own unique vision, a vision that burlesques religion as being a mindless, dangerous ritual (dangerous because it *is* mindless). The author's objective in "Pig Blood Blues" is an analysis of the human condition. He specifically investigates the beast-like nature of the human animal and finds a very cruel creature indeed. The pig is the predominant animal image in this story, a frightening—yet beautiful and attractive —beast. Transformations from human to beast to human punctuate the narrative's action. The animals of Tetherdowne, adults and boys and pigs, live within their prisons, and the final impression left with the reader is one of entrapment, a prison term with no hope of parole.

"Sex, Death and Starshine"

Clive Barker's early professional background in the theater is evident in "Sex, Death and Starshine." He populates this short story with theatrical personalities that, no doubt, are sketched from his real life experiences: the aging, but still boyishly virile director, the vain, sexually promiscuous soap opera actress, and so on. Barker employs his theatrical knowledge to good use, utilizing the short story as a vehicle to comment on the relationship between Apollo and Dionysus, a metaphor the author establishes in the story to express the conflict between money (Apollo) and art (Dionysus). Barker clearly favors art.

In "Sex, Death and Starshine," Clive Barker uses the opportunity to once again attack banality, in this instance represented by both Diane Duvall and television soap opera. By having Duvall a popular celebrity on television and a horrible actress in the live theater, Barker comments about both the mediocrity of television and about a mass audience willing to lionize such mediocrity. What is good is not necessarily what is popular, the author suggests, and the message is a profoundly interesting one when weighing Barker's ambivalent view of his own popularity as a genre writer. Barker loves the critical recognition he receives from his writings and films, but he dislikes the generic classifications his books are forced into, classifications that pander to the commercial mediocrity of the contemporary, crassly commercial book business.

Representing the crassly commercial—the Apollo metaphor of money— are the soap opera star, Diane Duvall, who is clearly more proficient at performing oral sex than she is at performing Viola's lines from Shakespeare's *Twelfth Night*, and Giles Hammersmith, who intends to betray the Elysium Theater—a wonderful choice for a name, having both a classical connotation and a direct reference to an ideal place arrived at only through death—by selling the theater to real estate mongers. Duvall is to be used, the author tells his reader, to draw an audience, an audience weaned on soap opera pablum. Her lack of true acting talent is destroying the production of the play. She befuddles Terry Calloway's sense of theatrical judgment by playing childish sex games with him. Like Duvall, Hammersmith is a mindless beast who worships money and possesses absolutely no sense of art or moral commitment to art. He secretly lusts for Duvall, since she represents the same level of banality as he does. Both Duvall and Hammersmith are destroyers, arrogant butchers of the theater. The author illustrates a just end for these two characters. Though they both could have been reborn through death, as Calloway was, instead they are destroyed by the fire that grips the Elysium. Their banality condemns them to the true death. The followers of Apollo, Barker implies, are not deserving of rebirth.

Barker occasionally frames his stories with other narrative traditions. For example, the "New Murders in the Rue Morgue" is modeled after the Poe tale, while "The Last Illusion" is influenced by the hard-boiled/Roman noir tradition. "Sex, Death and Starshine" is the author's tribute to Gaston Leroux's *The Phantom of the Opera* (1911), and Barker establishes several parallels in this short story to the Leroux novel. The character Richard Walden Lichfield is patterned after Leroux's "opera ghost," Erik. Like Erik, Lichfield's overriding passion is art, and this love of art stands in direct contrast to the protagonist's physical deformity. Also, like Erik, Lichfield disguises his deformity behind a mask, and moves mysteriously about the temple of art—in Leroux's novel the Paris Opera House and in the Barker story the Elysium Theater— as if he were a ghost. Lichfield intervenes in the theatrical production, as does Erik, when he senses a betrayal of artistic integrity, and finally, both narratives have their climactic "unmasking" scenes, where the vulnerable heroine fully comprehends the truly deformed physical nature of her captor.

But as Barker has often done elsewhere in his writing, he establishes a connection to a recognizable narrative tradition in "Sex, Death and Starshine," only to alter significantly that tradition later and thus return to a unique voice, a transformed story. Though the author pays homage to *The Phantom of the Opera*, "Sex, Death and Starshine" avoids being merely imitative. Barker meaningfully changes his version of Leroux's archetype by having his story end triumphantly — with Lichfield and his theatrical troupe optimistically confronting a future filled with performance and an existence dedicated to art, an existence that has conquered the mundane limitations of commercialism. *The Phantom of the Opera* does not conclude with such an optimistic vision, at least from Erik's point-of-view. In addition, where Erik madly loves the lead female performer, Christine Daaé, in Leroux's novel, Lichfield does his best to remove Duvall from Calloway's production of *Twelfth Night*. Indeed, Lichfield finally kills Duvall and then denies her resurrection through art by having her body destroyed in the theater's fire.

"Sex, Death and Starshine" is one of Barker's "happy ending stories," a tale that defies easy classification within the parameters of the horror genre. It is basically about a love — the inspiring love between husband and wife, Lichfield and Constantia — that denies the finality of death, contrasted with a purely lustful, adulterous relationship between Calloway and Duvall — that is narcissistic and self-destructive.

Ultimately, "Sex, Death and Starshine" is a tribute to the perfection of art. Barker's message is a profound one, one that applies to all human endeavors that strive to achieve a magical beauty in aesthetic creation. Starshine (or divinity) masters both sex and death when dedication to artistic perfection is the goal. The "Gods," as Barker ironically uses the theatrical term to describe the distant point from the stage where the resurrected dead sit and enjoy the Elysium's final performance, encompass both physical reality and fantasy. And Clive Barker would have us believe it's fantasy that really matters in the end.

"In the Hills, the Cities"

"In the Hills, the Cities" demonstrates the range and versatility of Clive Barker's storytelling in his *Books of Blood* collection. It is not a horror story, but more accurately may be considered an inventive fantasy. The focus of this story is not suspense, though there are some suspenseful moments, nor is the focus blood and gore, though there are scenes which are violently apocalyptic. For Barker, "In the Hills, the Cities" is more concerned with a physical representation of imagination: the two ambulatory city/giants of Podujevo and Popolac, constructed as they are of the interlocking bodies of thousands of people. The image that Barker utilizes here is composed of equal portions of the grotesque and the magnificent; his point is much like what's found in a great deal of Edgar Allan Poe's work, the notion that imagination is the greatest single achievement of humanity. But the price of that imagination, as in a number of Poe's tales, is sometimes terrible. Pragmatism dies as Judd dies at the conclusion of the story, while art, as an incarnation of imagination, is shown as providing a means to touch the heavens. Mick, the artist, is the one who hitchhikes a ride with a walking miracle.

Barker features as the protagonists of "In the Hills, the Cities" two English homosexual lovers on a "honeymoon." And the fact that Barker readily works with atypical protagonists supports the author's contention that he does not artistically discriminate against any single group of people, but that he kills everyone in his stories with equal abandon. These two lovers, Mick and Judd, represent the intellectual division between politics and art. Judd is a journalist, and as such, he is immersed in politics as a pig is immersed in mud and slime (the metaphor is Barker's). Judd cannot understand the less pragmatic worldview of Mick, who is a dance teacher. For his part, Mick frequently doesn't understand Judd's views. Mick's interests lie in "Renaissance frescoes" and "Yugoslavian icons," not in the current political situation of Europe. Judd thinks Mick is intellectually vapid, and Mick thinks Judd is boring and selfish. Barker implies in this relationship the incompatibility of art (Mick) and politics (Judd), of imagination and reason, of feminine and masculine instincts. The implication is that Mick and Judd make strange bedfellows — both figuratively and literally — and that this hand/heart dichotomy has profoundly negative connotations, unless it is tempered by the conciliatory agent of love.

Several other contrasts are established in the story: between great and small, between knowledge and ignorance, between the potential of imagination and the limits of imagination. The first of these contrasts, between great and small, is first seen when Mick and Judd are about to have sex in a country field.

As Judd follows Mick out into the field, he notices the field mice racing away from them in terror. Judd thinks about the hundreds of lives he is smashing with each of his steps (the numerous insects and rodents) and smiles at the thought. Of course, Barker is playing with irony at this point, foreshadowing Mick's and Judd's later encounter with the Popolac giant, in which the lovers themselves are the terrified, doomed mice. Like one of the many small creatures he has so callously destroyed with his strides, Judd is himself destroyed by the Popolac giant at story's end, his carcass ironically providing food and a new home for the animals of the field. Judd's destiny thus comes full circle. That which is great, the story suggests, is oblivious of that which is small. The great can destroy or create with equal ignorance.

However, that which is small is continually at the mercy of gigantic forces. And the final twist of this contrast is that great and small are relative concepts. Judd's huge steps in that field demolish the inhabitants of the small world, yet he himself is killed later as though he were nothing more than a mouse.

The contrast between knowledge and ignorance is seen in the detective-like work of Mick and Judd as they pursue information about what exactly is happening in that isolated backwash region of Yugoslavia. They attempt to distinguish between metaphor and actuality. At first, they think, for example, that the mortally wounded character named Vaslav Jelovsek is telling insane tales with his explanation of the Popolac and Podujevo contest. Jelovsek's comment about the giant's body being "the body of the state" (a political image which is echoed in the story "The Body Politic") is a wonderful pun of the phrase and is representative of Barker's fondness for wordplay. Mick's and Judd's pursuit of knowledge results in their encountering concepts previously undreamt of, such as the idea that the respective populations of two cities can harness themselves into the figures of giants that can move and do battle. The fact that literal fairy tale giants actually exist reinforces in Barker's story the author's desire to have miracles abruptly intrude into the world of the mundane.

A typical theme in Barker's work is that sometimes knowledge is bought at a great price. Judd pays with his life for his knowledge of giants and miracles. Yet the terrible expense is often worth the sacrifice, such as when Mick succeeds in catching a ride with the city/giant Popolac, and subsequently with imagination. Knowing what he knows, Mick would rather be part of the gigantic, part of the miraculous, and would prefer to die having touched an actual fairy tale than not. Once he hitchhikes his ride with walking imagination, the pedestrian aspects of his life fall away, such as ambition, sex, and memory. He knows that these things ultimately signify nothing.

"In the Hills, the Cities," finally, is a tale of fancy, about fancy. Edgar Allan Poe provides a guide for understanding Barker's use of imagination as a thematic concept. Poe typically places imagination as the single most important goal of human thought and emotion. To achieve this imagination and subsequent access to Heaven, the Poe protagonist must isolate himself and think deep thoughts of beauty and death, especially the death of a beautiful woman. However, there are dangers when one isolates himself from the company of society, contemplating melancholy thoughts of death. Thinking too much of death can lead to insanity, Poe suggests.

These same contrasts — between the limits of imagination and the potential of imagination, between madness and divinity — are what anchor "In the Hills, the Cities." Fantastic imagination spawned the twin wonders of Popolac and Podujevo. This dream, this flight of fancy, this fairy tale reality required generations of thought and creativity to achieve fruition. The resulting game contest — with the game being a frequent metaphor in Barker's work — is an event of the imagination, unlike anything else seen in the commonplace world. But if there is a flaw in the design of dreams, as there indeed was in the doomed Podujevo city/giant, then the resulting disaster creates insanity. When Podujevo dies because of internal structural weakness and, by implication, human inadequacy to give form to divinity, Popolac collectively goes insane. Madness is the price of reaching for Heaven and failing.

Imagination and imagination's disasters have their limitations for human comprehension. After Podujevo has fallen and Mick and Judd round the bend coming into sight of the recent tragedy, their minds are at first unable to comprehend the scope of the disaster. Barker writes, "This is a dream of death, not death itself." But as human vision improves, and as Mick and Judd move closer to the charnel pile of over thirty-eight thousand corpses that comprise the fallen and shattered debris of the city/giant Podujevo, cognitive limitations are overcome. The reality of things up close can be understood. Podujevo's miles of rope and harness and attached human carcasses provide adequate form for the otherwise indescribable.

But despite the consequences of the limitations of imagination, the power of realized imaginative potential is awesome and worth the dire consequences. The scene where Mick, Judd, and the husband and wife inhabitants of the country cottage are awaiting the arrival of the Popolac giant is both suspenseful and inspiring. As the monster approaches and, again, as their metaphoric vision of miracles improves, the lovers, Mick and Judd, witness the details of this walking marvel, this behemoth in the sky, such things as the giant's body and head, which is composed of thousands of living humans acting together as one being. Barker nicely blends the grotesque with the beautiful at this moment in the story. And for the author, both the grotesque and the beautiful are frequently part of the same thing (i.e. the image of imagination in its many aspects).

Those not possessing enough imagination are destroyed or mortally damaged by the confrontation with miracles in Barker's work. The husband relying on his impotent prayers, the wife relying on the protection of forest and nature — also equally impotent — and Judd relying on his faith in pragmatism: these are mental resources that lack true power. Of the group, only Mick catches a ride with the giant, but the price for this achievement is his sanity.

CHAPTER THREE

New Murders, Ancient Evils:
Clive Barker's Books of Blood, Volume Two

"Dread"

"Dread" is a concept story, philosophically exploring what constitutes fear and the individual's response to that emotion. Barker characterizes fear as a subtext of the human personality, and he constructs an extended metaphor relating the philosophy of fear to the image of the "beast." Barker also plays with verbal double-meaning regarding character and setting names, as evidenced with his use of the names "Grace" and "Pilgrim" Street. Barker reintroduces the Messiah figure (one of the author's favorite images) in Quaid. Quaid becomes the "teacher" of a new paradigm, one who would have impressed Descartes himself. What Quaid has accomplished is the marriage of science and philosophy, and his scientific method, though certainly perverse, is nonetheless effective in its results. In addition, photographs are an important visual theme in "Dread"; and one finds this theme of heightened senses and sensuality — as a form of transcendentalism — elsewhere in Barker. Finally, the transformation of the mild-mannered student, Stephen Grace, into the clown-like axe murderer (an unwanted by-product of Quaid's scientific experiment) establishes a typically paradoxical contrast between the humorous and the grotesque.

In an omniscient voice, Barker deliberates in the story's opening paragraph about the emotion of dread. The totality of one's life is a metaphor masking fear, the author argues, and thus the reader comes to understand that Quaid is a physical representation of Barker's philosophical point. Quaid's developing relationship with Steve Grace, as time progresses, reveals an interesting paradigm. Quaid is an iconoclast, someone who ridicules the history of philosophy. With Steve Grace, Quaid has an attentive student receptive to new, rebellious ideas. Quaid's ideas — *his* philosophy — are not only rebellious, but deadly. Quaid constructs his own metaphor that he believes is representative of truth. "*True* philosophy," says Quaid, "...is a beast."

Quaid, as Barker's voice, envisions the philosopher's role as being somewhat precarious. Quaid tells Grace, "We [as students of philosophy] should be walking close to the beast...don't you think? Reaching out to stroke, pet it, milk it —" The author once again returns to the animal image (see "Pig Blood Blues") to define the baser instincts — and the darker intellectual attitudes — of people. Quaid, unfortunately, is a sado-masochist. He wants to be "mauled" by philosophy. He embraces "mutilation by education." His notion of research leaves his hapless subjects humiliated, battered, broken.

Quaid's description of the "beast" in a sense typifies the word, not only as an illustration of philosophy, but as a definition of the horror story itself. Quaid says the beast is the "dark behind the door," certainly an apt example of the subject of the horror tale. Fear doubles as both Quaid's metaphor for the unknown and Barker's desired effect for his tales of horror. Quaid dedicates himself to touching the beast, though his own domestic breed of the animal (his fear of axe killings, for example) is still beyond his comprehension. The danger in closely examining the emotion of fear is that it's too powerful to understand fully, much less control. Quaid's pretensions about fear being an intellectual paradigm are hypocritical. He's not so much interested in studying the fear of others, but he *is* interested in learning how to control his own irrational paranoia. Quaid's sadistic side relishes others' pain, and that is the real reason he torments Cheryl Fromm and Stephen Grace. Barker's genius in this story is displayed in his twist ending, where the tormentor becomes the tormented. The beast is an impartial creature, willing to pleasure anyone. And as the author's voice proclaims, "There is no delight the equal of dread. As long as it's someone else's."

Barker also enjoys punning names in his satires, using them to define a character's personality or the setting of a particular scene. With Stephen Grace, the story's unwitting victim and eventual Frankenstein's monster, the character's surname has a religious connotation: someone in search of divine love or divine "grace," since he is the archetypal student, the apostle to Quaid's Messiah. Grace's name also suggests something that is a gift from God. For Quaid, Grace's gift is an unwelcomed thing, not a sacred present. Pilgrim Street, where Quaid lives and conducts his experiments in privacy, is indicative of religious and or educational meanings. Quaid is a pilgrim, seeking to know his fear. Fromm is an unwitting pilgrim, learning that Quaid's belief about the pervasiveness of dread is true. And Grace is a pilgrim, first at the feet of his teacher, and then journeying into madness. All the buildings on Pilgrim Street are demolished. It's a desolate landscape reflective of Quaid's personal worldview.

Barker returns to the Messiah figure with his character Quaid, lampooning the image. Barker ridicules unswerving faith in political or religious bureaucracies. As Christian history teaches us, Messiahs have been used in the past to foster much harm and much evil. Barker attacks this type of unconditional faith in religious teachers. After all, he terms Quaid as the teacher, and Grace — by inference — as the unfortunate lamb who follows. Both teacher and lamb are typical Christian stereotypes. Characters in search of transcendental knowledge in Barker's work frequently come to bad ends, as does Frank in *The Hellbound Heart*. Grace goes insane from his contact with his teacher, and Quaid literally loses his head in his zeal to instruct Grace.

Though Quaid preaches a new philosophy, his methods are scientific. Displaying no emotion, he torments Cheryl Fromm, treating her strictly as a laboratory animal, and he is indeed meticulous in his techniques and documentation. As does the scientist, Quaid develops a hypothesis, establishes a controlled environment to test that hypothesis, records his data so that other scientists can duplicate his experiment, and then, with data in hand, either refute, modify, or support his hypothesis. In Fromm's case, his hypothesis is correct. In Grace's case, Quaid has become a Victor Frankenstein, creating a monster which returns to torment his creator. The parallel here between "Dread" and Mary Shelley's *Frankenstein* is worth noting: the philosopher/scientist who isolates his work from any social conscience, from any moral responsibility. Such arrogance as Victor Frankenstein and Quaid demonstrate is akin to a god-like pride, and in Gothic tragedy, this pride ultimately results in self-destruction.

Of course, it can be argued that both Frankenstein and Quaid are transcendentalists, attempting in their efforts to know the face of God or, in Quaid's case, the face of the beast. For Barker, a heightened sensual experience usually leads to a transcendental state. Sometimes this transcendental state is for the better; sometimes it is not. The physical representations of the power of heightened senses in "Dread" are Quaid's photographs of Fromm. These photos, on the one hand, allow the philosopher/scientist Quaid to prove his thesis about fear. They are the tangible evidence of his work. On the other hand, the photos treat and pamper the sadistic voyeur, in Quaid, in Grace — and in us. They disclose Fromm's secret self, her vulnerable self, and they show insight into the dimmer recesses of the human id. And as Barker might joke, oftentimes it's not a pretty picture.

Quaid's creature, his Frankenstein's monster, is Grace, and with Grace the author offers the reader by story's end a grotesque and comical axe killer. This image is striking — the clown who deals in death rather than laughter. The author enjoys using such seemingly opposite emotions as fear and humor. A sense of irony is thus heightened, and the absurdity of life (and death) is championed. Barker returns to absurd and frightening carnival images in one of his more recent novels, *The Great and Secret Show*. There is a sense of retribution in "Dread," finally. Quaid gets what he deserves in the end. But with this retribution comes an education, a realization that, perhaps, Quaid might have gotten it all wrong. Barker concludes the story by writing,

> And Quaid knew, meeting the clown's vacant stare through an air turned bloody, that there was worse in the world than dread. Worse than death itself.
> There was pain without hope of healing. There was life that refused to end, long after the mind had begged the body to cease. And worst, there were dreams come true.

We see characters, doomed characters, later in Barker's work who neatly fill the above-quoted requirement for damnation. And, indeed, there are yet more dreams to come in the *Books of Blood*.

"Hell's Event"

Like "The Yattering and Jack," "Hell's Event" is lighter fare. Clive Barker's utilization of political satire in this story, counterpoised as it is against the contest of the foot race, offers some interestingly humorous moments. However, Barker interlaces this humor with some serious issues, such as the price of political freedom, the apocalyptic battle between good and evil (with the fate of the mortal world at stake), the noble sacrifice of the protagonist for humanity's sake, and the banality (and subsequent evil) of the organized mind. And though this is one of the several really fun stories in the *Books of Blood*, there are nonetheless some disturbingly horrific moments in it, like Cameron's basement encounter with the entrance to Hell, and Burgess's particularly nasty demise at the conclusion of the narrative.

A predominant theme in "Hell's Event" is gambling. Fashioned within the context of the game — specifically, the subtext of the sporting contest between Hell and humanity, which on the surface appears to be a foot race for charity — Barker reinforces the connection between Hell and the Devil's traditional love of wagering. Gregory Burgess explains to Cameron (the manager of the runner Joel Jones) at their meeting near the entrance to the Ninth Circle the details of the race and the implications of its outcome, that it is run every hundred years (usually clandestinely, in the middle of the night), but that this year it will be held in the light of day and under the nose of the world. The game controls both humanity and Hell, to Hell's immense happiness. The tables are turned temporarily as Cameron gambles that he can escape his captors. He does — for a short time anyway. He unfortunately makes the mistake of looking back at the demon rising out of the hole, seeing the demon's eyes. He thus forfeits his contest with life and loses the wager. But though the individual bet is made and lost by humanity, the game itself is later resoundingly won.

In addition to the use of the game metaphor—one of his favorite images—Barker once again demonstrates his knowledge of literature and archetype by establishing four central allusions in "Hell's Event." The first of these allusions is to Dante's *Inferno*. The scene where Cameron follows Gregory Burgess to the basement of the nondescript building in London, only to find a room there with an entrance to the Ninth Circle of Hell, pays tribute to Dante's epic poem. Burgess even quotes Dante for Cameron's benefit: "Lo! Dis; and lo! the place, Where thou has need to arm thy heart with strength." Barker adopts Dante—as he frequently does with other classic, literary authors in his work—and he then modifies Dante to suit his particular needs. Barker places this entrance to Hell in a nameless building in a nameless alley in modern-day London, and by implication suggests that Hell lurks behind the pasteboard facade of the commonplace, the seemingly normal. Clive Barker would tell us that the illusion that is our modern life is haunted by dark *bogeys* of our dark imaginings of centuries ago. Thus, Barker effectively juxtaposes classical metaphor with contemporary images. The plain and the commonplace can be effective emotional models of fear.

Barker's second literary allusion in "Hell's Event" is to the Faustian pact story (see also "The Yattering and Jack" and *The Damnation Game*). The pactmaker this time is the Member of Parliament, Gregory Burgess, who has apparently sold his soul to the Devil, not for knowledge, but for political power. Barker has some amusement with this character. Burgess's relationship with Old Scratch suggests that Hell is, no doubt, quite supportive of a number of the politicians in office, which then might explain some of the damned stupid legislation that emerges from time to time from the hallowed halls of power. When he introduces himself to Cameron as a Member of Parliament—one who maintains a "low profile," he blithely states—Burgess claims that he's "Independent. *Very* independent." Barker's humor with this remark is at the expense of the politician's partisan affiliations. Burgess is not attached to a political system that thinks in liberal or conservative terms, and consequently Burgess's reference to independence is meant to be satiric. Ironically, as the reader learns at the end of the story, Burgess is not "independent" at all, but instead must answer to his superiors, as we all must do in the business world, when he fails. And the price of his failure is severe.

With Burgess, Barker is addressing not only a satire of politicians, but is making a comment on the larger issue of politics. What's at stake in "Hell's Event," the prize of the foot race, is self-determination. Barker specifically uses the word "Democracy" to describe this concept. What Hell represents, and what it offers if its agent wins the race, we suppose is a dictatorship—tyranny. Hence, Barker obviously sides with the value of self-determination, playing it as he does alongside the fate of humanity, and he has his protagonist, Joel Jones, sacrifice his life for its continuation.

Burgess's sacrifice for political power is somewhat less noble. The author describes the learning process Burgess undergoes to become a good, damned person (as contrasted with a damned good person). His early sacrificial offerings with "kittens and cockerels" weren't sufficient; Hell thought these "ridiculous." What they instead wanted from him was self-mutilation, and in turn he offers them in oblation his nipples, his manhood, his thumbs. Typically in Barker's fiction, gross vivisection purchases dark power or transcendental pleasure, as in *The Hellbound Heart.*

The fact that Hell is interested in mortal politics bespeaks little of politics. As with pragmatism, with pedestrianism, Barker portrays politics as the product of an over-organized mind, of banal thought. And banality, for Barker, is evil, the very opposite of imagination and the liberating effects of imagination. In his chat with Cameron, Burgess talks about Cameron's wife, a woman he calls a "confirmed analyst" who provided (according to Burgess) much information about Cameron's Socialist political background. The person who wallows in politics, like Cameron's wife, is damned for his or her interests.

Burgess goes on to say that politics is the "...hub of the issue...Without politics we're lost in a wilderness, aren't we? Even Hell needs order. Nine great circles: a pecking order of punishments...We stand for order, you know. Not chaos. That's just heavenly propaganda." This "pecking order of punishments" remark is right out of Dante, and Barker implies in Burgess's discussion that Hell lacks original thought, that Hell fears to be inventive. The overtly planned is Hell's strength. In "Hell's Event," the ordered mind is the damned mind. It's amusing to note that Burgess's inability to prepare thoroughly for every possibility in the race—his overlooking of Lester Kinderman, for example, as the eventual winner of the race—leads to his doom. It seems that his mind wasn't quite ordered enough.

The third literary allusion in the story is to Stephen Vincent Benét's "The Devil and Daniel Webster" (published in *Thirteen O'Clock,* 1937). Like the Faustian pact tale, Benét's short story (and Barker's reference to it) is archetypal: the man who battles with the Devil, defeating evil with mortal cunning and intelligence. In "Hell's Event," the instant Jones recognizes the Malcolm Voight/familiar for what it is, and the moment he realizes what the outcome of the race might entail, he literally chooses to wrestle with the Devil, grabbing the Voight/familiar that is running in front of him and pulling it to the ground. He forces the demon familiar to reveal itself to the crowd, and he thus causes Hell to lose the race. He sacrifices his arm, his face, his very life, and with great pain. The narrative twist Barker gives to this essential story is that Jones cheats. He employs the very weapons of Hell against itself. Humanity (and democracy) wins by a fraud that would make the Devil proud, if he weren't on the losing end.

The fourth allusion in "Hell's Event" is taken from Genesis 19 in the Bible, which recounts the story of Lot's wife. God sends two angels to destroy the city of Sodom. Lot greets the strangers at the city's gates and offers them his home so they can rest and be protected from the evil in the streets. Hearing that Lot is housing strangers in his home, the men of Sodom plan to harm the strangers. The angels then blind the crowd and inform Lot of their mission. They tell him to take his family and leave, with the special warning that they flee to the mountains, not even stopping to look back. During their escape, Lot's wife does look back, and she is turned into a pillar of salt. The lesson in Genesis 19 is that God's warning should not be ignored.

Barker highlights three instances where characters in the story look back at something monstrous when they shouldn't. In each instance, vision serves to reinforce the author's artistic concern with heightened senses that typify a knowledge of death.

The first to look back at Hell is Cameron, and he is incinerated a few moments later. Before the fire ignites in his head (the "kiss" from the demon from Hell), Cameron remembers what happened to Lot's wife. This revelation comes a bit late to do him any good, however. The second to look back at Hell is Joel Jones. When Frank McCloud collapses during the race, he warns Jones not to look back. Without thinking, Jones does look back to check on Kinderman's progress and is doomed. He spots the ghost-like creature following him, and after he comprehends the significance of the race, chooses to wrestle with Hell and sacrifice his life. The third to look back, Gregory Burgess, does so unwittingly, and amusingly in a darkly humorous way. Burgess knows not to look back. He understands the message of Lot's wife, but this knowledge fails to save him.

Finally, Barker offers the reader several intriguing puns and jokes in the story: the "one hell of a race" comment from the play-by-play sports announcer (the other announcer calling the event a "revelation"); the nameless building imagined as "a dead man's bowel, cold and shitty" when Cameron stumbles across the entrance to Hell; and the final humorous paradox that concludes "Hell's Event" when the politician's head unnaturally looks ass backwards in death.

"Jacqueline Ess: Her Will and Testament"

"Jacqueline Ess: Her Will and Testament" is divided into four sections. Three of these sections are narrated, in part, by Oliver Vassi, Jacqueline Ess's lover. In this story, Barker examines the relationship between men and women. Specifically, he examines how the concept of power is manipulated by men and women, and is critical of what he finds. Men—as represented by Jacqueline Ess's husband, Ben, her physician, Dr. Blandish, and her wealthy lover, Titus Pettifer—all attempt to dominate Jacqueline specifically and, by implication, women in general. From the woman's standpoint, power takes physical form in Jacqueline Ess. She is able to destroy her tormentors in a very real sense, and thus her character functions as a means by which the author can address issues like sexual stereotyping, the deficiencies of marital relationships, and the motivations of a feminist mentality. There is, ironically, love (but little romance) with Jacqueline's indoctrination into the uses of power.

As mentioned elsewhere in this study, boredom is synonymous with evil and is the antithesis of imagination in Clive Barker's fiction. In the beginning of "Jacqueline Ess: Her Will and Testament," Jacqueline Ess is bored to death. She begs Christ for freedom, to be put out of her misery, and attempts to commit suicide. Her husband, Ben, arrives home early from work in time to prevent her death. Barker contrasts the horror of Jacqueline's misery and act of self-deprecation with the blandness of Ben's initial familial greeting, the "Hi, honey! I'm home!" of countless 1950s domestic sitcoms. Barker's point is that Ben's stereotypic treatment of (and condescending attitude toward) his wife (the "little woman of house and home") is suffocating.

Of course, Ben isn't the only man who is condescending to her. When Jacqueline Ess revives from her suicide attempt, her doctor/therapist, Dr. Blandish, talks in generalities to her, not really looking at her in the process. He treats her as a female stereotype. With Blandish, again, Barker presents the "doctor" figure as a villainous character, as someone who hurts rather than heals. Barker also suggests that embodied in Ess is a larger representation of how men frequently dominate women. Power is what's at issue in the war between the sexes, with women generally being the victims. However, with Jacqueline Ess, Barker turns the tables by having the female victim discover within herself a previously unknown, formidable, supernatural ability, a power that she can turn against men with devastating results.

For example, when Dr. Blandish antagonizes her with his insulting attitude, she thinks the man into a woman, literally. His chest sprouts breasts and his pelvis metamorphoses into a woman's. The shock of this "fairy-tale transformation" (Barker's phrase) is devastating and kills him. Though Jacqueline is, at first, sickened by what she has done, she later realizes — and embraces — his death. Her newly discovered power has become a mighty tool for her revenge against men. She also kills her husband — who is still patronizing her — as he tells her about his affair and his love for another woman, mentally compacting his physical body into the size of a suitcase.

The metaphor for men's supercilious attitude toward Jacqueline, and women overall, is that of the father figure who patronizes his little girl. Such an attitude, Barker implies, does women more harm than good. At one point, Jacqueline contemplates why all the men in her life, except the lawyer Oliver Vassi, call her nicknames other than her full name of Jacqueline. By implication, Barker shows the father figure to be destructive, in a much more subtle way than Ess's supernatural ability. Men's power resides in their capacity to dehumanize women. And Jacqueline's retribution, in a sense, then, becomes particularly apt when she mutilates her male victims' bodies.

The traditional power that men usually wield proves impotent against Jacqueline Ess. Her doctor and her husband are quickly disposed of, and the one man in the story who should represent indestructible male authority and vigor, Titus (which is Barker's pun of the name, "Titan") Pettifer, when stripped by Ess of his knowledge of how to use power properly, is little more than a vulnerable old man. His paranoid concern about being blackmailed by his personal secretary, Lyndon, and his fear of his wife, Virginia, finding out about his affair with Ess indicate that he is subservient to Lyndon and his wife, controlled by them. After Ess obtains all the information that Pettifer has to offer, she discards him while he begs for his life. Later, Pettifer tracks Ess down, imprisons her temporarily, and in his subsequent meeting with her begs her to kill him. She is nearly goaded into doing so, once again almost manipulated by a man. She does transform Pettifer—after he verbally attacks her woman-*ness* repeatedly—into an aberration, something that looks like a "four-legged crab." Ultimately, Pettifer's power is illusory, his personal weakness profound. He is truly a feeble man, and less than a woman.

Images of androgyny appear elsewhere in Barker's work, such as in the short story "The Madonna." Barker uses these images to demonstrate the efficacy of female strength. It's difficult for Barker's characters sometimes to understand or communicate with their opposite gender. When Dr. Blandish tells Jacqueline that he knows that women "have certain needs," she quickly dismisses this remark, thinking how does he know what a woman needs when he isn't a woman? Androgyny is a physical/emotional balance between male and female, and it's this gender relationship equilibrium that's severely lacking in "Jacqueline Ess: Her Will and Testament." With her eventual lover, Oliver Vassi, Ess lets slip early in their relationship the comment stating that "...there was a balance to be redressed between men and women." Vassi, the lawyer trained to detect lies and innuendo, senses there's more to Ben's death than what Ess initially discloses. The point here is that men and women are out of synch with each other, out of touch. Jacqueline Ess is tormented by this imbalance, seeking retribution first and self-punishment later. Vassi rhetorically comments about Jacqueline Ess's secrets, saying that everybody has them. The secret self is an important theme in Barker's writings, so important that he explores the concept substantially in his novel, *The Great and Secret Show*. Jacqueline's supernatural power to transform others *is* her secret self. Her story is about a rite of passage, where she attempts to harness tremendous power, does harness it, and then allows it to destroy her. Vassi also comments on this notion of the potential of the secret self, stating, "How little we know—I mean *really* know—about our capabilities." Knowledge of one's secret self can reveal power in Barker's work, but as in Jacqueline's case, having tremendous power is a mixed blessing, and there is always a heavy penalty exacted for its use.

Vassi derides himself at one point about assuming that Jacqueline is unaware of her secret self, or her power. He recognizes his chauvinistic assumption that "power must be in male hands." He witnesses several demonstrations of Ess's abilities, both controlled and uncontrolled. He thinks of her like the sea, using such terms as "boundless" and "deluge" to describe her. For him, this sea is "sublime."

The sea and water also serve as dominating images in Barker's "The Madonna," establishing as they do the setting of that story. Vassi talks about his loss of Jacqueline as if it were a fall from grace, and in the final section of his first-person narrative, he describes a graffiti picture of Ess as a "burning Madonna."

Graffiti is a recurrent image in Barker's writings, and surfaces again in "Jacqueline Ess: Her Will and Testament." When Vassi tracks down Jacqueline at story's end, he stumbles across the house in Surrey where Pettifer kept Ess prisoner, and where she transformed the financier into a crab-like creature. A sexually charged graffiti illustration there greets Vassi, one obscene in its exaggeration of female genitalia. Vassi learns that the picture was drawn by one of the men who was hired by Pettifer to guard Jacqueline (his companion bodyguard was the individual who shot and killed the Pettifer crab-creature and who later himself committed suicide in prison). The graffiti not only represents the object of Vassi's search, but it symbolically anticipates his final meeting with his lover.

When viewed in retrospect, "Jacqueline Ess: Her Will and Testament" is a love story. Vassi's narrative dominates a significant portion of the tale, and his quest, his Holy Grail, is an unconditional love of Jacqueline Ess. Ess's mortal weakness is that she fails to embrace this love. She desires more in life. She wants to know how to use power to revenge herself upon men. Such desire is her tragic flaw, and eventually leads to her self-imposed degradation as a whore, though, granted, a rather deadly whore. Vassi's final reconciliation with Jacqueline is mutually beneficial in a desolate sort of way. Vassi's devotion to Ess is his life, and that devotion is doomed. Jacqueline's inward journey to her secret self is equally catastrophic, and so when they perish in their romantic/destructive embrace, their love for each other halts the great pain and suffering that they are experiencing. Barker describes this scene as a literal coming together of bodies, male and female. Elsewhere in his work, Barker depicts the therapeutic effects of love (see both "The Book of Blood" and *The Great and Secret Show*). Typically for Barker, love is the one force greater than evil, greater than suffering, and in "Jacqueline Ess: Her Will and Testament," love soothes the deep wounds of two tragic lovers with the only remedy possible: death.

Jacqueline's "Testament" is the feminist struggle for social equality, what the author terms a balance, and her "Will" bequeaths the reader a hope, housed in love and in pain.

"The Skins of the Fathers"

Clive Barker uses the Genesis myth as the focus of "The Skins of the Fathers." He envisions an origin of mankind that is both faithful to the Classical Western cultural tradition and outrageously contemptuous of that paradigm. Western religious tradition has man as the center of creation and woman as the agent of man's fall from grace. In Greek mythology, Pandora releases the plagues upon mankind, and thus introduces man to mortality. In Genesis 3, Eve seduces Adam, and thus dooms the children of Adam to a life deprived of the Garden of Eden. Barker also shows humanity to be a failed moral experiment in "The Skins of the Fathers"; however, he has woman as the symbol of grace and man as the harbinger of evil and destruction. There also is a Christ symbol in "The Skins of the Fathers," a potential savior named Aaron (Aaron's name providing another Biblical tie), but Barker again employs the traditional image to debunk that image, thus making a new artistic statement in the process. Finally, the author returns to a favorite theme in "The Skins of the Fathers": the persecuted race of bizarre, grotesque, and profoundly beautiful creatures. These "monsters," for Barker, serve as a physical representation of imagination, and their persecution acts as a kind of mini-narrative detailing the attack of the conventional world upon imagination.

As with a number of Barker's other stories, "The Skins of the Fathers" makes use of verbal puns and jokes. The title itself is intended to comment upon the literal, alien, physical differences of the race of monsters known as the "father." And yet, the author puns the religious phrase "the sins of the fathers," as well, implying as he does the mismatched moral stances of the humans from the town called Welcome and the divine monsters. Barker also experiments, through religious implication, with characters' names. Davidson (the son of David) is the hapless witness of upcoming events in that Arizona desert. His name literally means son of the beloved one, and yet his anti-heroic stance in the narrative acts in sharp contrast to the religious authority implied by his name. The boy, Aaron (meaning "exalted one"), though not Moses (Aaron's brother in the Bible), is the next best thing, and if given half-a-chance to survive, could become the new Messiah, the new Law Giver. What's ironic with Aaron is that the townspeople of Welcome, though cast as the villains of the story (and they *are* a nasty group, the real monsters in the narrative), falsely invoke righteousness as a justification for their violent actions. Barker features the fathers as the true divine beings in the story. They gave humanity the gift of life, but the present was squandered. Man, in particular, is the root of all evil in "The Skins of the Fathers."

When Davidson first encounters the fathers at the beginning of the story, Barker describes the event as something akin to a carnival procession, resplendent with bizarre music and grotesque forms marching in a parade. As seen elsewhere in the author's work, Barker is fond of the carnival image. He enjoys counterpoising the ridiculous with the deadly, the humorous with the humorless. Behind the clown's mask is death, as Davidson quickly learns when one of the comical monsters breaks from the parade to attack him. Death *is* ridiculous; death *is* humorless. And by clothing death in the garb of merriment, the irony of the contrast is thus more fully pronounced. With the carnival image, Barker is working within the tradition of Ray Bradbury's *Dark Carnival* (1947) — later revised and re-titled as *The October Country* (1955) — but whereas Bradbury initially and loosely constructs the dark fantasy carnival image, Barker fully explores it in the totality of his imaginative work, both in his film and his fiction (and to such a great extent that I am reminded of the carnival-like music in the film, *Hellraiser*, that accompanies Frank's dramatic physical reconstruction in the mortal dimension).

As Barker did in his short novel, *Cabal*, he fashioned as the protagonists of "The Skins of the Fathers" what would normally be the antagonists in tales of dark fantasy: the monsters. Obviously, Barker uses monsters in his work as things that represent a good deal more than creatures of nightmares that desire to rob people of their sanity and their lives, though at times, this image is still at work. His monsters are literal representations of imagination, and despite the fact that they embody both positive and negative aspects of this imagination (people can either die from or become miraculously transformed by imagination), on the whole Barker views the fathers, the creatures of grotesque (yet beautiful) imagination, as being procreative, procreative, not destructive. The fathers are described as having the physical appearance of devils, but surface appearance is only a metaphor for a deeper subtext of meaning. What seems evil (the fathers) is in reality good, and what seems good (the townspeople of Welcome) is actually evil. A new future for humanity is potentially embodied in the character Aaron, the hybrid child of the monstrous and the commonplace, but his and, by implication, humanity's future legacy is quickly terminated by ignorance and mindless violence.

In both *Cabal* and "The Skins of the Fathers," the symbols of destruction, of the ultimate form of banality, are the "redneck" humans, people like Welcome's Sheriff Josh Packard (a very *un*welcoming fellow). Packard is arrogant, bombastic, and profoundly ignorant. When he pays the price for his ignorance with the loss of the fingers on his hand, he is not educated by the experience. Instead, he seeks to instigate new mindless violence, new hatred for things not easily understood. His method for dealing with the unknown involves the use of rifles and grenades and bazookas. On another level in the story, Barker comments about the evil of wife and child abuse. The abuser is a man named Eugene, Aaron's stepfather and a character who expresses his own inadequacies with the back of his hand. Eugene is infinitely more monstrous than Aaron's true fathers because of the way Eugene violently abuses his wife and stepson. The fathers treat Aaron and his mother, Lucy, with gentleness. Eugene, on the other hand, could easily kill either one of them in a fit of anger. Both Packard and Eugene are frighteningly destructive because of their lack of imagination.

Barker returns to a favorite thematic image in "The Skins of the Fathers": the Messiah figure. By having Lucy's rape at the hands of the god-like fathers, he is refashioning the Virgin Birth story from the Biblical New Testament. And though Lucy's rape is by no means immaculate—Barker describes the physical act in imaginative detail—it is certainly as wondrous. The "Joseph" of Barker's narrative, however, is much less sympathetic toward this miraculous birth. Aaron suffers great misfortune, and he becomes a literal embodiment of the Christian sacrificial lamb. Aaron ultimately dies, but not for our sins in the traditional sense. He dies *because* of our sins, because of our love of ignorance and violence. And whereas Christ provides a symbol of hope and redemption, Aaron becomes a symbol of what could have been, of what was tragically lost for humanity.

Two lesser themes that Barker employs in "The Skins of the Fathers" are his parody of the American Western myth and his portrayal of people as a language metaphor. From the perspective of the ineffectual—yet objective—narrator, Davidson, Barker describes the marshalling of Welcome's population to do battle with the fathers as something out of a Western movie. Davidson sees in the townsfolk a correlation to "watching settlers, in some movie, preparing to muster paltry weaponry and simple faith to meet the pagan violence of the savage." Davidson understands this metaphor as being indicative of failure—the savages will triumph once more. Later, Sheriff Packard (another of the author's debunking of Western myth images: the sheriff who is fool and coward rather than hero) addresses his mob of followers as they're on the trail of the fathers. His speech is trite—and meaningless. The highlight of his speech is the line, "You've nothing to fear but seeming less than men, men." Packard implies in his speech that the fathers are like Indians, thus encouraging for his men, and for the reader, a cultural mindset that is as recognizable as it is clichéd. He concludes his speech by ordering "Wagons roll!" to the vigilante convoy, and the picture is complete. In a recent conversation that I had with Clive Barker, Barker indicated his dislike of the traditional American Western movie, and this dislike is obvious as the Western formula is debunked in several of his stories (see: "Son of Celluloid").

Clive Barker concludes "The Skins of the Fathers" with one last powerful image. After the fathers have defeated their human tormentors by causing the floor of the desert to become like lethal quicksand, and as Lucy leaves the scene to try and get help (which the reader understands to be a futile act) through her eyes, Barker writes,

> She [Lucy] glanced round once more at their trivial forms, dwarfed by the bloody sweep of the dawn sky. Little dots and commas of human

pain on the blank sheet of sand; she didn't care to think of the pen that wrote them there. That was for tomorrow.

After a while, she began to run.

The authors of such a punishment—the fathers—who are the owners of the "pen" of retribution composing the text of humanity's doom, are indeed formidable and tragic.

"New Murders in the Rue Morgue"

"New Murders in the Rue Morgue" is Clive Barker's homage to, and sequel of, Edgar Allan Poe's famous tale of detection. But Barker takes his sequel in a different, startling direction. Poe's "The Murders in the Rue Morgue" (1841) is considered by many critics to be the first published example of the modern detective story. Indeed, the tale contains most of the elements that the diehard classical detective fiction reader has come to expect in the formula: a mysterious crime, a brilliantly intelligent and somewhat eccentric detective hero—named C. Auguste Dupin—and a rational solution to the crime. Though Clive Barker begins *his* version of the Dupin formula very much as Poe would have done (i.e. a detective hero attempting to solve a puzzle-like crime), Barker changes course mid-way through his narrative, producing a story that highlights the emotive, the sentimental, and the irrational. Clive Barker's "New Murders" is just that, a new version of a traditional genre—a twentieth-century update of a nineteenth-century conceit.

The setting plays an important role in "New Murders in the Rue Morgue." Barker carefully selects the proper mood for this story. It is more of an atmospheric tale than a conceptual tale. The seventy-three year old protagonist, Lewis, is described as hating the wintery Paris ("Winter...was no season for old men") and the people, both children and lovers, who frolic in the snow. Lewis thinks of the snow and children and lovers as a "curse." During Lewis's first meeting with the incarcerated Phillipe Laborteaux, Barker shows Lewis—who contemplates his friend's situation specifically and the condition of the modern, twentieth-century world in general—as thinking "of the snow, and the ice-floes." Lewis then sees the "sense in dying." Images of winter and ice are also used as metaphors for Catherine's emotional state. She is unwilling or unable to thaw out, to become more of a feeling human being. She is cold and still beautiful, but, ultimately, she is representative of death. The irony of Barker's story, for Lewis, is that the winter and ice that he so despises finally serve as the medium of his self-destruction. He jumps "from the parapet of the Pont du Carrousel" into the cold river filled with ice floes in order to destroy both his bleakly realized present and his idealized past.

That idealized past is as much responsible for Lewis's death as is the icy river in which he commits suicide. When Lewis returns to Paris at the beginning of "New Murders in the Rue Morgue" to help his friend, Phillipe, who is charged with the murder of a young woman named Natalie Perec, he prepares himself for "another desecration," another building torn down, another street obliterated by the bulldozer. Lewis loves the past, fantasizes about it even, and this obsessive love frames his paranoia of the modern world. Lewis sees 1937 Paris as a "pleasure-dome," where he and his friends thought they lived an endless life of "perfect leisure." The idealized world is first tarnished by the atrocities of World War Two, and then destroyed by the march of modern progress. Lewis yet perceives Phillipe as a "breath of a lost age," a physical representation of the past, a past unable to conform to the present. Phillipe is not understood by contemporary Paris. He is laughed at, mocked. The author's voice expresses, through Lewis, the contrast between the quaint evils of nineteenth-century mystery fiction (as represented by the murderous ape in Poe's "The Murders in the Rue Morgue") and the very real modern day evils ("there were far greater atrocities to be accounted for, all committed by human beings"). Clive Barker revisits this thematic notion of the nineteenth-century/twentieth-century contrast between horrors of the past and horrors of the present day in his short novel *Cabal* (in *Cabal*, the traditionally perceived monsters of the past, called the "Nightbreed," are involved with a terrible battle with a modern-day serial killer named Decker). These conflicts between ice and warmth and between past and present are ultimately embodied by the larger conflict between fact and fiction in the story.

Barker tells us early in "New Murders in the Rue Morgue" that Lewis sees no sense in distinguishing between fact and fiction. He does not care about truth and falsehood, and this attitude sets up an irony where Lewis—the character who thinks the distinction between fact and fiction as being "academic"—is nonetheless unable to face the reality of Phillipe's man/ape creature's existence. His very inability to distinguish between fantasy and reality causes him to take his own life.

Part of Lewis's problem is that he embraces too closely the fictive myth of Poe and Poe's tale, "The Murders in the Rue Morgue." Lewis thinks of these as being "part of his heritage." Every family has its own traditional legends. For Lewis, he was told that his grandfather had given Poe the raw material for Poe's famous detective story, "The Murders in the Rue Morgue," and that the genius detective hero featured in this tale, Dupin, was, in fact, Lewis's grandfather's brother—Lewis's great uncle. Barker is unclear whether this tradition is true or not (prefacing his remarks with the cryptic comment "If the stories he [Lewis] had been told as a young boy were correct...."), but he is very clear about the tragic outcome of an all too powerful faith in such a belief. Lewis's friend, Phillipe, fascinated by Lewis's stories of Poe and Dupin and Rue Morgue murders and razor-wielding orangutans, creates fact from fiction. The fact (or reality) of Phillipe's efforts—his Frankenstein's monster creation—destroys both Phillipe and Lewis. Fiction taken too seriously can be a destructive thing indeed. However, to the world at large, which is usually oblivious to such intellectual conceits, fact and fiction are meaningless, insignificant. The redheaded whore at story's end, for example, views Phillipe's man/ape as being Phillipe himself, as being nothing more than another lover, one willing to supply her drug needs. At the conclusion of the story, Paris society takes no particular note of the ugly beast and young woman leisurely walking together as a loving couple to the steps of the Sacré Coeur.

Eventually the man/ape comes to accept its condition, its existence, while the intellectuals, Phillipe and Lewis, cannot or will not. Clive Barker implies in "New Murders in the Rue Morgue" that sometimes a total, sensual acceptance of things is best and that the reality of so-called "facts" may be difficult to judge. In an interview with the police inspector in charge of Phillipe's case, Lewis is told by the inspector,

> "*Merci*, Monsieur Fox [a derogatory reference to Lewis and Lewis's conceptualization of the detective sleuth hero]. I understand your confusion, *oui*? But you are wasting your time. A crime is a crime. It is real; not like your paintings."
>
> He saw the surprise on Lewis's face.
>
> "Oh, I am not so uncivilized as not to know your reputation, Monsieur Fox. But I ask you, make your fictions as best you can; that is your genius, *oui*? Mine; to investigate the truth."

Indeed, Lewis is an artist of two different types. He is first a painter who is past his days of painting, and who is now enjoying the monetary rewards of his earlier labors. However, Lewis is no longer actively painting, and thus has become sterile, and non-productive, which, from Barker's standpoint, is a terrible condition. Lewis is also a second type of artist: one who apparently inspires others to create from fact, fiction. Phillipe was motivated by Lewis's stories of Poe and Dupin to re-create from fantasy or legend Poe's famed ape killer. The part-fiction, part-fact product of Phillipe's amazing creation unfortunately succeeds marvelously in its design. Phillipe's man/ape becomes as successful a murderer as the fictive model. For example, in a sexually excited state, the man/ape kills a redheaded prostitute named Monique Zevaco, and, in addition, he kills the investigating snoop, Jacques Solal. Along with being a killer, however, Phillipe's man/ape during the course of the story becomes, ironically, a lover as well.

Barker toys with the notion of sexual bestiality in "New Murders in the Rue Morgue," not only in having the man/ape make love to a whore toward the end of the narrative, but also by having the beast's creator become jealous of his monster when the monster is seduced by nineteen-year-old Natalie Perec. Did Phillipe kill his mistress in a jealous rage? Barker is not totally clear about this question. Phillipe claims that the man/ape murdered the girl because of jealousy, but by showing us Phillipe's tirade when Lewis questions him about the strange beast, the implication is that Phillipe actually *is* Natalie's murderer and it was a crime of passion. Thus, the beast is perhaps more appealing than the man. Sexual obsession — or the lack of it — and guilt are at the bottom of "New Murders in the Rue Morgue." Catherine, for example, is too sexually aloof; Phillipe is too sexually preoccupied; and Lewis is too much the voyeur, as demonstrated by Lewis's spying on the man/ape's lovemaking. The moral imbalance created by sexual obsession in the story directly leads to the characters' sense of guilt. And, guilt in Barker's story is quite destructive. Phillipe and Lewis both kill themselves, and Catherine becomes more dead than alive in her feelings about others.

Yet, the supposedly abnormal sexual partners in "New Murders in the Rue Morgue" — the man/ape and the whore — through love find love and a type of normality. Barker suggests that the act is greater than the individual and that love most certainly conquers all, for better or for worse. The man/ape is another of the author's creatures of imagination, created by imagination, who finds some measure of happiness in the end.

CHAPTER FOUR

Confessions of a Dark Fancy: *Clive Barker's Books of Blood, Volume Three*

"Son of Celluloid"

As "Sex, Death and Starshine" pays homage to Clive Barker's interest in the theater, "Son of Celluloid" highlights another of Barker's great loves: the cinema. The story contains a number of motion picture metaphors—clichéd scenes from films and images of movie celebrities; and yet Barker constructs these cinematic images as a monster story or, more correctly, as a ghost story (the ghosts of flickering images and celluloid fantasies). In addition, as he did in "New Murders in the Rue Morgue" and as he would do more thoroughly in his novel, *The Great and Secret Show,* Barker explores the relationship between reality and illusion, between fact and fiction, in "Son of Celluloid." Finally, Barker features another of his strong-willed female protagonists in this tale: a thirty-four year old overweight woman named Birdy—who not only overcomes her negative self-image about her physical deformity (her weight problem), but uses this deformity to combat and destroy evil.

The author divides "Son of Celluloid" into three sections, and it is the only other story up to this point in the *Books of Blood* collection, besides "Jacqueline Ess: Her Will and Testament," having such pronounced breaks in the narrative action. Each section title has a film designation attached to it.

The escaped convict named Barberio provides yet another vehicle for Barker to comment on one of his favorite thematic images—prisons. In the beginning of "Son of Celluloid," Barberio vows that he'll never go back to jail, that he would rather kill himself than be captured again. Of course, he *does* kill himself because of his inattention to a gunshot wound and stomach cancer in his persistent flight from the law, but his death only serves to transform him, specifically his disease, into a monstrous parasitic entity. Barberio makes reference, in particular, to his fear of spending time in prison, where he would be subjected to the mind-numbing monotony of the place, and where he would do nothing more than spend his days obsessively counting hours, minutes, seconds. Even the escaped con's personal deity is linked with a prison. It's an invented god the convict calls "Sing-Sing," envisioned by Barberio as being "a fat guy with a grin that hooked from one ear to the other, [holding] a prime salami in one hand, and a cup of dark coffee in the other." Barberio's intense fear of prison establishes in the narrative a sense of entrapment that leads to the character's ultimate metamorphosis into evil. Barker implies in this story that once Barberio makes the wrong choice in escaping prison, his wrong choices progressively multiply (e.g. shooting the cop, hiding in the back of the "Movie Palace" cinema) until they not only doom him, but they serve to doom innocent people as well. Obviously, Fate is not kind in this tale.

The "Movie Palace" setting of Barberio's death and transformation illustrates several of Barker's other favorite notions. The first of these is the deteriorating condition of the building and or neighborhood. What was once thriving is now dying, as is seen in the Movie Palace's dilapidated structure itself, and thus the image of death dominates the action of the story. Barberio's locating his secret hiding place in the Movie Palace — a secret place possessing great power (note the similarity with the underground settings of *The Great and Secret Show*) — is emblematic of the building's hidden nature (it was once a "Mission Hall"), a nature that disguises both the religious trappings of the original structure (a temple to the Christian God) and the secular power of the cinematic reservoir of life (a temple to the movie gods). The fact that the building's original owner could have made the place either a church or a cinema implies the crassly commercial attitude held by Barker toward the former and the morally elevated nature of the latter.

The predominant metaphor of "Son of Celluloid" (as the title indicates — a reference to the Universal Studios' monster movie sequels of the 1930s and 1940s) is the cinema. Movies, as the author implies in his story, have a life of their own, a life that feeds on the emotions of their audiences. Barberio becomes an actual representation of that parasitic relationship between movies and their audiences. His cancer (another parasite) is magically charged by the pent-up emotive power of countless films. And once the cinematic ghost/monster haunts the Movie Palace (the theater's name serving as a wonderful reference to those famous historical locations where feature-length films first attracted a middle-class audience) it literally begins to transform the theater into a motion picture.

For example, in the men's toilet where the ghost kills Dean and attempts to kill Ricky, the ghost transforms the location into a generic scene from a Western movie. The place even has a generic John Wayne (in true homicidal form) that is the ghost's particular incarnation in this illusion. Ricky has to not only recognize the movie illusion for what it is, he has to combat the Wayne doppelgänger in order to survive. Barker is teasing his readers at this point through this parody of the traditional American Western movie. From Ricky's point-of-view, the character confronts the John Wayne illusion,

> Ricky had never had a taste for westerns. He hated all the forced machismo, the glorification of dirt and cheap heroism...This face [Wayne's face], so mock-manly, so uncompromising, personified a handful of lethal lies — about the glory of America's frontier origins, the morality of swift justice, the tenderness in the heart of brutes. Ricky hated the face. His hands just itched to hit it.

It's not coincidental, from Clive Barker's standpoint, that the real-life setting of the story's Western movie illusion is the men's toilet.

The reader briefly sees in this scene, as well, Barker's dislike of drugs. As Ricky takes visual stock of the Western illusion in the men's toilet (of the "Zane Grey's nightmares"), and after his earlobe has been shot off, he searches his jeans pocket for some drugs to "improve the situation." Ricky, however, has to face the reality of his unreal situation, and the author implies that drugs are an unsuccessful method of doing this. Drugs are a crutch that won't save Ricky's life; at this point only his own initiative with his fists gives him a temporary respite. The comparison between the effects of a drug-induced fantasy and the mental fantasies created by Barberio's cancer ghost is a valid one for the author. Both rely on a function that is parasitic — they each take something from their users — and both are deadly.

But Barberio's movie ghost is not so easily thwarted in its attempts to feed on Ricky. It eventually gets what it wants from him (his emotions first, then his life in a process reminiscent of past science fiction monster movies), using a more powerful — and much more sexual — film image as its weapon: Marilyn Monroe. The ghost/monster also snares Dean's date, Lindi Lee, with a cinematic trap. In the pursuit of its final victim, it terrorizes Birdy with movie personality voices on the telephone and with an image suggestive of the huge eye creature from the 1958 science fiction monster invasion film, *The Crawling Eye*. The ghost's parade of movie scenes and celebrities nearly works in capturing her. But the creature makes one fatal mistake. It tries to use Dumbo as one of the cinematic images to terrify Birdy, and this backfires.

Dumbo — the elephant who could fly, as featured in the 1941 Walt Disney animated motion picture — had been part of Birdy's torturous past where she was teased about being fat like the elephant. This pain causes Birdy to not only resist the illusion, but to conquer it, using her weight abnormality as a weapon against the monster. Birdy is the only protagonist to overcome the Movie Palace nightmare, and though she initially appears to be the weakest of the four characters, her inner strength, forged in the crucible of pain and humiliation, eventually takes control. She survives and wins her battle with death where the others fail. Birdy is typical of the Barker female protagonist. Though possessing human faults, his women nonetheless achieve great personal power *via* their gender.

One of the most interesting comparisons that the author makes in "Son of Celluloid" is between cancer and movies. As Birdy confronts the real, physical manifestation of the ghost ("It was a filthy thing, a tumor grown fat on wasted passion. A parasite with the shape of a slug, and the texture of raw liver"), the monster/ghost/cancer states, "[I am] His cancer. I'm the piece of him [Barberio] which did aspire, that did long to be more than a humble cell. I am a dreaming disease. No wonder I love the movies." When Clive Barker describes motion pictures as a "dreaming disease," his allusion is a powerful one in the story. And though for the most part the author views dreaming and imagination as the high points of our existence, there sometimes exists a dark side to the dreams, a side that with the muddling of the boundaries between fantasy and reality is subversive. Barker ends the *Books of Blood, Volume Two* with this message in "New Murders of the Rue Morgue," and he begins the *Books of Blood, Volume Three* with the same message in "Son of Celluloid." But the author would no doubt tell us that "Son" is a comedy, a story with a happy ending. After all, the monster *is* destroyed in the end. After Birdy wrestles with the creature at the Movie Palace, using her weight to kill it, she later tracks down the possessed Lindi Lee in Seattle; as the Barberio parasite discards Lindi Lee's body, Birdy shoots it and then uses acid to totally eradicate the monster. Birdy, indeed, has triumphed over the dreaming disease and will confidently live her future.

"Rawhead Rex"

Simply put, "Rawhead Rex" is an intense story. Like "The Midnight Meat Train," "Rawhead Rex" is a powerful tale of terror, pulling no punches in its graphic description of violence and gore. This is basically a monster story. The monster here, the creature called Rawhead, is primordial, essential, a force of nature's evil side, and this is what makes the ogre truly frightening. Rawhead is the ancient bogeyman made real, and made in frightening detail. Barker symbolically paints Rawhead as the literal embodiment of death. Rawhead's story presents a conflict between death and life, or more specifically between male (as image of destruction) and female (as image of creation).

This male/female dichotomy is evident in Barker's other work, but in "Rawhead Rex," the conflict is stated most fiercely. The author establishes connections *via* the male/monster destructive force of nature to an antediluvian age where the mother goddess held great sway in primitive society, where her bounty provided the season's crops, and where she symbolically represented an insurance of a continued life. "Rawhead Rex" is an autumnal horror story. It takes place in September during the time of harvest festivals that have their origins in the distant past. Before recorded history, in a number of agrarian societies the fall harvest anticipated winter, the time of dying and death, and was ruled over by the harvest king whose blood sacrifice guaranteed the return of spring and the new crop. Rawhead is a wicked interpretation of the harvest king. The monster's imposing face is portrayed by Barker as looking "like the harvest moon." Rawhead harvests people like the farmer harvests wheat, a comparison that the author also fosters in this story, and the bounty of Rawhead's crop is wholesale destruction; specifically, he enjoys eating the flesh of young children. Children are emblematic of youth, of fresh, vibrant life, and of women's reproductive power. They are representative of the future, so it's appropriate that Rawhead, a monster from the dim past, finds them uniquely satisfying.

Rawhead is the archetypal bogey man character, the bogey man of children's nightmares "who'll get you if you don't watch out." Among the more terrifying moments in the story is when Rawhead captures children and feeds them into his moon-faced mouth, vividly described at one point in the story when the monster captures and devours Ron Milton's son, Ian. Barker underscores his description of Rawhead, and the monster's voracious appetite, with the language of the fairy tale. But it's not the variety of fairy tale with a happy ending. Though Rawhead is eventually destroyed, the havoc he creates during the course of the narrative is indeed tragic.

Clive Barker fashions "Rawhead Rex" in military images. He describes the village of Zeal — the setting for the frightening events that are about to unfold — as being invaded by various armies through the years, from the Romans to the Normans to the modern-day English themselves. The most recent variety of conquerors has descended from London, the tourists and developers who search in Zeal for a haven from their urban lifestyle. With tongue in cheek, Barker labels these tourists the "new barbarians," and calls their weapons "courtesy and hard cash." He also says in a caustic aside, which is a profound comment about war in general, "Like the Romans before them, like the Normans, like all invaders, the commuters made their profoundest mark upon this usurped turf not by building on it, but by being buried under it."

Zeal is located, the author tells us, some forty miles southeast of London, in the "orchards and hopfields of the Kentish Weald." It is an ironically pastoral setting for a vicious war between human and monster. Ron Milton and his family, some of these "new barbarians," will unwillingly partake in a fight for their very lives as the story unfolds. Clive Barker no doubt draws reference in Ron Milton's surname to the epic English poet, John Milton (1608–1674), and to the apocalyptic *Paradise Lost* (1667), one of the greatest battle narratives ever written.

Before the author introduces the central protagonists in "Rawhead Rex," he first shows the reader several minor "battles" in the story after the monster, Rawhead, is released from his tomb prison. Farmer Thomas Garrow, for example, is waging war with a large rock lodged in a corner of his field. As Garrow labors, he wonders why his father left this part of the field unplowed. Garrow's backbreaking work reminds him of the labor his father had put him through as a child. Such memories are not pleasant, and as Garrow removes the boulder which has trapped Rawhead through the years, his inadvertent birthing of the monster is fostered amidst hateful memories. Barker is being a bit sardonic at this moment. The king of death emerges from his slumber, *via* hate for fathers and the past, to wreak havoc upon both fathers and sons once more. Garrow wins his battle with the rock as he finally topples it, yet he loses the war with his life as he becomes the first bloody sacrifice for the creature. Rawhead's rebirth is thus consecrated by violent death.

Elements in the story are both politically and morally reactionary. Perhaps the reason why Thomas Garrow died in such hideous fashion, stuffed as he was headfirst into Rawhead's former tomb, was because Garrow failed to keep in touch with tradition. He was unable to read the warnings of his cultural tradition, of the past, and his ignorance costs him his life. Of course, there exists in numerous horror tales this notion that ignorance is deadly. Many characters have met their doom because of stupidity, or a false notion of bravery, or a fanatical desire to learn the truth of something terrible. And in the horror tale, once a supernatural interdiction has been ignored, disaster soon follows. Barker designs this motif to satisfy his own voice. When his characters are unable or unwilling to "read" the subtext of the world, those characters suffer as a result of their ignorance.

Besides the fool Thomas Garrow, the police in "Rawhead Rex" are a pathetic lot, and are used as satiric images. Detective Sergeant Stanley Gissing, for example, is described unsympathetically. The police set up a "murder squad" unit at "The Tall Man" pub following the Nicholson killings, and Gissing is in charge of the investigation. Ron Milton spends some time talking with Gissing in the hotel bar. Detective Sergeant Gissing discusses the horror of the recent killings, the worst he's ever seen, Gissing claims, but Milton cannot himself see the horror of Gissing's secret self. While being driven to file his report, lounging in the back of the car, Gissing is having sexually provocative dreams of little girls, and when Rawhead attacks Gissing, killing him and his driver, it's as if one perversity is destroying another. Typically in Barker's fiction, good and evil are not neatly defined. Nearly every character possesses qualities of both. Evil in "Rawhead Rex" comes in several different varieties. Gissing is a lesser evil who gets what he deserves when he becomes the victim of an even greater evil.

The other policeman in the story, Sergeant Ivanhoe Baker, is also a satiric figure. Barker says of Gissing's replacement, "Ivanhoe was not a heroic man, either by inclination or education." With Ivanhoe Baker, Barker is not only able to parody the stereotypical heroism of the cop figure, he is also able to mock the paradigm of the romantic hero—as embodied in the name "Ivanhoe," a brave knight from Walter Scott's famous historical romance.

Traditional masculine bravery is not relevant in "Rawhead Rex"; it is simply ineffectual when confronted with Rawhead's overwhelming destructive power. In this story, the dragon is stronger than the knight in shining armor. Ironically, the damsel is the one who saves the day, as the reader discovers by story's end. Thus, when Barker debunks the police, he makes them rather unimportant contestants in the battle between life and death.

Barker also ridicules religious fanaticism in "Rawhead Rex," and has in Declan Ewan, the verger of St. Peter's Church, yet another example of the depraved cleric, which is an important thematic concern for the author. When Rawhead is released by Garrow, Declan Ewan feels an unusual excitement, "It was like being a child again. As if it was Christmas, and any minute Santa, the first Lord he'd ever believed in, would be at the door." It turns out that Ewan's "Santa Claus" is Rawhead, and the cleric worships the monster like a god. One of the most striking, and horrible, moments in the story is when Ewan undergoes a type of grotesque baptism in Rawhide's urine. Ewan perverts religion, embracing as he does sensual lust in the place of God, while at the same time worshiping something older than Christianity. Ewan's villainy in the story is made that much more perverse because of his violation of traditional Christian symbols: the Church and the hierarchy of the Church. When he assists Rawhead, he is assisting death incarnate, and Barker has a terrible death at the cruel hands of Rawhead as Ewan's reward for services rendered.

The power of Christianity has no effect upon Rawhead. Even the tormented Reverend Coot—the only positive, though still ineffectual, religious figure in Barker's tale—is less the savior and more the victim. The problem for those protagonists representing good in "Rawhead Rex" is that the monster they battle is older than Christ, and thus older than Christian good or evil. Barker tells us that Rawhead is the last of his immortal kind, that loneliness over the years was his lasting torment as he was trapped in his underground prison, a concept that provides an interesting parallel to John Milton's Lucifer in *Paradise Lost*.

Rawhead's battles are ancient ones, especially his battles against women. At one point, the monster remembers when he and his brothers would capture and rape women, "They would die having the children of those rapes; no woman's anatomy could survive the thrashing of a hybrid, its teeth, its anguish. That was the only revenge he and his brothers ever had on the big-bellied sex." Whereas Christianity does not intimidate Rawhead, the fertile, procreative power of woman—representative of the oldest type of religious worship—does. The true power in St. Peter's lies not with the altar and what the altar represents, but with what is beneath the altar. The female fetish hidden there is the only thing primal enough and strong enough to best Rawhead.

A minor, yet significant, battle skirmish in the story occurs when the newly liberated Rawhead terrorizes a nearby farmer named Denny Nicholson, his wife, and his little daughter. But despite Rawhead's formidable power, the monster has a mortal weakness. In the terrifying scene where Rawhead attacks the Nicholson family, he is temporarily thwarted in his attack when he encounters Gwen, the wife, who is menstruating. The "blood cycle" offends him, sickens him, represents a power diametrically opposite to his own. The larger war, then, in "Rawhead Rex" is between man and woman. Barker portrays man, represented by Rawhead, as destructive, consuming, horrifying, as the howling chaos of wilderness. Barker describes the feasting Rawhead — while he is enjoying a bloody repast of pony flesh in the Nicholson's barn — as considering himself the king of the earth.

Rawhead's very existence thrives on senseless destruction. He kills and devours children, because children are symbolic of reproduction, life, and the future. He burns cottages and villages because these epitomize civilization. He spreads chaos because anarchy pleases him. Indeed, he loves the reverse of those things which provide security and social order. If Nature is mother earth, then Rawhead is father death.

Yet, as powerful and frightening as Rawhead is, the procreative force of woman can beat him. The climactic moment, toward the end of the story, when Ron Milton, aided with the ancient earth mother fetish unearthed in the altar at St. Peter's, confronts and helps to defeat Rawhead is vivid indeed. Rawhead is consumed by his own nihilistic nature. While in the process of setting Zeal ablaze, Rawhead inflicts self injury. The author writes, "The beast [Rawhead] had been careless in the enthusiasm for destruction: fire had caught its face and upper torso. Its body hair was crisped, its mane was stubble, and the flesh on the left-hand side of its face was black and blistered." Rawhead is literally blinded by a love of violence, and is finally defeated in his apocalyptic battle with Woman.

The townspeople of Zeal subsequently overwhelm Rawhead in a scene that is reminiscent of those Boris Karloff Frankenstein movies from Universal Studios. We are made aware at this moment of Barker's cinematic sense, a sense that is founded, in part, in the horror genre, but which is profoundly revised by Clive Barker's quest for a unique artistic voice. Clive Barker's love of film evidences itself in "Son of Celluloid," and will reappear again in his epic novel, *The Great and Secret Show*. The townspeople of Zeal (aptly named Zealots) unknowingly revert to past tradition as they kill their ancestral nemesis, Rawhead. Barker writes, "Their [the townspeople's] hatred was old; in their bones, did they but know it." The so-called modern citizens of the twentieth century, when confronted by a creature evocative of their ancient past, embrace that past as they essentially become a group of witch hunters, violently exorcising the pagan devil.

The inhabitants of Zeal are unable all along to read the signs of their heritage — such things as the purpose of the boulder in Garrow's field, or the significance of the name of their local tavern: "The Tall Man," or what's underneath the altar at St. Peter's, or the remote history of Rawhead's existence—and their ignorance leads to Rawhead's release. Their prospects for future enlightenment are slim, since they can't (or won't) understand their "old" hatred of what Rawhead represents. They are as blind as ever to their secret selves.

"Confessions of a (Pornographer's) Shroud"

Ronnie Glass's confession that frames the narrative structure in "Confessions of a (Pornographer's) Shroud" is a ghost story, but unlike those Victorian chain-rattlers that stereotyped the form in the nineteenth-century popular press, Clive Barker's variant is quite contemporary. "Confessions of a (Pornographer's) Shroud" details Glass's physical transformation from commonplace accountant to supernatural spirit, a transformation that begins in banality and ends in imagination. Important themes are reintroduced in this tale, such as Barker's criticism of the Church and of law enforcement agencies, and his debunking of belief systems, like the Horatio Alger "rags to riches" myth. Barker has also returned to his use of sensual images—such as sight and sound—and sensuous images, sardonically describing the products of the pornography business and how those products relate to the shattering of hypocritical puritanical mores. Indeed, this is a ghost story like no other.

The senses prevail in "Confessions of a (Pornographer's) Shroud." At the beginning of the story when Glass's ghost begins his confession, his memories of his past life and of his family are subtly visual ones. Barker's descriptions of the pornographic magazines stored in Maguire's warehouse are visual, and are depicted in a ludicrously obscene manner. When Maguire tortures Glass, he literally destroys (among other things) the man's sense of sound—his eardrums, and when the gangster finally kills Glass, he shoots a "third eye" in Glass's forehead. This third eye provides the ironic means of Glass's spirit exiting from his corpse. The vice-loving Father Rooney at story's end is taking sexually suggestive photographs of the prostitute, Natalie (photos from a religious perspective, of course), no doubt to appease his voyeuristic secret self. And as the story concludes, the vile smells of Glass's discarded shroud thrill Father Rooney with forbidden thoughts of vice and sin. The use of senses as thematic images is intended to be both comic and sublime. Sight, sound, smell, these can reveal the marvelous, the ridiculous or the grotesque—and sometimes for the author, all three. Even Glass's name hints at the character's illusionary appearance. He is after all a ghost, an illusion himself, something transparent and hard to define.

While he was alive, Glass's life was meaningless. Described as initially being preoccupied with neatness (that's why he "enjoyed accountancy"), Ronnie

Glass's sexless, lifeless existence was founded in banality. Death gives Glass a new body, a marvelous form, one that rebels against the confines of the commonplace. For example, as the two mortuary technicians hover near his corpse, they are discussing the most banal of subjects—shoes. And as they talk on and on about cheap shoes, Glass's spirit becomes more and more offended, more outraged. Though Glass was himself, until recently, a mundane individual living a pedestrian lifestyle, his journey from life to physical death to spiritual life has now changed his outlook. As representative of imagination, as a being beyond rational explanation, he rebels against that which is not imaginative, not marvelous.

At a diametrically opposite point from the marvelous for Clive Barker is institutional authority, and the two examples of this authority in "Confessions of a (Pornographer's) Shroud" are the police and the Church. Inspector Wall from Scotland Yard is as brutal as he is dishonest. His close association with pornography gangster Michael Maguire (a "drinking companion of many years' standing") naturally subverts the policeman's superficial, yet official, function as society's guardian. He actually undermines the integrity of society *via* his hypocritical secret self. He not only protects the interests of the pornography business, he has a deep-seated and basic love of brutal, meaningless violence. When Inspector Wall interrogates the innocent Lenny about the murder of the pathologist at the mortuary, he and his associates attempt to beat a confession out of the hapless eye-witness that doesn't sound so ridiculous, something other than the idea that a shroud can be alive. "Wall of the Yard" is not only incapable of dealing with imagination, he attempts to batter the thought of it into submission, hammering it into a version that will make sense in his report. Wall doesn't care if he harms the innocent. He simply wants to prove Lenny the primary murder suspect. The concepts of mercy or justice are unknown to him. And when Lenny is absent-mindedly playing with his genitals through a hole in his pants pocket, this gives Inspector Wall further justification to begin beating him again. The Inspector needs little encouragement to feed his lust for blood. Wall (along with Maguire) is a terrible symbol of evil in "Confessions of a (Pornographer's) Shroud."

One of the great ironies of the story presents itself in Father Rooney. Glass's final, great act of contrition is to "confess" that he was not involved in pornography, that he was not the "Sex-King" that Maguire framed him as being. For Glass, pornography is a terrible sin, obviously much more vile than murder for him since he kills several times in the story with abandon. What Glass doesn't realize—because he doesn't survive long enough in his linen shroud form to find out—is that the religious figure that he seeks to confess to gleefully indulges in the same vice (i.e. pornographic photography) that Glass finds so reprehensible. Father Rooney, we are told, enjoys his work in Soho because it provides him with "Something new every day. Mysteries on the doorstep, on the altarstep." Barker puns the use of the word "Mysteries," which is intended to have a double, paradoxical meaning, blurring as it does the distinctions between the Mysteries of the Church and the mysteries of the street. Barker also plays with characters' perceptions. Glass perceives mysteries in a sexless light, in the light of the official Church. His notions are sterile, not breathing with the sensual power of Father Rooney's mysteries: the tangible artifacts of sin that smell of blood and corruption. But Father Rooney, with his passion for the street, is nonetheless a traitor to his Church. He is not what he represents. He absolves sins that he himself wallows in. Even the photographs he takes of the prostitute Natalie (his snapshots for his "private collection") betray his moral hypocrisy. "[Natalie was] A daughter of vice," writes Barker, "somebody had told him [Father Rooney], but he couldn't believe that. She was too obliging, too cherubic, and she wound a rosary around her pert bosom as though she was barely out of a convent." The contrasting images are striking here—the prostitute, the rosary, and the convent. Barker's joke about the Church official being consumed by perverted sexual desire is a lively one.

Barker also has some fun playing with the "rags to riches" myth. He inverts its significance by having the gangster, Michael Maguire, succeed within the parameters of its definition. Barker understands that the promise of the Horatio Alger myth is a promise that works both ways, the notion that both good and evil people can become successful through hard labor and perseverance. It's not accidental that Barker selects a gangster, albeit a British gangster, to debunk the myth, since criminals have always represented the dark side of the success story. Gangsters, because of their dedication to an ideal or goal, can be admirable, as perhaps best illustrated in America's fascination with the likes of Al Capone and John Dillinger. In fact, Maguire's collection of portraits in his "fortress" include those of Dillinger, Louis B. Mayer, and Winston Churchill—a group of men idealized by Maguire and reflective of his personal view of himself.

The scene near the conclusion of "Confessions of a (Pornographer's) Shroud"—where Maguire attempts to thwart Glass's supernatural retribution by cloistering himself within the estate of his fortress home, his "'Ponderosa'" as he likes to think of it—is predictive of *The Damnation Game*, which is not only Barker's first novel, but is also one of the most intense fantasy/horror stories to have been published during the past several years. In this novel, Clive Barker is able to expand more fully upon that sense of entrapment and paranoia that he initially only spends several pages examining in his *Books of Blood* tales.

"Scape-Goats"

In "Scape-Goats," Barker returns to the ghost story, but this time there are no traditional haunted houses. Instead, he uses a haunted island as the setting, and places in this setting two shipwrecked couples who unfortunately happen to violate the law of the dead by being disrespectful. Once this law is violated, the dead enforce their retribution in typical horror tale fashion. What is untypical here is that the author deliberately blurs several important social definitions. For example, Barker shows us that at least one of the shipwrecked characters in the story, Jonathan, is as brutally violent as any spectral antagonist. He uses sex as a weapon—specifically against the narrator of the story, Frankie—and when sexually impotent, he resorts to mindless destruction. Frankie is symbolically compared to the captured sheep penned-in on the island, while Angela is a brainless woman. Counterbalanced against the characters' personal shortcomings are the rigorous expectations of the dead, who tolerate no disrespect. Politically, "Scape-Goats" is conservative, reinforcing as it does the inflexibility of Fate, but then, most horror fiction tends to be located right of center. Ultimately, this ghost story is a *Gilligan's Island* tale gone wrong, where the games of the dead punish mortal lust and senseless violence.

"Scape-Goats" is one of the few *Books of Blood* tales narrated in the first person, and as the story begins we are told by the female narrator, Frankie, that the yacht—aptly named the *Emmanuelle*—that she and three others are sailing has beached on an uncharted, seemingly deserted island located somewhere in the Inner Hebrides. Sharing the yacht with Frankie are Raymond (or Ray), Jonathan, and Angela. This group is a collection of "beautiful" people; however, though they may appear beautiful on the outside, their appearance disguises violent, egotistical and or vapid personalities. Ray is obtuse, Angela is stupid, and Jonathan is mean-spirited. Frequently, they argue among themselves about silly, meaningless things. Indeed, with these self-centered yuppies, there is no love to be found anywhere.

A sense of sterility—and of death—pervades the setting of "Scape-Goats." In the first paragraph of the story, the narrator, Frankie, depicts the island that she and her companions have beached upon as a "lifeless mound of stones," and a "hunchbacked shit-pile." She particularly notes the lack of life in either the sea around or in the air above. Frankie feels the power of the island and her own powerlessness in the face of the island as a symbol of the great unknown by stating, "I can think of no use for a place like this, except that you could say of it: I saw the heart of nothing, and survived." Of course, Frankie's mentioning of survival here is tinged with irony since this survival depends upon her ultimately dying. She indeed discovers peace in the end, but it is the peace of the dead. Barker's story itself is a vacuum tale. The island's nihilistic setting is invaded and violated by four souls who lack souls. These vapid people are human aberrations and must be killed to preserve the graveyard harmony of the island burial mound. The four travelers are more dead inside than out as the narrative begins, and the island's offended dead move to rectify this terrible anomaly.

When Ray examines his charts to locate their position, all he sees is an empty spot. And after Frankie's initial view of the island, things go downhill from there. In the light of the mist-shrouded sun, the narrator tells us the place is "bleached-out gray," the color of "over-boiled meat," which provides the reader a powerful visual image of decay. As the sun pierces the mist, the landscape changes in color to "somber green, and, deeper, a hint of blue-purple" — no doubt, the shades a corpse may exhibit while in the process of decomposition. At one point in the story, Frankie is negotiating her way through the garbage-strewn beach. Her detailing of the refuse is sickening, as is her description of the swarm of flies buzzing about the place. Flies are the carrion creatures of death. They go hand-in-hand with the smell of decay that hangs about the place, a smell that Frankie effectively recounts as being like the odor of "rotting peaches," or worse, like the aroma of "an open drain clogged with old meat." Extending our examination of the story's grim setting, a setting that is a larger metaphor for death and dying, it's ironic that Jonathan first notes the "total silence" of their surroundings, ironic because Frankie says, in an aside, that they "might as well have been deaf": perhaps deaf as the dead are deaf to life, Barker implies. Jonathan is arguably the most deaf of the four when it comes to the finer graces of the human spirit. Like their "empty space" island prison, this empty space is not only an appropriate description of the island's setting, it is also an apt expression of Jonathan's and the crew's overall moral attitude.

Jonathan is himself like an animal. Devoid of romantic feelings for his lover, Frankie, he uses her for sexual satisfaction alone, an animal's satisfaction. Jonathan's intercourse with Frankie aboard the yacht is a sterile expression of love. Frankie lets Jonathan have his way with her, not so much because she loves him, but because she is indifferent to him. When Ray becomes a voyeur of this lackluster copulation, Frankie wonders if Ray can see that she is dispassionate. In fact, she would rather her love-making partner be Ray. Ray, however, is blind (as well as deaf) to Frankie's thoughts. When finished, Frankie desires a kiss, some expression of tenderness, but Jonathan, losing interest and pulling up his shorts, says that he's "always sensitive when...[he] come[s]," a good play on words here since Jonathan is anything but sensitive when he comes. Jonathan then inquires of Frankie if "it" was good for her, and though she nods in assent, she thinks to herself, "It was laughable; the whole thing was laughable." Jonathan's attitude toward sex here is much like a rapist's, one of violence rather than affection, one that is destructive rather than constructive.

Jonathan is not only an inconsiderate lover, he is also a boorish, violence-loving lout. He is the antagonist of the defenseless. For example, when the group discovers three penned-up sheep on the island, Ray considers the situation "odd," while Angela and Frankie feel sympathy for the pathetic creatures. Frankie recognizes in the animals' eyes the sense that nobody really cared if they lived or died. She thinks, "I'd thought that about myself an hour earlier. We had something in common, the sheep and I." Jonathan, on the other hand, views the defenseless animals in a somewhat less sympathetic light. Being the brute that he is, Jonathan considers passivity a weakness, as something to be exploited, just as he has exploited his sexual relationship with Frankie.

After discovering the sheep—and telling Frankie that if the creatures "had any decency, they'd slit their ugly fucking throats"—Jonathan wants to repeat his sexual conquest of the passive narrator. However, he quickly finds that he's impotent, and his response to his inability to inflict sex upon Frankie is to terrorize the sheep. Frankie is appalled at hearing Jonathan's "whoops of satanic glee" as he kills one of the sheep by crushing its skull with a stone. Frankie describes Jonathan's smile as,

> Oh, that grin: it served so many purposes. Wasn't that the same smile he charmed women with? The same grin that spoke lechery and love? Now, at last, it was put to its true purpose: the gawping smile of the satisfied savage, standing over his prey with a stone in one hand and his manhood in the other.

Expressing the author's voice, Frankie recognizes the connection here between sex and violence. For Jonathan, sex is nothing more than an extension of his violent nature. He feels no compassion for either the sheep or for Frankie, and thus Jonathan embodies those worst qualities of human nature, qualities that require a moral purging. Frankie wants to run away from the scene. She perhaps is again reminded how very much she herself is like the sheep. And though Jonathan eventually returns to his senses—vomiting his "half-digested gin and toast over the grass"—his violations have gone too far. Punishment, indeed, is about to be enacted.

Ray learns in a book about the Hebrides that their desolate island is a type of memorial to the soldiers and sailors killed at sea during the two World Wars; the bodies of the war dead were brought there by the currents of the Gulf Stream. These dead souls of the island take offense that Jonathan has desecrated their offerings. The sheep were intended to placate them, to honor their memories. They give Jonathan the same treatment that he inflicted upon the sheep, causing a stone to sheer off the top of his head much the same way in which he brained the one animal. In "Scape-Goats," Barker returns to his "The Book of Blood" framing story with his emphasis upon the thematic notion of reactionary horror. The dead are not to be messed with in either story, Barker suggests, and when they *are* messed with, the dead enact a frightful retaliation. The penalty for Jonathan's crime, according to the reckoning of the angry dead, requires more than Jonathan's life in compensation. They kill the *Emmanuelle*'s entire crew.

Even the intervention of the story's potential savior, the Gaelic man who cares for the sheep and, in essence, is the caretaker of the island burial mound, does not provide Frankie, who is the only sympathetic character, safety. The dead pursue their attack against the both of them as they attempt to flee the island in the Gaelic sheep-feeder's boat. The vengeful dead play a type of morbid game with them, scratching the planks of the boat with their nails and using Ray's mutilated corpse to splash about in the water, frightening them. This morbid game playing reinforces in the reader's mind Barker's thematic interest in the game as a metaphor, representing as it does heightened dramatic conflict that is powerful and, at the same time, ironic. In several of the tales appearing in the *Books of Blood,* and in a number of scenes in his novels, Clive Barker uses the game metaphor to suggest that characters frequently are merely pawns in the larger scheme of things, that Fate, in its many guises, is a difficult opponent to defeat. Certainly, the dead are omnipotent in "Scape-Goats," and their anger cannot be escaped.

Yet Barker mutes the horrifying impact of the story in the end. When Frankie is finally claimed by the island's dead, she finds a type of tranquility that she perhaps never knew in her life, a peace that she certainly never had with Jonathan. She joins Ray in a watery grave. By writing "Scape-Goats" in the first person, Barker forces the reader to identify with the victimized Frankie. We suffer with her as Jonathan abuses her, and we sense her emotional release as she becomes one with the sea in the story's conclusion. Frankie tells the reader that "A kind of peace was on me," and we believe her. Life without love is not really living, Barker suggests to us.

"Human Remains"

If "Rawhead Rex" is a cautionary tale that warns about the dangers of a society ignoring its past, then "Human Remains" is a tale that argues that the past sometimes should remain buried and forgotten. The pathetic antiquarian, Ken Reynolds, learns this harsh lesson the hard way. Reynolds, when the narrative begins, displays to Gavin, the twenty-four-year-old male prostitute and central protagonist of the story, his collection of artifacts that he has on display in his Livingstone Mansions flat (another of Barker's puns, since the monster that Reynolds resurrects is literally living stone). Reynolds tells Gavin that Roman Britain is his "personal obsession." This personal obsession leads to his reviving and succoring an ancient, vampire statue, which is representative of tremendous evil. And by the conclusion of "Human Remains," after he has fully realized what he has let loose upon the world, Reynolds smashes his collection of historic artifacts, as if this act alone can undo the damage. The antiquarian explains his actions to Gavin by stating, "It's a sickness. ... Needing to live in the past." Reynolds's shattered artifacts—his "ruins of Rome," as Barker coins the phrase—illustrate the appalling psychological condition of Reynolds himself in the end. He pays a terrible price for his thoughtless actions. Unfortunately, his crime cannot be forgiven because his deeds cannot be reversed.

But Reynolds is not really an evil character. Quite the contrary, as he is about to feed the vampire statue (which he is housing in the bathtub in his flat) Gavin's blood, he feels guilty about being a potential murderer, and he tries to warn the young man to leave the place before it's too late. Gavin ignores Reynolds's warning, and becomes an eventual victim of the statue. In "Human Remains," evil is not human-made, though a case could be made that Gavin—lacking humanity—is certainly not Snow White. Instead, evil is supernatural and historical in nature. This story is a vampire tale of the Bram Stoker variety. It features a creature that rejuvenates itself with the life force of its victims. Like Dracula and his literary progeny, the ancient statue is immortal, living through the centuries.

But here the comparison between the formulaic vampire tale and Barker's interpretation of that tale ends. The statue feeds on much more than the blood of its prey; it robs its victim's very identity. Thus, when the creature selects Gavin as its next target, the dramatic action in "Human Remains" details Gavin's wasting away, a metaphoric death that involves the loss of his identity along with the loss of his life force. Although Gavin's body is still technically alive at the conclusion of "Human Remains," his soul has been stolen from him.

Of course, Barker implies that Gavin didn't have much of a soul to begin with. The author describes Gavin as pursuing a zombie's existence. Gavin makes his living as a male prostitute, yet his indifference to sex, or any sort of real human contact, is pathological. His is a self-centered world, a world of narcissistic love where his most important daily ritual is when he grooms and preens himself for the next hustle. He is cynical about other people's emotional needs, callously pigeonholing his hustling targets into various objectified classifications. Gavin dehumanizes others because he himself is not all that human. Amusingly, upon reflection, Barker offers us a pun in the story's title, since by the end of the narrative, not very much of Gavin remains human.

Gavin's single quality is his great beauty. His face is the standard of this beauty. The author writes, "He was wonderful. People told him that all the time. Wonderful. The face, oh, the face, they would say, holding him tight as if they could steal a piece of his glamour." Gavin's good looks eventually get him into serious trouble. The vampire statue is attracted by them when the creature first sees Gavin in Reynolds's bathroom. However, unlike the other pitiful men and women in Gavin's superficial existence, the vampire statue is certainly able to steal his "glamour." When the police, at one point thinking that Gavin is responsible for several brutal street murders (murders actually committed by Gavin's doppelgänger), investigate the prostitute's apartment, they are like the statue in that they also attempt to steal some of

Gavin's life. Yet, Gavin rationalizes what the police have done, since there wasn't very much of his existence to be had in the first place. And as the statue feeds on the young man's body and soul, Gavin at one point dismisses the loss of his soul. He is more outraged that the monster is stealing his face.

Such a superficial attitude is reflective of Gavin's lack of emotion. There is nothing inside that beautiful head. When Gavin is at Reynolds's flat early in the narrative, examining the antiquarian's collection of artifacts, Barker describes the young prostitute as knowing nothing about art and history. If the subject doesn't involve hustling, then Gavin isn't interested. He's a vapid character, having no real substance. This is illustrated several times in the story when Barker shows Gavin in front of the mirror. Early on, what's reflected in the mirror is Gavin's good looks, but as the creature begins to plunder the young man's beauty, all that remains without that beauty is shadow. While Gavin is in his apartment, sickened by the vampire statue's feasting upon his identity, Barker depicts a transformed character,

> As he [Gavin] crossed the room to where his dressing gown hung on the back of the door he caught sight of himself in the mirror, a freeze frame from an atrocity film, a wisp of a man, shrunk by cold, and lit by rainwater light. His reflection almost flickered, he was so insubstantial.

Barker refers to a cinematic image at this point in the story, as well as a visual one. In "Human Remains," Gavin's biography is little more than an empty-headed film romance, a motion picture telling of a silly life. In addition to these visual references of movies and mirrors disclosing double images and ghost-like, insubstantial reflections, the story abounds with images of water. The statue is in a tub of water when Gavin first sees it, and later returns to the bathtub in Gavin's apartment when the creature is wounded in the chest. As Gavin is wasting away in his bed, his body is drenched in water; a parallel reference is thus made to the water-loving vampire who is siphoning away his life. It also seems to be raining throughout the narrative, which subsequently presents a melancholy backdrop to the action.

Despite his lack of emotional substance, Gavin does, however, entertain a dream in the beginning of "Human Remains," a promise that he has made to his secret self. He seeks to raise his social position in the world, albeit in meager fashion. His plan is to rise "from street hustler to gigolo, from gigolo to kept boy, from kept boy to husband" of some wealthy widow. Ironically, Gavin's evil counterpart in the tale, the statue incubus, has its own dream as well — to rob Gavin's face and his identity. The monster is a statue having aspirations for humanity. Gavin fails himself from the start, dreaming a hustler's fantasy. Later, his dream becomes a very real nightmare. The vampire statue, on the other hand, achieves its goal, and becomes a better version of Gavin. What Barker has outlined here is an unusual Horatio Alger story, a reverse "rags-to-riches" adventure in which the bad guy succeeds in the end.

But the statue does not truly achieve total success in its designs to be human. For example, when Gavin returns to Reynolds's apartment, the archaeologist is about to attack the prostitute because he thinks Gavin to be the vampire statue. Gavin tries to prove his identity to the hysterical and violent Reynolds without much success, until Reynolds notes that Gavin is sweating. This fact convinces him that Gavin is who he says he is, and not the statue facsimile. States Reynolds, "It could never sweat. . . . Never had, never would have, the knack of it." Barker is suggesting that during the everyday processes of living, such things as sweating are important; indeed, these are proof of reality. Since the statue is not actually a living person, the creature has difficulty imitating the little things, the things that we take for granted but which are proof of our biological identity. Yet sooner or later, with hard work the vampire statue will no doubt fully succeed in its "playacting."

In a wonderfully staged scene toward the end of "Human Remains," Gavin, losing his interest in living, wants to pay his final respects to his departed father, whom he never really cared for. When he arrives at the cemetery where his father is buried, he encounters there his double, the statue. The doppelgänger is weeping. Gavin is impressed with how real his double looks, and when he asks the monster why it's crying (because it's sad being in the cemetery, of course), the double aptly responds, "I don't see any tears on your face." The statue has thus become better at living than has Gavin, and the reason for this is because the doppelgänger understands something that Gavin never did, that human existence is more than just a pretty face, that a meaningful life incorporates more than just simple pleasures. The creature has not yet perfected the details of his newly acquired identity. The vampire, which had brought flowers to the father's grave, does not know, for instance, that Gavin's father did not like flowers. But still, the vampire statue is trying harder at being human than Gavin ever did. The creature dearly loves *all* aspects of living, the good and the bad, even the toothache it has stolen from Gavin.

"Human Remains" is ultimately a dark fable of the "Me" generation. It admonishes the contemporary yuppie's fixation with surface beauty and surface pleasure. The story warns that the penalty of such a fixation is the loss of one's soul, of one's identity. Certainly, in the beginning, Gavin is living a waking dream. His identity lacks substance. His recurring dreams in the story are either failed ambitions or nightmares. If "Human Remains" is not, technically, a horror story (after all, the statue is a rather polite monster), what makes it so potentially frightening is that there really *are* people like Gavin out there, people with beautiful faces and no minds living the existence of the walking dead.

CHAPTER FIVE

Sexual and Political Puzzles: *Clive Barker's Books of Blood, Volume Four*

"The Inhuman Condition"

"The Inhuman Condition" features an important conflict in its narrative. This conflict, at one level, is an ongoing physical confrontation between a psychopathic derelict, named Pope, and Karney, the youngest member of an urban street gang. Throughout the course of the story, Pope and Karney fight for possession of a magical knotted cord. Clive Barker employs this struggle between Pope and Karney as a metaphor representing, at another level, the conflict between religion and science over the proprietorship of knowledge. The knotted cord serves as a type of mystical icon, and as a puzzle that, when deciphered, will reveal the mysteries of life, the mysteries of the *human* condition. Throughout the story, Barker utilizes metaphors emblematic of subtextual meaning. Generally in Barker's work, another reality exists beneath the surface of things, beneath appearances, a reality that is quite different from what is initially perceived. For example, as seen with both Pope and the knotted cord, appearances can be deceiving; what seems mundane can indeed prove to be fantastic. Karney, like a number of other Barker protagonists, searches for the fantastic. He seeks life's meaning in life's miracles, though he can barely understand either, and the key that unlocks miracles in Barker's stories often is a riddle or a puzzle. As Karney certainly discovers in "The Inhuman Condition" when he deciphers the puzzle of Pope's knots, beautiful and terrifying creatures may lurk in the shadows of life's riddles.

The story begins with Karney and his three gang member friends—Red, Brendan, and Catso—accosting a street derelict, a bum named Pope. Though Karney enjoys being with his older friends, he does not enjoy this "particular game." Barker's use of the term "game" here is ironic. Children do indeed play games, but not the type of games where they humiliate and batter helpless vagrants. The members of Karney's gang are mean-spirited, violent, and stupid. They fail to see what Karney does, that there is more to Pope than his derelict appearance. And all three eventually pay the price for their ignorance with their lives.

While Pope is being accosted, Karney deliberates about the bum's past, wondering what the man had been before becoming a derelict. Unlike his friends, who only perceive the surface of things, Karney is interested in deeper meanings, in the past, in what is beneath the dirt and grime. Barker's turn-of-phrase is striking when he describes Karney's thoughts about the color of Pope's blood, "There was more color [blood] where that came from, Karney knew. He'd seen pictures aplenty of spilled people — bright, gleaming coils of guts; yellow fat and purple lungs — all that brilliance was locked up in the gray sack of Pope's body."

The "gray sack of Pope's body" is representative of surface appearance. It is dull, banal, of little visual interest. But located beneath that gray surface is wild, brilliant, terrifying color, the color of life and death, the stuff of miracles. Pope's appearance parallels that of the knotted cord. Catso discovers as he empties Pope's pockets that there are many "filthy" layers to the man, that, indeed, there is a great deal more to Pope than what one first thought. Karney is ordered to search Pope's "trash," and eventually locates the cord with three knots. Catso also locates a bottle of vodka — what he was searching for in the first place — and steals it. Karney himself takes Pope's knots. Karney alone is intrigued with puzzles, while his friends are merely interested in satisfying their baser wants. Karney is more cerebral, more reflective, than his friends. He feels sorry for Pope, and embarrassed at invading Pope's privacy. Red, Brendan, and Catso possess none of these qualities. They lack Karney's sense of imagination, limited though it may be.

After much effort, Karney succeeds in untying the first knot. He is rewarded with a miracle. A reptilian creature is released, born in a pyrotechnic light display, and Karney begins to comprehend the imaginative reality that exists beneath the surface of the commonplace. Yet, in Barker's literary world, miracles can be wondrous, and they can also be deadly. The reptilian-like monster frightens Karney's friend Catso to such an extent that Catso literally kills himself by running in front of traffic trying to get away from it. Indirectly, Pope thus has his revenge upon the first of his youthful tormentors.

Frequently, Clive Barker experiments with a concept in one of his short stories in the *Books of Blood* and later more fully develops that concept in a longer, more complex work. His motif of the puzzle, for example, that, when solved, releases its terrible secret (most often some sort of nightmarish, violent aberration that is emblematic of a rational world gone awry) upon the puzzle solver, initially seen in a short story like "The Inhuman Condition," is again employed by the author in his short novel, *The Hellbound Heart*. The puzzle in *The Hellbound Heart* isn't a knotted cord; it's something called "Lemarchand's box," an elaborate device that rewards the individual who successfully deciphers its riddle with a visit from the Cenobites, sadists who practice the fine art of torture. Frank, one of the central characters in *The Hellbound Heart*, is the unlucky equivalent of Karney. Obsessed with the promise of exquisite sensations, Frank opens Lemarchand's box, and is most certainly introduced to exquisite sensations, but not the variety that he bargained for. *The Hellbound Heart* is an intricate tale, and its story of evil, twisted, convoluted passion is an excellent mirror image of the puzzle box that so dominates the narrative action and that serves as Barker's symbol for human sexual ambition.

The puzzle in "The Inhuman Condition" is the knot of evolution. It's initially possessed and held in check by Pope, but once the knot is loosened, once it is removed from the hands of the Church, then marvelous secrets are released, secrets such as the knowledge of man's origins. However, sometimes knowledge can be dangerous, even deadly. Catso is killed when Karney unties the first knot. Red—the leader of Karney's gang—dies next when his girlfriend, Anelisa, unties the second knot, after which Barker describes her as literally beginning "to see the light," the light released when knowledge is unfettered. Each knot becomes progressively easier to solve. Conversely, when knowledge begins to unfold, it becomes more difficult to control, to halt.

The knot of evolution, the puzzle of humanity's past, when unraveled discloses a progression of stages of animal development. Karney releases the reptile creature. Anelisa releases the ape creature ("There was something simian in its flayed, palpitating form..."). With fanatical determination, Pope tries to regain possession of the cord and the final knot. He threatens Karney with Brendan's life. Karney meets with Pope at a "wrecking yard," and as Karney is about to return the cord to Pope, the ape-like beast appears "with a haunted stare" to prevent the transaction. Pope kills Brendan in anger, Karney escapes with the cord and is provided with just enough time to untie the third knot. Frantically, Pope pleads, then cajoles, then threatens Karney not to unravel the final puzzle. But despite the verbal persuasiveness of Pope's entreaties, Karney liberates the third creature, the most evolutionary advanced of the three: a human-like infant.

The three creatures, then, begin the process of reassembling themselves into a new, more human-appearing entity, and a new puzzle,

> They were tying another knot, random and yet inevitable; more elaborate by far than any Karney had set fingers on. A new and perhaps insoluble puzzle was appearing from the pieces of the old, but, where *they* had been inchoate, this one would be finished and whole.

Despite the serious danger from Pope, the creatures of the knot succeed in gaining their liberty. The rebellion of knowledge triumphs. Evolution has freed itself from the clutches of the Church. The *real* miracle of life extricates itself from the pasteboard truths of hypocritical, ineffectual religious dogma. Pope attempts to escape the evolutionary being, but evolution is too strong to be avoided once it breaks out of the prison of its past. Pope, rather than his marvelous antagonist, is defeated, killed.

However, even a defeated Church is not without some measure of power. Throughout "The Inhuman Condition," Pope time and again surprises us. He is initially seen as a drunk and helpless victim brutalized by young hoodlums, yet during the course of the story, Pope wreaks a violent revenge upon his youthful antagonists — the victim becomes the victimizer, the hunted becomes the hunter. During the first confrontation between adolescent and old man, Pope demands from Karney the return of the knotted cord. Karney is amazed, as is the reader, at Pope's transformation. Pope is indeed powerful, and is indeed persuasive. Midway through the story, when Karney resists returning to Pope the magical string ("Karney was loath to give back the only fragment of mystery that had ever come his way"), the reader observes through Karney's eyes,

> The speech — so measured, so scrupulous — startled Karney, coming as it did from Pope's lips. Two weeks ago they had caught Pope in his cups — confused and vulnerable — but now, sober, the man spoke like a potentate; a lunatic king, perhaps, going among the hoi polloi as a pauper. King? No, more like *priest*. Something in the nature of his authority (in his name, even) suggested a man whose power had never been rooted in mere politics.

In this passage, Clive Barker makes obvious his use of the character Pope, both as a reference to organized religion and to the greater efficacy of the Church over the State. Barker insinuates that secular power is second rate when compared to religion. Religion, after all, demands not only an obedience to its laws and governance, but it also seeks to capture an individual's sense of wonder; and that, for Barker, is a much greater conquest than servitude to a mere political government. Government seeks to control people's actions, Barker might suggest, while religion seeks to control people's very thoughts, their imaginations. During Pope's and Karney's desperate encounter toward the end of "The Inhuman Condition," Pope physically abducts Karney. Despite the fact that the tramp has been severely wounded in his showdown with evolution, Pope still retains enough strength to drag Karney into following him to his hideaway in the wrecking yard: a "car which was buried behind a heap of rusted vehicles." Like Pope, his hideaway is not what it seems to be. It is an altar housing a book of great power.

At Pope's decrepit sanctum, he reveals some of his secrets to Karney. Pope calls the now unified creature released from the knotted cord his "brother." He tells Karney that his brother was "spellbound," until Karney's interference, and when Karney, with images of reptile and ape on his mind, utters the word "beasts," articulated as a type of question, Pope replies, "Human...Evolution's the knot, boy." Interestingly, Barker parallels the Holy Trinity of the Christian Church with his own variant in "The Inhuman Condition," a holy trinity delineating the stages in humanity's evolution, from reptile to ape to human. If there is a "human" condition to be found in this tale, Barker might tell us to look in a place where the miracle of humanity's origin is not made cryptic, such as in the knowledge of scientific fact. For Barker, the Church is where the "inhuman" condition is really located.

Pope's purpose in bringing Karney along is to use the adolescent as a type of defensive shield to be employed against the evolutionary creature. Karney overhears Pope saying to himself, "He won't harm me...not with you. Always had a weakness for children." The tramp then retrieves a book from "its niche beneath the passenger seat," and attempts to escape — but to no avail. Pope's revelations given to Karney are the last thing the old man accomplishes in life, as his "brother" finally catches up with him, attacks and kills him. Karney is thus left in sole possession of a book that Pope risked, and lost, his life in obtaining.

Karney locates Pope's book next to the old man's body, opens it, and discovers "the stained pages more rewarding than he'd anticipated."

> Here, copied out in a meticulous hand, and accompanied by elaborate diagrams, were the theorems of Pope's forgotten science: the designs of knots for the securing of love and the winning of status; hitches to divide souls and bind them; for the making of fortunes and children; for the world's ruin.

Karney is thus given a fresh puzzle to solve, a puzzle that, when more fully investigated, will grant Karney, the master puzzle solver, access to the making of puzzles, or more specifically, to the making of knots. Barker implies in the final paragraph of "The Inhuman Condition" that Karney will become a new "Pope" ("he [Karney] looked forward with rare exhilaration to the pilgrimage ahead"). Though the Church is temporarily thwarted in its attempt to control knowledge, the old, impotent regime of the past has now been replaced by youth and vigor, and religion's future looks promising.

Pope's book of knots is analogous to the Bible. Both are print texts which preserve the history and rituals of their creators. Both possess mystical information, and both are documents representative of great force, force that can be used destructively or to manipulate others, literally to tie other people's lives up in knots. A recognition of the importance of text and textual images is crucial when approaching Clive Barker's fiction. Certainly, the central metaphor for his six-volume *Books of Blood* collection is the book, and in the short stories in this collection — and elsewhere in his longer works — a close reading of Barker's fiction reveals a deep and abiding love of books. For Barker, books are emblematic of imagination. They provide the text and subtext of wonder and the wonderful. They are the essential documents of imagination. And yet, like people, books can either be good or evil, constructive or destructive. Pope's book, though remarkable, is nonetheless evil. The knowledge that's to be found in its pages is intended to obscure knowledge, to mystify what should otherwise be demystified.

"The Body Politic"

"The Body Politic" is one of Clive Barker's more ingenious short stories. The language of politics dominates the narrative, and the story itself is constructed as an extended pun on the clichéd expressions of political systems. "The Body Politic" is also one of the most frightening tales in the *Books of Blood* collection, exploiting as it does one's fear that events in life are not rationally ordered, that what at first glance appears whole and substantial is actually fractured and insane, and that paranoia dominates one's very existence. Yet underpinning the tremendous physical and emotional horror of the story is a sense of wonder. In addition to being a terrifying spectacle, the army of amputated—and subsequently liberated—hands is also a miraculous vision, something unique and bizarre, something beyond the commonplace drudgery of daily life. Thus, Barker once again blends horror and miracle in his writing, creating a type of fantasy-like allegory in the process in which he pokes fun at politics, at modern-day humanity's psychological dependence upon reason, and at the meaning of a banal, unexamined lifestyle.

In the opening paragraphs, Clive Barker quickly establishes a sense of paranoia in "The Body Politic" by stating that Charlie George's hands were "still" when he was awake, but when he was asleep, they began "their secret lives again." The notion of the secret self is perhaps Barker's most fascinating literary device. Throughout his fiction, a number of his characters engage in a dialogue with the secret side of their personalities, a side which often reveals previously untapped sources of great power. For Barker, the power of the secret self can either be constructive or destructive, depending on the point-of-view of the protagonists in the narrative. The secret self can provide either a paved avenue to Heaven or to Hell, or simultaneously to both. Barker's ability to be flexible with this literary device is a tribute to his skill as a writer of imaginative fiction. In "The Body Politic," for example, the hands' physical liberation from the body of Charlie George—from the hands' perspective—is a positive thing, a fulfillment of the promise of their secret selves. However, from Charlie George's perspective, the rebellion of his appendages is a horrifying revelation. The secret lives of his two hands serve as a brutal introduction into the world of paranoia.

Since "The Body Politic" *is* a horror story, Barker directs much of the reader's sympathy in favor of Charlie George. Charlie appears in the opening of the story to be a normal person living a normal life, and when the events of the narrative conspire to wreck his life, to kill his wife, and literally to make him into someone who is not whole, either physically or mentally, then these are truly tragic occurrences. If Charlie George is to be blamed for anything, then he should be reproached for his ignorance of the miraculous, for his not knowing of secret lives and the power of imagination to animate what is otherwise taken for granted, like the use of one's hands.

Indeed, what makes "The Body Politic" such a shocking tale is not the blood and gore that's found in the story (though the scenes in which the hands amputate themselves from their various host bodies are certainly appalling). Instead, it's that sense of paranoia, the knowledge that what was once taken for granted is now hostile and homicidal, the idea that nothing in life is "safe," and the feeling that everyone (and even more frightening, *everything*) is "out to get you": these are what make "The Body Politic" so outrageously macabre, and arguably, the finest dark fantasy story published in the twentieth century. Barker takes the obvious, external paranoia of the story (i.e. the revolt of human hands against the "body politic") and integrates this with an even deeper, more complex personal paranoia found in the protagonist, Charlie George.

The eerie passages describing the marauding army of hands are certainly intense, possessing as they do a surrealistic, nightmarish quality, but it's those moments in the narrative when Charlie George discovers that his identity and psychological well-being are at risk that provide the real emotional punch of Barker's story. Charlie's feeling of sexual inadequacy with his wife, Ellen (i.e. his growing sense of dislocation with "the act" of lovemaking), is a scary thing, especially since it involves such a personal tract of the modern ego. He is not responsible for his wife's sexual fulfillment, but his alien hands are. The reader is told that Ellen had recently begun to fix her amorous attentions upon Charlie's hands, and thus Charlie's revolting appendages (revolting in two ways) function as a provocative image for the modern-day, adulterous lifestyle that is so common in contemporary Europe and America, a lifestyle that has fostered an assortment of sexually transmitted diseases (the next person you sleep with may actually be the death of you), and that has significantly contributed to the modern high divorce rate. Barker's ambulatory hands are but a fictive illustration of a much larger social ill. Charlie's hands end up murdering Ellen before they attempt to sever themselves from his arms, and Charlie must then deal with two shocks — the death of his wife (as a symbolic extension of his sexual inadequacy) and the physical loss of an important part of himself.

Charlie George's identity as a worker is also attacked. Barker tells the reader early in the story that Charlie "was a packager by trade; he worked with his hands all day long." When Charlie felt an "uncomfortable ache" in his wrists and hands when he woke up in the morning, he merely thought his condition was a side effect of his occupation. Of course, Barker is foreshadowing in this scene the astonishing events that will soon follow. Yet Barker is making a subtle point regarding Charlie's hands, and Charlie's occupation as well. When one takes for granted the gift of life, the gift of motion and of being, then he or she is in danger of losing the gift. The unexamined life deserves its punishment, and this frequently happens in Clive Barker's fiction. Thus, early in the story when Barker describes Charlie as feeling "cut off from common experience," the reader senses that such a feeling is undeniably alarming because it is emblematic in a sociological sense of the contemporary, alienated individual, of people seeming out-of-joint with their world.

The predominating image, of course, in "The Body Politic" is politics. The entire story is an extended pun of the idiom: "plotting against the body politic," which expresses the author's own choice of words to describe the activity Charlie George's hands engage in as they clandestinely communicate with each other in the night when Charlie is asleep. The metaphor of this phrase is political. Its common meaning obviously refers to a political faction's—most probably a subordinate faction's—conspiracies against another. Barker has added humor to the phrase by writing about a literal rebellion of a person's hands against the rest of the body in "The Body Politic," a rebellion that is political as well as physical.

Clive Barker's political joke is an elaborate one. He has Charlie George's subversive hands mimic a *coup d'état*. The "Left" hand and the "Right" hand initiate their conspiracies covertly, at night, beyond the sight of the ruling government, which in this case is represented by Charlie's conscious thought. Though the rebels initially plot in secret, the unrest they foster is subconsciously felt by the political mainstream. In Charlie's case, his wrists ache, his fingers "beat out martial rhythms on the boxes he was sealing up at the factory," and his hands, of their own accord, intimately clasp total strangers' hands, all of which makes Charlie quite embarrassed. These unusual, but otherwise innocuous, occurrences proclaim the beginning of the end of Charlie's wholeness, his individual identity, just as in the political world where such endeavors herald the beginning of the end of the ruling class's power. When a revolution does eventually take place, it is frequently a bloody affair, resulting in great loss of life and tremendous hardships for the rebels and ruling class alike. Barker pursues this parallel in "The Body Politic" when he portrays those scenes where people's hands are amputated. The army of hands create their freedom through horrible, violent acts, permitting Barker in his story to have some amusement with the concept of an idealistic political revolution. By implication, Barker intimates that *all* rebellions are foolish, that they are little more than violent exercises of childish fury, and that they most often merely replace one tyranny with another.

Clive Barker, in addition, frequently incorporates religious imagery with his political satire. When Charlie's hands plot their liberation from his body, they both agree that the Right hand will manipulate the weapon that will amputate — and thus free — the Left. Right tells Left that it is the "Messiah," that without Right's charismatic leadership, "there will be nowhere to go." By having Charlie's right hand claim a religious title for what is an obviously secular, political function, Barker is parodying the political role that many religious leaders assume. Historically, as today, when these religious leaders establish a divine rationale or justification for their less-than-religious aspirations, they enhance their authority and have a greater chance of achieving their goals. After all, Christ is sometimes used by unscrupulous despots as a political — as well as religious — figure. Barker sees humor in this and drolly castigates the self-styled Messiah as being nothing more than a political boss in priest's clothing.

However, if we only saw "The Body Politic" as a criticism of politics, violent revolutions, and hypocritical Messiahs, then we would be engaging in an overly simplistic reading. There is little doubt that the author is having some amusement censuring the clichéd images of revolutionary ideology, but, more important, Barker is using his political metaphor in the story as a stepping stone to what is, for him, a more crucial matter: that being the intrusion of wild imagination into the world of reason. When Charlie is attempting to sort out his growing sense of alienation early in the story, he takes the advice of one of his acquaintances he knows at his work — a man named Ralph Fry "from Accounting, a sober, uninspiring man, whom Charlie trusted" — and calls upon Dr. Jeudwine, a "headshrinker," for help. It's ironic that Charlie's impotent quest to discover emotional stability in his life occurs because he seeks assistance from the world of science and medicine, an overly rational world unequipped to deal with armies of ambulatory hands. Unfortunately, Charlie gets his referral from a fellow worker who is sober and uninspiring, not the type of qualities that will help Charlie discover the true nature of his impending doom.

Indeed, what Charlie needs — and fails to get — at this early moment in the story is an imaginative outlook, an outlook that will cognitively prepare him for miracles. The world of science is unsympathetic to Charlie. For example, the reader is told that Dr. Jeudwine is a "good" man, but because he presents Charlie with a significant memory about his father's hands without helping Charlie to interpret correctly that memory, Dr. Jeudwine fails to equip his patient for the truth, a truth which is beyond Dr. Jeudwine's limited, scientific comprehension. At the climactic moment in the story, when Charlie's hands have just killed Ellen and are about to liberate themselves from the "tyrant" body, Charlie calls Dr. Jeudwine on the telephone late in the evening, desperately seeking assistance. The psychiatrist — the twentieth-century symbol of intellectual rationality and so-called healer of body and soul — is confused by his patient's frenzied pleas for help, and blithely tells Charlie to contact his office tomorrow. Charlie's grim fate is thus sealed. Later, after Dr. Jeudwine begins to discern that he has incorrectly diagnosed

Charlie's condition, he finally starts to doubt the veracity of his profession. Dr. Jeudwine's guilt about his failure with Charlie is humorously framed by his professional outlook about his own future. Even as he loses his professional reputation because of his blunder, Jeudwine thinks that he can still salvage something from the mess, such as a best-selling book detailing his association with "wife-murderer Charles George." When Dr. Jeudwine's death quickly approaches (by his own hands, of course), his faith in his mentor, Freud, is sorely tested. He mourns just before he dies "the efficacy of Freud and the holy writ of reason." As represented by Dr. Jeudwine, Barker's critique of the Freudian mindset is acrimonious and effective.

Another intriguing character in "The Body Politic" is the "black kid" named Boswell, a tenant of the Monmouth Street YMCA and hapless witness to an awful scene of butchery as the army of hands begin their reign of terror, capturing victims and assisting in the liberation of the other YMCA residents' hands. With this character, Barker is drawing reference to the famous James Boswell (1740–1795), companion and chronicler of Samuel Johnson (1709–1784). Like his namesake, Barker's Boswell is a chronicler of sorts, a biographer of the new revolution. Clive Barker intends Boswell to be another one of his translators, a character who is asked to read unusual texts or strange events and to serve as an objective narrator who seeks to interpret what he or she has witnessed. In fact, the entire six-volume *Books of Blood* anthology is a collection of ghost tales, or more correctly, of ghosts' tales. Barker has this eclectic congregation of stories, in total, serve as texts within texts, stories within stories, books within books. Boswell's particular tale is, unfortunately, not a pretty one, but it certainly is singular. And his role radically transforms when he becomes someone who is more than mere biographer. The incident, for example, in which Boswell's legs are amputated at the train tracks provides Barker with the opportunity to develop an ironic ending to the story. At the conclusion, Boswell is recovering in a hospital from his amputation. As he revives from his unconscious state, he hears the "shuffling of . . . intruder's feet" in his room. When he demands to know who is there, he becomes painfully aware of the loss of his legs, which are standing in front of him, "still alive and kicking." Barker writes,

> And did his [Boswell's] eyes envy their liberty, he wondered, and was his tongue eager to be out of his mouth and away, and was every part of him, in its subtle way, preparing to forsake him? He was an alliance only held together by the most tenuous of truces. Now, with the precedent set, how long before the next uprising? Minutes? Years?
> He waited, heart in mouth, for the fall of Empire.

Boswell is henceforth a witness to a new uprising, one in which he is an active, if unwitting, participant, and though Boswell wins the battle and succeeds in escaping his hand attackers at the YMCA, he ultimately loses the war when he becomes a victim of the new leg insurrection.

Charlie George also wins his particular battle, luring the mob of rebellious hands to self-destruction. This army of carnage pursues him because its beloved Messiah is still attached to his arm. After Charlie escapes from both his hospital room and his nurse (who tries to comfort him by saying that he's "in good hands"), in a chilling scene Charlie interrogates his still attached right hand and tries to strike a bargain with it. But to no avail, for at that moment the marauding hands descend upon Charlie's hospital, and the Messiah wants to go out and greet the disciples. Barker's description of the tree in the garden outside the hospital where the hands have gathered "chattering away like a manual parliament" typifies the author's intent in his work to fuse the grotesque with the miraculous. The sight is meant to be both frightening and beautiful. With his right hand—the Messiah hand—as hostage, Charlie entices the army of pursuing hands into chasing him to the hospital roof. He subsequently destroys the army when they follow him as he leaps to his death. As the hands literally rain down upon the empty parking lot below, Barker writes, "To the patients and nurses crammed at the windows it was a scene from a world of wonders—a rain of frogs would have been commonplace beside it. It inspired more awe than terror. It was fabulous." Barker highlights this miraculous scene with a puzzle, Charlie's final puzzle. While he is being pursued by the mob of hands, Charlie frantically contemplates the meaning of a Buddhist enigma, which begins "What is the sound. . .?" Charlie solves the formulation of this riddle the moment he sacrifices his life—"What is the sound of one hand clapping"—and thus he finds some measure of satisfaction before he dies; yet he doesn't solve the riddle itself. Charlie's mind can handle only so much miracle at one time, and the riddle's answer requires divine inspiration.

In "The Body Politic," Charlie George's life is tragic. His meaningless existence is punctuated by a marriage that lacks true companionship, a job that is blandly physical rather than imaginatively cerebral, and by bizarre events that are beyond his meager understanding. His body and mind are tortured relentlessly during the course of the story's plot, and his two greatest accomplishments are the articulation of a riddle he can't possibly answer and the destruction of a miracle. Yet we sympathize with Charlie because we recognize in him an image of ourselves. Like Charlie, we, too, are limited and limiting in our lives. Charlie's brush with imagination, though abusing and ultimately destructive, nonetheless provided him with a singular experience, one in which he touched the stuff of fantasy with his very hands.

"Revelations"

As with "Confessions of a (Pornographer's) Shroud" and "Scape-Goats," "Revelations" is a ghost story highlighting a powerful sense of moral outrage and subsequent moral retribution. "Revelations," in addition, reinforces Clive Barker's framing story entitled "The Book of Blood." "The Book of Blood" advances the notion that the entire six-volume *Books of Blood* collection is a compilation of tales told by the dead, tales explaining how the dead got to their present dreadful, yet marvelous, condition. The spirits in "Revelations," like the vengeful spirits in "The Book of Blood," desire to re-enter the mortal sphere of their previous existence, but instead of simply telling us dark stories, the ghosts named Sadie and Buck Durning seek answers to elusive questions, answers that might reveal what went wrong with their lives when they were alive.

The process of discovering answers to questions (or of unearthing revelations) is not limited to the efforts of Sadie and Buck to learn the truth of their relationship. The living have their lessons to learn as well. Barker counterpoises a mortal couple, the hellfire preacher John Gyer and his abused wife Virginia, with Sadie and Buck. Like Sadie, Virginia desperately yearns to find answers to important questions about her life, although at the beginning of the story she does not recognize her desperate need for self-awareness. Both women, one living and the other not, covet freedom from their brutal husbands' terrible mental and physical abuse. At one level, "Revelations" recounts a feminist narrative, a story of two women who take it upon themselves to end harassment by men, no matter what the cost.

At another level, "Revelations" is a biting satire of religious fanaticism. As seen many times in his fiction, Clive Barker objects to the institutionalization of fanatical organized religions, in particular when those institutions mask human evil with a hypocritically pious face. Though the critique of organized religion is a frequently used theme with Barker, in "Revelations" he generates his most piercing attack yet in his *Books of Blood*. Barker effectively personifies the evils of the Church—specifically the charismatic, born-again, holy-roller Church—in the character John Gyer.

What at first starts out as an intolerance of the human frailties (and, it seems, basic humanity) of others, by the end of the story transforms into an exercise of pure hate, and John Gyer is an important catalyst for other people's misery. His personality, like a terrible storm, devastates those around him, especially those who should be emotionally close to him. When Barker writes about the "vehemence" of the rainstorm early in the narrative, he is drawing reference to the vehemence of John Gyer's Biblical rhetoric. Gyer's compassion for others, especially his wife, is as barren as the landscape that they are traversing. Barker describes both the barrenness of the country, and also his wife's response to it,

> There had been talk of tornadoes in Amarillo; of cattle, cars, and sometimes entire houses lifted up and dashed to the earth again, of whole communities laid waste in a few devastating moments. Perhaps that was

what made Virginia so uneasy tonight. Either that or the accumulated fatigue of traveling so many empty highways with just the deadpan skies of Texas for scenery, and nothing to look forward to at the end of the next leg of the journey but another round of hymns and hellfire.

Early in "Revelations," Barker uses this approaching storm as a metaphor reflecting the repressed feelings of three people traveling on the Amarillo-Pampa highway. Locked in a love/hate relationship with one another, the three travelers include John Gyer, his wife Virginia, and Earl Rayburn—who serves as both general manager to John Gyer's traveling tent-revival meetings and traveling companion. Earl is driving the car, while Virginia and John are sitting in the back. Virginia is hot and uncomfortable, yet only a portion of her discomfort is due to the inclement Texas weather or the long drive in the car. She is equally distressed sitting next to her husband, John. Though physically close to each other, "to all intents and purposes a million miles' distance" separated the two. John, as usual, is oblivious to his wife's discomfort. Barker describes Virginia's state-of-mind as being like the coming storm, "She sat, the unease growing in her with every mile they covered to Pampa, listening to the vehemence of the downpour on the roof of the car, and to her husband speaking in whispers at her side." Though John is speaking in "whispers" as he obsessively reviews the Epistles of St. Paul, his incantations are spoken with hostile zeal, and identify him as a man—a fanatic—who squeezes from the Bible all the hate and anger that's to be found there, without preserving any of its lessons of love or compassion. For a man of God who is supposedly interested in people's salvation, he is less than concerned with his own wife's well-being.

On the other hand, Earl Rayburn, the Gyers' traveling companion, is much more sympathetic to Virginia's emotional needs and to Virginia's great emotional suffering. He clandestinely slips Virginia tranquilizers for "her increasingly jangled nerves" so that she can better deal with her fanatical husband. There is a "subtext" to Virginia's and Earl's relationship with each other, a secret kept from the fanatical husband, a secret not unlike a love affair that cuckolds the ignorant, unsuspecting spouse. Like a devoted lover, Earl is closely attuned to Virginia's sensitivity and sensibilities. Unlike Gyer, Earl Rayburn is truly compassionate with Virginia, and his compassion doesn't flow from sterile Biblical scripture. Unlike Gyer, Earl is not beyond the range of true redemption and ultimate salvation. Earl redeems himself through the act of loving Virginia platonically, and then Laura May Cade physically (though Earl pays for both of these relationships with a blood sacrifice). Earl is one of the few truly alive people in a story that features the dead. John Gyer, on the other hand, is as emotionally dead at the beginning of "Revelations" as he is physically by the story's conclusion.

The setting for Barker's confrontation between the living and the dead in

"Revelations" is the Cottonwood Motel, which "lay a half mile west of White Deer, in an area of waste ground south of U.S. 60." Because of fatigue and the worsening storm, the three travelers decide to stay at the motel for the night. Barker's descriptions of the rooms of the motel are used to provide a contrast to the fantastic sequence of events that will soon follow. The author writes, "The interior of the two rooms was a hymn to banality. They'd stayed in what seemed like a thousand cells like these, identical down to the sickly orange bedcovers and the light-faded print of the Grand Canyon on the pale green walls." Virginia sees these rooms as being like Purgatory (of course, Gyer is insensitive to his surroundings, as usual), and in a sense they are. The rooms are not only symbolic of Virginia's imprisonment at the hands of her husband, they are also emblematic of Sadie's and Buck's Purgatory, their life-in-death existence. Clive Barker injects fantastic mystery into banality with the motel scene. He contrasts miracles (i.e. the miracle of Sadie's and Buck's ghostly resurrection, the miracle of ghosts becoming whole and solid, and the miracle of Sadie's and Virginia's discovery of their female identities, a "revelation" quite out of keeping with what John Gyer would preach) with the commonplace, and shows that both wonderful and frightening things can happen when such a combination between imagination and pedestrianism occurs.

Barker also utilizes this blending of banality and the fantastic in his portrayal of Laura May Cade's bedroom and in his description of Laura May's avocation: the collecting of trivia. At one point in the story, Laura May invites Earl Rayburn to her bedroom at the motel for an illicit romantic interlude. Earl steps into the room and witnesses the following, "The bedroom was a mausoleum, founded, it seemed, in the name of Trivia. Laid out on the shelves, hung on the walls and covering much of the floor were items that might have been picked out of any garbage can." Yet, all of Laura May's trivia is arranged and catalogued with such "meticulous care" that Earl initially thinks her to be insane. If Laura May is insane, it's a wondrous insanity. Barker imbues her desire to make special what is otherwise "garbage" with a reverent quality. Laura May is special, Barker implies, unique, different, someone who sees miracles in the mundane. Earl Rayburn soon discovers this special quality as he enters into a sexual relationship with her, a sexual relationship that helps him to break with religious hypocrisy and with the righteous evil of John Gyer. In addition, Laura May's curatorship of the gun Sadie used to shoot and kill Buck makes the weapon available for Virginia's use later on in the story.

Clive Barker employs the traditional ghost story as a narrative vehicle by which he can examine the problem of marital violence — and also the promise of the women's rebellion against the male dominated world, a rebellion not without its price but an act that leads to an understanding of inner power (and inner peace) that is not dependent upon masculine consent. The frame of the larger ghost story encompasses two parallel sub-plots that ultimately converge. The one sub-plot recounts the ghosts' (Sadie and Buck Durning's) attempt to "retrace the journey they'd taken thirty years before, to see if they could discover how and why their marriage had ended in murder." Exactly three decades earlier, on June 2, 1955, Sadie had shot Buck to death with a Smith and Wesson .38 pistol, and then she herself was executed for Buck's murder. Sadie willingly goes to her execution. She is prepared to pay the price for her liberation, and her bravery makes her an admirable (and perhaps even heroic) protagonist. On the auspicious anniversary date of Buck's murder, both he and Sadie are given the opportunity to reexamine past mistakes. They are given a second chance. Unfortunately, despite her noble efforts, the callous, brutal Buck seems unwilling or unable to change, and this causes problems once more, not only for his tormented wife, Sadie, but also for another tormented wife, Virginia Gyer.

The second sub-plot narrates the growing, destructive tension between John Gyer and Virginia. Like Sadie, Virginia is brutalized by her husband, a victimization that denies Virginia not only her integrity as an individual, but also her very sanity. When the Gyers and Earl Rayburn stop for the evening at the Cottonwood Motel, they are given the only two rooms left in the motel, and one of the rooms ("Room Seven") is where, precisely thirty years earlier, Sadie had killed Buck. The two sub-plots convene into one when the two ghosts begin to gain substance, and also begin to interfere with the lives of the living.

Sadie recognizes the fact that as she and Buck become more substantial they are beginning to terrify the already emotionally devastated Virginia. It's revealing about their respective personalities — and about the author's deliberate contrast between male brutality and female victimization — that Sadie is sensitive to Virginia's discomfort, while Buck thinks of only a selfish need for sexual fulfillment. When Sadie spurns him (she is, after all, more amazed than Buck with the miracle of their transformation from ghost to person), Buck then turns to the hapless Virginia. He nearly rapes Virginia, until, like Sadie, she discovers a sense of identity, a powerful feminine identity that savagely rebels against the male brute. With Sadie's .38 pistol in hand, she shoots the near-solid specter of Buck. The bullet divides Buck's "smoky body," passes through him and into her husband, John Gyer, killing him on the spot. Virginia has effectively eliminated both of her oppressors with one shot. She has done this against great odds and in heroic fashion, as Sadie had done thirty years before.

Even though Sadie was unable to heal the old wounds of her past relationship with Buck, she is able to have a positive impact upon the world of the living by advising Virginia to give herself up to the authorities, and not to commit suicide. Virginia takes Sadie's advice. Pretending that she is insane, Virginia surrenders to the police, and thus the woman as victim has taken an additional step past rebellion and independence, a step toward self-preservation and reintegration with herself. She accomplishes what Sadie had accomplished earlier, her independence from her male victimizer, but she also has done better than Sadie in that she wants to live her life.

Because of her capacity for kindness, her empathy for a fellow sufferer, and because she was able to heal the catastrophic injuries of others (though she failed at this with herself), Sadie completes the transformation begun early in the story; only this time, she does not change physically. She is changed spiritually. Sadie evolves during the course of her life and death from victim, to rebel, to ghost, and finally to angel. Her nobility ultimately triumphs against great odds, first against the man who so brutalized her, and then against the male-dominated system which executed her without regard for the extenuating circumstances.

All in all, there are several things disclosed to the characters (and the reader) in "Revelations." The first revelation is that professed goodness — in the grim form of the hypocritical John Gyer — can be turned into an ugly weapon, that religious ritual can be used to bind others in the chains of evil. John Gyer claims an understanding of the Bible, but he only comprehends the words of the book and not the meaning, or subtext, behind the words. What little he does know of Christianity is the grim stuff, the fire and brimstone rhetoric of the Book of Revelations. The second revelation in the story is the understanding that domestic violence against women by men is a terrible, cruel act, one that denies the identity of women and leads to a cycle of unreasoning chaos. The failure of both Virginia Gyer's and Sadie Durning's respective relationships is an apt demonstration of how men — who embrace the notions of emotional robbery and sexual greed — can be blindly destructive of others, and most interestingly, of themselves. Such blind destruction introduces us to the final revelation in Clive Barker's "Revelations": that a valid and truly pious vision of human sin and redemption is difficult to achieve. Those who profess such an understanding the most vociferously, Barker implies, are usually the ones who are the most blind.

"Down, Satan!"

"Down, Satan!" is one of the shortest tales to appear in the *Books of Blood*, yet, despite its brevity, it is a fascinating story. Following in order of publication as it does "Revelations," "Down, Satan!" effectively reinforces the author's thematic discussion of the evil and the pervasiveness of religious fanaticism while contributing to his game metaphor (i.e. the injurious consequences of playing nefarious games). In addition, Barker echoes images from literature and classic film in "Down, Satan!" His tale plumbs the depths of our collective artistic consciousness in order to both mirror and parody those artistic images, and in order to provide his story with a cognitive base of meaning that is far greater than the story's brief length implies. "Down, Satan!," in essence, thus departs from the narrative limitations of the short story form and functions more like an existential philosophical tract, one that advances a powerful moral allegory about a godless man who in his desperate efforts to find a god becomes himself that for which he so desperately searches.

Gregorius is but one of two characters named in "Down, Satan!," both of whom are quite insane (the other character identified in the story is the mad architect, Leopardo, who is enlisted by Gregorius to build a literal Hell on earth). Gregorius is described as being "rich beyond all calculation." Gregorius reminds the reader of an interesting cross between Aristotle Onassis and Charles Foster Kane (from the Orson Welles's film, *Citizen Kane*, 1941).

In fact, Barker relies heavily upon several images found in *Citizen Kane*. Gregorius, like Kane and Onassis, possesses the wealth and the power to create anything he desires. He has the ability—as few do—to manufacture either wonderful dreams or terrifying nightmares, but since Gregorius is a man who owns a great deal yet lacks the one thing that is beyond his reach (i.e. happiness), his efforts to achieve the one ultimately result in his forfeiting the other.

Barker tells us that before his "dizzying rise" to wealth and power, Gregorius "found succor" in the Catholic faith that he was raised with as a child. However, Gregorius is a protagonist who discovers later in life that, due to neglect, he lacks faith as well as happiness. Barker writes, "it was only at the age of fifty-five, with the world at his feet, that he woke one night and found himself Godless." Barker employs this great contrast between faith and godlessness as the larger frame of the story in which Gregorius's fanatical quest to build a literal emblem of his desire for the sublime ironically actualizes desire.

Gregorius becomes that which he so desperately seeks, but not in an anticipated way. Barker tells us in a slightly sarcastic tone that Gregorius initiates his quest to rediscover God, to "make good his loss," by performing benevolent acts, such as the founding of "seminaries and leper colonies." Gregorius's efforts naturally fail, and he then develops the notion that if he places "his soul into the direst jeopardy," if he can somehow concoct a meeting between himself and the archfiend Satan, then that would evoke some response from God.

Gregorius, like John Gyer from "Revelations," is a zealot who will go to any extreme to achieve his desires. He is someone who subverts the means to attain the end, no matter what the moral cost. Barker thus suggests with Gregorius's character that though the desire for miracles is a noble crusade (perhaps the noblest crusade in Barker's eyes), if one becomes obsessive in his or her quest, then the virtuous goal may become debased, transformed into the very antithesis of one's aims. Hence, the pursuit of the divine, if overdone, engenders the demonic. In his search for a faith, Gregorius sacrifices much of his wealth and the very commercial stability of his business empire. Gregorius's obsessiveness is destructive, but this means little to him if he can attain his single-minded ambition. With this character (i.e. the fanatic seeker of Truth) Barker echoes in "Down, Satan!" the imaginative writings of Edgar Allan Poe.

Poe's premise in a number of his tales is the protagonist's attempt, through isolation and the contemplation of beauty (preferably, the death of a beautiful woman), to achieve revelations into the nature of Truth or of Heaven, as perhaps best illustrated in the poem "Israfel" (1831). Unfortunately, this process may sometimes go afoul, and the protagonist's isolation then leads to madness, such as seen in the poem "The Raven" (1845) and the short story "The Tell-Tale Heart" (1843). Like Roderick Usher's predicament in Poe's "The Fall of the House of Usher" (1839), Gregorius's adventure is one that recounts a descent from emotional instability into darkest insanity. Gregorius's descent is both figurative (his growing madness) and literal (he lives in his "suite of chambers on the ninth level" of his self-created Hell, a reference to Dante's *Inferno* [transcribed circa 1320] where the deepest tier of the underworld is the ninth level).

"Down, Satan!" also resounds with allusions to another Poe story, "The Masque of the Red Death" (1842). In Poe's tale, the ironically named Prince Prospero gathers about him one thousand knights and ladies in his abbey stronghold to escape the Red Death plague that is ravaging the countryside. Prospero's aristocratic mockery of death is turned back upon himself and his followers when the "Red Death," in costume, makes an appearance at Prospero's masquerade and forces all the revelers to confront the reality of both their own mortality and the Red Death's omnipotent power. As does Prospero, Gregorius—because of his tremendous vanity—creates his own tormented version of an isolated stronghold, though rather than serving as an escape from the evil of the Red Death, Gregorius's "New Hell" (as it is termed in the story) is meant to attract evil.

Gregorius is very thorough in his fanaticism; his New Hell draws inspiration from the finest authoritative texts available. Barker writes, "The finished designs owed something to de Sade and to Dante, and something more to Freud and Krafft-Ebing."

Barker also makes reference in "Down, Satan!" to Orson Welles's motion picture, *Citizen Kane*. Welles's *Citizen Kane* is a thinly disguised interpretation of William Randolph Hearst and Hearst's rise to power in the newspaper business. In Welles's film, Charles Foster Kane constructs a sprawling Gothic residence in Florida which he calls Xanadu, where he stocks the great art treasures he has acquired from around the world. Kane's Xanadu is a grotesque place, one that is uninviting and cold despite its palatial splendor. Xanadu is emblematic of the tormented mind of Charles Foster Kane. He never finds happiness there, and it serves as a forceful reminder that wealth does not always buy happiness. Gregorius's version of Xanadu is no less fantastic than Kane's in its design. Intended as a lure to tempt Satan into a meeting with Gregorius, Gregorius's New Hell is a folly of magnificent proportions, reflective of a monstrous ego and an equally monstrous will. Both Xanadu and New Hell are the residences of tormented and tormenting beasts, animalistic characters who destroy others in their desire for a narcissistic self-gratification and who are also tragic because they ultimately destroy themselves.

Along with Barker's use of cinematic and literary references, images of games and game playing appear in "Down, Satan!" Specifically, Barker employs the game of hide-and-seek to illustrate Gregorius's steadily increasing madness. After he has built his New Hell, Gregorius awaits the arrival of Satan. His vanity refuses to believe that the Prince of Darkness will not be sorely tempted, "His plan could not fail. The Devil would be bound to come, if only out of curiosity to see this leviathan built in his name, and when he did, Gregorius would be waiting." Gregorius, residing in his clockwork underworld, thinks he hears noises, various "disturbances" that he fancies as proof of Satan's occupancy of New Hell. He races around his creation expecting to confront the Devil, but he always seems to be a bit late. The author writes, "The Prince of Darkness was here, Gregorius could have no doubt of it, but he was keeping to the shadows. Gregorius was content to play along. It was the Devil's party, after all. His to play whatever game he chose." Gregorius's childlike belief that Satan is in residence with him reinforces his adolescent reliance upon the game. It may be the Devil's party in "Down, Satan!," but it is Gregorius who is the major player. Interestingly, through Gregorius's observations the reader sees clues to support Gregorius's contention that Satan is indeed present in New Hell. However, Barker leaves a great deal of room for doubt as to whether these clues ("Wasn't that his [the Devil's] fingerprint on the door handle? His turd on the stairs?") really exist at all, except in the deranged mind of New Hell's owner.

Yet the ambiguity of Gregorius's so-called proof of the Devil's presence, and even the ambiguity of the Devil's (and God's) actuality in general, reinforce Barker's idea in "Down, Satan!" that gods and devils are personal creations, that divinity or the devilish are internal constructs, originating from within rather than without. When Gregorius is finally caught by the authorities, though he has never physically met with "the Serpent," the reader discovers that Gregorius himself has become the Devil incarnate. Gregorius's nefarious quest has transformed him into that which he so desperately sought—the master of torture and death in Hell. Gregorius has become his own Satan. After he has been caught and his ugly deeds are brought to light, Gregorius refuses to atone for his sins and even brags about his deeds to the world as if they were marvelous accomplishments. Barker writes at the conclusion of the story,

> But there were those, even among the cardinals [of the Church], who could not put his [Gregorius's] unrepentant malice out of their heads, and — in the privacy of their doubt — wondered if he had not succeeded in his strategy. If, in giving up all hope of angels — fallen or otherwise — he had not become one himself.

Barker's moral in "Down, Satan!" is an existential one. "Good" and "evil" are relative concepts and do not filter down from Heaven above or bubble up from Hell below. Instead, good and evil are created by people, not gods, and the efficacy of morality is thus determined by an individual's actions. Because Gregorius practiced evil, he became the embodiment of evil. Barker's existential argument implies that the individual is solely responsible for the creation of Heaven and Hell. The fanatically naïve belief in the existence of God and the Devil, Barker implies, allows criminal acts to be committed and the responsibility for those acts to be pushed off upon some abstract religious construct that is beyond the obligation of the individual. Barker's "Down, Satan!," then, belies its brief length with a thematic sophistication rarely duplicated in other horror stories.

"The Age of Desire"

Clive Barker has never been one to shy away from using explicit sexual content in his horror fiction, and the final story in the *Books of Blood, Volume Four*, entitled "The Age of Desire," takes an outrageous "what if" sexual premise as far as it will go. Barker asks the question in this story: what would happen if the ultimate aphrodisiac were discovered? Barker answers this question for us, in part, by writing a monster story, one that establishes references to Mary Shelley's *Frankenstein* (1818) and to Robert Louis Stevenson's *The Strange Case of Dr. Jekyll and Mr. Hyde* (1886). Like Shelly and Stevenson, Barker knows that the plot frame of the monster story, if done well, is perhaps the best equipped formulaic device to handle moral allegory. "The Age of Desire" purports to be an apocalyptic fantasy, but actually ends up being a critique of the relationship between sex and death. "The Age of Desire" also reintroduces us to several of Barker's favorite themes: the fanatical Messiah character (in the guise of Dr. Welles) and the intellectually limited policeman (as seen with Inspector Carnegie). In "The Age of Desire," Barker accentuates his mix of monster story and apocalyptic fantasy with a strikingly powerful conflagrative image. Fire, both physical and emotional, consumes people and places in this tale; human sexual lust is colored bright flame-red, and the metaphoric light created is quite revealing of human (and inhuman) nature.

Basically, "The Age of Desire" is a monster story. The so-called "monster" of the narrative is a character named Jerome. Jerome was used as a guinea pig for a clandestine experiment to discover an effective aphrodisiac that could be marketed for commercial purposes. He is given an injection late one evening by Dr. Dance, the director of the experiment, and her assistant Dr. Welles. The experiment not only succeeds, but it transcends all expectations by changing the hapless Jerome into a ravenous sexual monster, a libidinously perverse creature who attempts to rape and kill everyone he comes into contact with. Barker has patterned both Dr. Dance and Jerome after Victor Frankenstein and his monster from Mary Shelley's Gothic novel. Barker borrows Shelley's philosophical premise from *Frankenstein* — the notion that certain realms of knowledge are best left to God, and that crossing the boundaries of these realms (even for scientific purposes) can be a destructive thing — and makes effective use of it in his version of the Frankenstein myth. As in Shelley's novel, the laboratory as evil icon dominates certain scenes of the story. It is employed by Barker as the site of a vile murder (and worse). The images of Jerome's injection with the "Project Blind Boy" serum, Jerome's subsequent rape and murder of Dr. Dance — who literally dances with death in the story — and the cruel experiments with the laboratory monkeys: these reinforce our stereotyped notions of the mad scientist's lair. Jerome, like Frankenstein's monster, has his revenge upon his creator, in essence serving as a tool of divine retribution against the scientist who dared to tap the forbidden reservoir of God's knowledge. Dr. Dance and Victor Frankenstein are Promethean figures, punished for their profound arrogance. Barker's intent in "The Age of Desire" is to be outrageously Gothic in his laboratory scenes. As in the traditional Gothic tale, he wants to establish a narrative situation in which the social order is violated. He encourages his reader to envision the connection between evil and science-gone-wrong that is such an integral part of the Gothic novel: best illustrated in *Frankenstein* and in the popular series of "Frankenstein" horror films adapted from Shelley's novel that were released by Universal Studios during the 1930s and 1940s.

If the setting and narrative frame of "The Age of Desire" are loosely patterned after Mary Shelley's *Frankenstein*, then Jerome — the so-called monster of Barker's story — is equally suggestive of Robert Louis Stevenson's Henry Jekyll/Edward Hyde. In Stevenson's short novel, the respectably Victorian Dr. Jekyll develops a potion that will release his otherwise suppressed evil nature. Stevenson meant *The Strange Case of Dr. Jekyll and Mr. Hyde* to be a criticism of moral hypocrisy, an attack against those people who showed a socially respectable front but who otherwise engaged in debauchery. Whether he also intended it or not, Stevenson's narrative is a sexual fable. It admonishes against the temptation to give in to one's ignoble, sexual (read: beastly) instincts. It warns the reader about the dire consequences of seeking escape from moral constraints, and it serves (at least it did during Stevenson's era) as a type of ethical/religious propaganda; it was quoted often in both the church pulpit and in ecclesiastical newspaper articles of its day (Dalby 403).

The events surrounding Barker's protagonist, Jerome, in several significant ways match those surrounding Stevenson's Jekyll/Hyde. Both characters partake in a doomed experiment, one that involves a scientifically created, yet magically endowed, serum that deteriorates the moral responsibilities of the individual, while simultaneously heightening the baser drives. In both stories, once the protagonist is injected with the serum, the evil effects of the drug assume total control of the person and eventually lead to the protagonist's death. Jerome and Jekyll/Hyde, following their respective transformations from man to beast — from respectable to despicable — become outcasts of society and are persecuted by society. They are both perceived by the reader as being monstrous, as something inhuman and deviant. Yet, unlike Stevenson, Barker sees his character's monstrous aberration as being a blend of miracle and affliction, rather than only an affliction. Barker's monsters generally tend to be rather non-traditional, and Jerome follows this pattern.

Granted, once Jerome has begun his metamorphosis, his actions are vile and reprehensible. After his injection with the "Blind Boy" serum, he becomes the supreme rapist, one who not only violates his victim through sexual intercourse, but who violates the life of his victim as well (he wants to rip the beating heart from his victim's chest). Barker illustrates the extreme degenerate nature of Jerome's transformed character by having him at one point in the story lustfully rape a brick wall. He is a man who is totally out of control of his physical *and* mental sexual identity, and despite his many severe crimes of passion (including sodomy and murder), he is nonetheless a pathetic individual, someone who is tragically and thoroughly alienated from his new life ("I'm dying of *terminal* joy," Jerome thinks to himself at one point in the story). Jerome's inhuman lust takes its inevitable toll upon his body. It rapaciously feeds upon him as he attempts to quench his insatiable desire, eventually turning him into a mere shell of his former self.

Yet along with acquiring the rudiments of the disturbing, the pathetic, and the vile, Jerome gains, after his change, several wonderful qualities. For example, his physical senses have radically changed, evolving into a higher, nearly superhuman state. Jerome returns to his apartment (after he has been injected by Dr. Dance with the "Blind Boy" drug and after he has raped and killed Dr. Dance, providing her with undeniable proof of the potion's vitality) in a daze, and when he regains consciousness, inspecting his bizarre wounds and trying to piece together what had happened, he turns on his radio and hears music in a totally new way. Barker writes,

> It was as though he were hearing the words and music for the first time, as though all his life he had been deaf to their sentiments. Enthralled, he forgot his pain and listened. The songs told one seamless and obsessive story: of love lost and found, only to be lost again. The lyricists filled the airways with metaphor — much of it ludicrous, but no less potent for that.

This passage suggests the new Jerome is now able to comprehend metaphor, the meaning behind the songs. Vision, as well as hearing, is affected. In addition, Jerome is now able to see amazing illusion,

> He began to tremble. His eyes, strained (or so he reasoned) by the unfamiliar spectacles, began to delude him. It seemed as though he could see traces of light in his skin, sparks flying from the ends of his fingers.
>
> He stared at his hands and arms. The illusion, far from retreating in the face of this scrutiny, increased. Beads of brightness, like the traces of fire in ash, began to climb through his veins, multiplying even as he watched.

Like Stevenson's Edward Hyde, Jerome's animalistic senses have dramatically improved, have dramatically elevated his cognitive understanding of reality to a new, fantastic level, but this is a terrible gift. For Jekyll, it eventually brings ignominious death. For Jerome, it immediately leads him to lustful thoughts of his landlady, Mrs. Morrisey, and his inevitable downward spiral toward death accelerates.

Barker creates an amusing pun in "The Age of Desire" by naming Dr. Dance's aphrodisiac the "Blind Boy." This appellation is used by Dr. Dance as the code phrase for the project. Her intent is to be facetious, parodying the trite expression sometimes told to adolescents by their parents about how self-abusive sex leads to blindness. Barker's pun of Dr. Dance's scientific code name occurs at two points in the story. The first is when, after Jerome's injection with the "Blind Boy" serum, he indeed becomes blinded by an inhuman passion. That blindness, however, is tempered by his equally inhuman transformed senses and is later radically reversed when Jerome can see things that others cannot. The second instance of Barker's punning happens at the very end of the story when Jerome, while dying, senses the absurdity of his death (and perhaps of life in general) and laughs. The intellectually lacking Inspector Carnegie, who is always one step behind Jerome's movements, after hearing the tormented man's dying laughter, asks the just expired (and forevermore unresponsive) Jerome a pointed question,

> "Tell me..." Carnegie whispered to the man, sensing that despite his preemption he had missed the moment; that once again he was, and perhaps would always be, merely a witness of consequences. "Tell me. *What was the joke?*"
>
> But the blind boy, as is the wont of his clan, wasn't telling.

Barker humorously implies in this final scene that we all sooner or later will become blind boys, that death will inevitably blind everyone's vision. The dullard Carnegie is too dim-witted for sophisticated jokes, especially those jokes involving a subtext of meaning. He (like Jerome and like us), when all is said and done, is blind in the end as well.

Inspector Carnegie, in fact, is an additional example of Barker's dislike of blind, institutional authority, such as the police, and this dislike reinforces one of the author's important thematic interests in his *Books of Blood*. Carnegie represents, for Barker, the image of banality. He is described as being accustomed to boredom and as being more than accustomed to the mind-numbing bureaucracy of his profession. His best quality, the author states, is that he has learned over time "the art of going with the flow." He lacks imagination and initiative, two cardinal sins in Barker's fiction, and like most of the other policeman characters in Barker's novels and short stories, Carnegie is single-minded in his slavish devotion to duty. Barker writes, "All that mattered [to Carnegie], in the fullness of time, was that the finger be pointed and that the guilty quake."

Clive Barker attacks religious fanaticism, as well as professional fanaticism, in "The Age of Desire." He utilizes Dr. Dance's laboratory assistant, Dr. Welles, as a humorous, yet pathetic, Messiah figure in the story. Welles views the invention of the "Blind Boy" drug as the heralding of a new age of mankind, a literal "Age of Desire," and he envisions himself as the prophet of this new age. Welles's monstrous ego is only matched by Jerome's monstrous sexual passion. Both characters are dominated by lust: Jerome is controlled by a lust for sex, and Welles by a lust for power. Though Dr. Welles initially had only a professional interest in the development of the "Blind Boy" project, his attitude changes. Barker writes, "But his [Welles's] motives had matured through their months of secret work. He had come to think of himself as the bringer of the millennium. He would not have anyone attempt to snatch that sacred role from him." Barker describes Welles at one point as being "blinded" (another reference to the "Blind Boy" phrase) by the thought of becoming the new "Apostle of Desire." Hence, Welles's religious thirst, like that of many of Barker's other Messianic characters, is catastrophically self-serving and can only be quenched in the waters of destruction. Ultimately, Welles is even more pernicious than Jerome, because Jerome's madness is tempered, even muted, in the end by an expanded vision of compassion for suffering and Welles's fanaticism is not. Jerome would have made for an infinitely better Messiah than Welles, except that Jerome could not discuss the miracle of his transformation.

Along with Dr. Dance's ambivalent gift (in the guise of the "Blind Boy" drug) of heightened senses, Jerome, near the conclusion of "The Age of Desire," also experiences heightened emotional sympathy for fellow sufferers. When he returns to the laboratory scene where his tragedy began, he encounters the fanatical Dr. Welles, who is in the process of destroying all evidence relating to the "Blind Boy" experiment, including several laboratory monkeys. The aphrodisiac serum has been tested on monkeys, turning them into sexually tortured creatures. Eventually, as with Jerome, they will all die hideously of terminal lust. While observing Dr. Welles as he kills one of the remaining surviving monkeys, Jerome is engulfed with feelings of sympathy. The author writes,

> *Sentiment*, Jerome thought, muddily remembering the songs on the radio that had first rewoken the fire in him. Didn't Welles understand that the processes of heart and head and groin were indivisible? That sentiment, however trite, might lead to undiscovered regions? He wanted to tell the doctor that, to explain all that he had seen and all that he had loved in these desperate hours. But somewhere between mind and tongue the explanations absconded.

In the above passage, Barker shows us that Jerome has finally made the transition in his new-found emotional perceptions from the mere gut-level experience to a rarefied level, a level where he can understand the pain in others. He is able to strip away the plain surface of popular music (and, by implication, reality) to mine the core of genuine emotion underneath. Jerome's journey may have begun in the blinding fire of mindless passion, but toward the end of his life, like the phoenix rising from the ashes of its own fire, his passion has become ennobled. His great tragedy in "The Age of Desire" is neither his wasted life nor his imminent death, but that he can't communicate adequately his new, heightened understanding of love to others. Indeed, love for Jerome early in the story acted as blind, brutal, murderous lust, but in the end he understood it to be a philosophical quality that transcends the physical. His education into the nature of love began in death and destruction, but it concluded in hope and compassion. Unfortunately, Jerome is not a competent storyteller. The text of his evolved passion will remain indecipherable, unreadable, and thus lost.

Destruction is an integral part of Barker's "The Age of Desire." Images of fire engulf the story—the fire of Jerome's lust, the fire of Welles's monomania, the fire of Dr. Dance's greed (after all, the reader is told that she rushed her experiments to achieve quick results), and the fire of apocalyptic destruction that looms as a possible outcome if Welles has his way. Jerome's metamorphosis is magical, and his subsequent visual illusions involve light and fire. Welles builds two "bonfires" to destroy the "Blind Boy" material in Dr. Dance's laboratory, and in his physical confrontation with Welles at the conclusion of the story, Jerome wishes he could "ignite" both himself and Welles (whom he is embracing in physical conflict), thus "consuming maker and made in one cleansing flame." Jerome's very life after his injection has acted as a terrible, bright flame, incinerating his physical being to mere ash. The brighter the passion, the more intense the sensual experience, the faster the fire of life is spent. Jerome's flame was short-lived, fearsome, but intense.

In becoming something less than human, Jerome became something more than human. Before he could comprehend the significance of the human condition, in particular the emotion of suffering, he had to act as a monster and cause great suffering in others. This paradox is a crucial point of reference in Barker's fiction and highlights his delight in establishing incongruities. There also resides a subtle anti-drug message in this story. This message, though not overt, is certainly in keeping with the author's own expressed dislike of drugs and their effects. Finally, "The Age of Desire" is another example of Clive Barker's fascination with subtext and secret lives. Dr. Dance, for example, attempts to keep her "Blind Boy" experiments a secret, and the scientific laboratory therefore hides an ugly mystery. The banal exterior of Dr. Welles's character obscures the seething prophet within, and the supposedly competent Inspector Carnegie is nothing more than an inglorious fool. When the mask hiding Jerome's passions is removed, he is enlightened, ultimately, about both the complex metaphor of sentiment and the subtext of suffering. He leaves this world with a joke on his lips, a joke with a meaning that will forever remain undeciphered.

CHAPTER SIX

Mother's Fine Children: *Clive Barker's Books of Blood, Volume Five*

"In the Flesh"

"In the Flesh" is a pivotal tale in the *Books of Blood* in that it brings together into one story a number of significant themes that appear elsewhere in Clive Barker's short fiction; in addition, it articulates a theory of the horror genre that functions as the philosophical basis for much of Barker's imaginative work. Barker employs a prison setting for "In the Flesh," a setting that highlights his interest in the "trap" as narrative metaphor. He also relies upon visual imagery in this tale. He examines the relationship between shadow and light, night and day, and interprets this imagery as being a moral reflection of the characters' motivations in the story. In an intriguing twist, Barker sees the murderer as a type of populist figure, and murder as a democratic act, but perhaps most importantly, Barker scrutinizes in detail a unique interpretation of the afterlife, and of damnation. He proposes within the plot frame of "In the Flesh" a theory of the cognitive effect of horror fiction, one that persuasively argues the point that a person's lack of control over events in his or her life engenders the sensation of horror, both in his characters' motivations and in his reader's understanding of what is actually frightening. Finally, "In the Flesh" serves as a linchpin for the *Books of Blood* anthology; appearing in the middle of the six-volume anthology, it helps support the unity established in the beginning and end framing stories by alluding to Barker's "highway of the dead" idea.

With "In the Flesh," Barker returns to a favored thematic setting: the prison. But unlike "The Yattering and Jack" or *The Damnation Game*—other stories that employ prison imagery—"In the Flesh" is physically set within a prison. The protagonist of the story is a small-time convict named Cleveland Smith. As the narrative begins, Cleve is serving time—his third visit—in the

Pentonville prison for "handling marijuana." Cleve is a veteran survivor of his environment. The author writes that though he might look like an attorney from a distance, a closer inspection reveals "the scar on his neck, the result of an attack by a penniless addict, and a certain wariness in his gait, as if with every step forward he was keeping the option of a speedy retreat." However, Cleve possesses a compassionate heart that seems to contradict his tough exterior. Early in the story, Cleve tells his cell-mate Billy Tait that he's nobody's friend and that he doesn't want to be burdened with the responsibility of looking after Billy. Cleve, without expressing much enthusiasm, tells Billy, "Seems I've been volunteered...to keep you from getting mauled," yet, throughout the remainder of the story, Cleve acts as young Billy's protector and confidant (up to the point, at least, when Cleve recognizes Billy for the tragic monster of shadow that he is, and at that moment Cleve is alienated by his fear of Billy). For example, early in the narrative Cleve attempts at his own peril to protect Billy from the sexual advances of an inmate named Lowell, who is a cruel and violent man.

Thus, Barker has in Cleveland Smith a sympathetic protagonist, a character whom the reader identifies with and someone whom we can feel for. By placing this sympathetic criminal in several different types of prisons (and traps) — from the commonplace to the unearthly — during the course of the story, Barker encourages us to fear for Cleve's safety, and his very sanity. At the mundane level, Cleve is able to deal with those problems that confront him at Pentonville. In fact, the reader senses his general comfort with his lifestyle there. Cleve thinks of himself as "a leopard born and bred." He is content living a life of crime ("Crime was easy, work was not"). He is not disenfranchised or embittered, but instead seems to be able to cope with those otherwise normal obstacles that one might expect to find in a penitentiary. However, as Cleve begins to confront the unusual — specifically the supernatural — during the course of the narrative, his self-assurance starts to falter. It eventually disappears altogether.

Cleve really doesn't feel trapped until he begins to understand better exactly who, or what, his cell-mate is. Midway through "In the Flesh," Cleve witnesses Billy's communication with his dead grandfather, Edgar Tait. He also views Edgar's and Billy's visit to the city of the dead and witnesses Billy's subsequent metamorphosis from shadow monster to human. These events are quite frightening for Cleve since he is trapped in the same cell with Billy and does not fully understand what is happening to Billy (or to him). After Edgar is aware of Cleve's meddling with Billy, the most tense moment in the story occurs when Cleve is awaiting the diabolical Edgar's judgement about his fate. Barker's use of the trap image is terrifying here. Cleve screams for help when Billy transforms into the shadow monster and summons his grandfather, the vile Edgar Tait. But will help arrive in time for him?

Barker has as his most fascinating use of the trap image the city of the dead—or the afterlife necropolis—that Cleve first views in his dreams. The purpose of this city, the reader learns by the end of the story, is to imprison murderers in the exact scene of their crimes so that they can face what they have done and eventually come to grips with their guilt. At first glance, this necropolis is a horrifying place, a place that darkly boggles the imagination. To be trapped with one's crime for all eternity is a vastly appalling notion, a cosmic profanity, the ultimate prison (one that dwarfs into insignificance the mundane Pentonville). But Barker offers his characters an escape from these traps. Cleve survives his confrontation with the supernatural in his jail cell. He eventually gets out of Pentonville (only to be killed on the outside), and Barker gives us the promise that Cleve will eventually escape from his afterlife prison, to be reborn into a new life and to have a new chance at living free of traps.

Along with his use of the trap metaphor, Clive Barker creates a contrast between light and shadow in this story that reflects what is happening to the characters and also emphasizes the dream-like quality of the narrative. At one point midway through "In the Flesh," Cleve fakes sleep to observe if anything unusual will happen to Billy. But Cleve views more than he can believe. As he waits in the dark trying not to fall asleep, he begins to sense that something is amiss. He sees that the shadows in the cell are wrong, specifically that "the shadows in the corners of the cell, and on the opposite wall, were not empty." The invasion of shadows, an invasion of the otherworldly into the grim reality of the prison, is a symbolic as well as physical manifestation of evil.

There are two shadowy evils in this story. The first is the thoroughly vile Edgar St. Clair Tait, a mass murderer and consummate liar. His corruption is absolute, as absolute as is the murkiness of his shape-shifting (or more correctly, his shadow-shifting) ability. Edgar is Billy's dead grandfather, a former inmate executed and buried at the prison. He attempts to seduce his grandson with the promise of a nefarious education—the ability to transform into a shadow monster—but what grandfather Edgar is really after is someone to replace him in the eternal prison of the afterlife. Edgar's shadow, in both a moral and a physical sense, is the darkest in the story. He professes an altruistic motive (the attempted destruction of his so-called evil family), but, in actuality, his motivations are thoroughly self-serving; he simply wants to escape from a prison—and his fate. And he is willing to sacrifice his naïve grandson Billy in the process.

The second shadowy evil is Billy Tait. Billy, during the course of "In the Flesh," is learning how to become corrupt. With his grandfather's guidance, he is mastering his ability to transform into the shadow monster (an apparent genetic trait). His grandfather, Edgar, also teaches Billy how to murder, and Billy has learned this talent quite well, as is demonstrated by his mutilation killing (*via* supernatural means) of his former tormentor, Lowell.

Edgar encourages Billy to murder because he wants his grandson to assume his place in the afterlife prison. However, Billy is not an intrinsically bad person. He is more the victim than the victimizer. He has been subverted by his crafty grandfather. When Cleve witnesses Billy's several transformations, Billy's physical body appears to fight its metamorphosis from and into shadow. At a subtextual level, Barker is showing in Billy's obvious torment during the process of this miraculous transformation the conflict in Billy's character between good and evil, between man and monster, between ego and id. When Cleve is questioned about the disappearance of Billy, he attempts to tell the truth by saying that Billy has gone "To the [afterlife] city ... He's a murderer, you see." But Cleve is not believed, thus implying that the authorities are so intellectually encumbered by their limited modes of thought that they cannot comprehend a miracle when it happens. Cleve suspects where Billy's physical body is located, and he directs his wardens to the prison graveyard where Edgar Tait is buried. They open the grave, only to discover Billy's corpse locked in an embrace, as in a final trap, with his grandfather's well-preserved corpse.

Barker contrasts episodes of shadow and evil with visions of light. But light is not always necessarily a good thing in the story; rather than revealing the nature of reality, in Barker's "In the Flesh" it is described as blinding, as obstructing true vision. Following Cleve's voyeuristic eavesdropping of Billy's meeting with Edgar (a meeting which almost drives Cleve to the brink of insanity), Barker writes a brief aside in which he philosophically comments on the nature of light. This passage functions as a contrast to the images of shadow and night in the scene immediately preceding, and it also informs the reader of the subtext of evil in the story,

> Sunlight was a showman. It threw its brightness down with such flamboyance, eager as any tinsel-merchant to dazzle and distract. But beneath the gleaming surface it illuminated was another state; one that sunlight—ever the crowd pleaser—conspired to conceal. It was vile and desperate, that condition.

Barker describes Cleve as being cognizant of "the state of sunlessness." Cleve knows that dark evil lurks in the shadow of sunlight. He knows that terrible dreams of bizarre cities are more than mere dreams. And the author gives us the impression that Cleve's knowledge of the meaning of light is a tragic thing. Barker writes about Cleve, "and though he [Cleve] mourned the loss of his innocence, he knew he could never retrace his steps back into light's hall of mirrors." Night follows day as shadow follows light as dream follows reality, until all are a confusing mixture. Barker implies with this mixture a blending of moral images as well as visual images.

Barker postulates an intriguing theory with "In the Flesh." Toward the end of the story when Cleve is abducted by Edgar Tait into the "murderers' metropolis" ("He was still only *dreaming* his presence here [in the afterlife city]. His corporeal self was still in Pentonville; his dislocation from it informed his every step"), he views the inhabitants — or the incarcerated murderers — of the city who are "appearing at the doors and windows of their cells." Barker describes the scene,

> So many faces, and nothing in common between one and the next to confirm the hopes of a physiognomist. Murder had as many faces as it had occurrences. The only common quality was one of wretchedness, of minds despairing after an age at the site of their crime.

The author's point with this scene is that the act of murder knows no social class, no gender or racial distinctions. Barker might humorously quip that murder is an equal opportunity employer. Hence, despite their obvious suffering, the inmates of the murderers' metropolis are a democratic lot. No one is superior to the rest. Grim fate is equally applied to all. Murder is the great equalizer, Barker amusingly suggests; it is perhaps the only workable populist ideology. And by implication, the murderer — through the act of killing — becomes a type of inverted populist figure, someone who supports through his (albeit violent) acts a legitimate democracy.

In addition to his notion of murder as a democratic act, Barker advances a unique interpretation of life after death, and also of the nature and function of "sin." Barker's intrepid explorer of the afterlife, Cleveland Smith, harbors within his personality a powerful sense of inquiry. Content and secure in his life at Pentonville, Cleve "needed a problem to occupy the days." The problem he selects is sin, and he spends his time reading books about the subject, philosophically contemplating its source. Barker again shows Cleve to be intellectually sensitive to a theoretical understanding of sin when Billy questions Cleve about the texts he reads and questions him specifically about his belief in damnation. Cleve distractedly replies that he reads those types of books because no one else checks them out of the prison library. Cleve tells Billy that he doesn't believe "a word" of what he reads (about "damnation and all"), but then the conversation takes a more confessional route when Billy then asks Cleve if he ever is afraid, to which Cleve answers that, indeed, he sometimes is afraid. The subtext of this conversation is that Cleve is becoming very afraid of Billy. Ironically, during the course of "In the Flesh," Cleve is granted a great deal more than philosophical insight into the origin of sin. He witnesses its source firsthand. He then dramatically changes his opinion from that of an intellectual skeptic to that of a true believer.

Before his death, we are told that Cleve is an agnostic, that he learned not to believe in God when his prayers for his father's life went unanswered. Even his terror experienced in Pentonville could not reinstate his belief. Cleve is thus a secular inquirer into divine mysteries, a "show me" individual who has to see the process of redemption to believe in redemption. He gets this opportunity at the conclusion of "In the Flesh" when, after his release from Pentonville, he becomes involved in drugs and then murders to "earn him a fee the equal of his [drug] appetite." Following this murder (which makes him an acceptable inmate in the afterlife murderers' metropolis, his final prison home), Cleve is chased and mortally shot by the police. The room in which he killed is awaiting him upon his arrival at the necropolis. After a period of time, he leaves his "cell" to go beyond the city's perimeters into the surrounding desert. He subsequently witnesses a startling event. He sees a man come to the city's edge, drop the gun he is holding into the sand, and then wander further out into the desert, there to be greeted by "the makers of the voices ... loping and wild, dancing on their crutches." The man is picked up by one of the "celebrants." Barker writes,

> [The man was] taken on to its [the celebrants'] shoulders as a boy, thence snatched into another's arms as a baby, until, at the limit of his [Cleve's] senses, he heard the man bawl as he was delivered back into life. He [Cleve] went away content, knowing at last how sin (and he) had come into the world.

Barker's description of Cleve's final contentment in his understanding of the source of sin underscores the fact that "In the Flesh," though sporting many frightening elements, is on the one hand not a horror story at all, but instead is a tale in which the author discusses with his reader both his theory of the afterlife and of how sin is created and redeemed. Barker's explanation of how evil got into the world is certainly logical in its conception, very secular in its construction, and profoundly sympathetic in its rendering. There is no damnation in Barker's vision of the afterlife (damnation is an invention of the Church). Instead, people are punished with the scene of their crime so that they can work out their sense of guilt over time, and once this guilt is purged, they return afresh as a babe to the world of the living. For Barker in this story, guilt with a capital "G" is not divine (or satanic) in origin, but is rather produced by human hand and heart, and thus may be purged by human will. The true miracle of Barker's necropolis is that everyone (since murder is a great democratizer) has the chance of forgiveness and a new start, and sin with a capital "S" is not forever: it is a state-of-mind that can be cleansed from the soul. However, Barker's afterlife not only explains how sin is partially redeemed, it also shows how sin came into the mortal world, a piece of it being carried beyond the afterlife with the birth of each new child.

On the other hand, "In the Flesh" typifies both the contemporary horror story and Barker's interpretation of the tale of horror. The most frightening thing that happens in this narrative, Barker suggests to us, is the characters' sense that they are not in control of events in their lives. Billy Tait once asks Cleve if he ever is afraid. When Cleve replies to Billy, "What have I got to be scared of?," Billy answers, "Things that happen. . . . Things you can't control."

Ever the perceptive observer, Cleve notes in Billy's inquiries about fear that the boy himself is afraid, and that what he fears specifically is a lack of control over events (the same thing that Cleve fears as well). Billy is afraid of what he's becoming—the shadow monster—and Cleve is afraid of being with Billy during his bizarre transformation. They both are fearful of the unknown (another basic precept of the horror story), but their fear is larger than this. It extends to the lack of control over one's life, and one's fate. Not knowing what will eventually happen to them—this is what really scares Billy and Cleve. What hides behind that closed door? What evil shadows lurk at night in the corner of the room? What happens to us after death? These are questions that establish the fundamental essence of the contemporary horror story.

In the traditional horror story published prior to the twentieth century, evil was perceived as being external. The individual was attacked by eternal forces: the lab-created monster, the blood-sucking vampire, the vengeful ghost. Evil was thus definable, understandable within a socio-religious context. But with the advent of psychological horror—as seen in Stevenson's *The Strange Case of Dr. Jekyll and Mr. Hyde* and James Hogg's *The Private Memoirs and Confessions of a Justified Sinner* (1824)—evil became internal, human-made, and subsequently less comprehensible and more problematic. It might be argued that when the horror story became psychological, it also became more frightening because it argued that evil is relative in nature, that it lacks definition, and by lacking definition it is terrifying by virtue of its incomprehensibility. What scares characters most in Barker's fiction, or in the contemporary horror story, or what scares us with our own life in general, is the state of not knowing things, not knowing the origin of evil, not knowing what lies beyond death, not knowing what motivates people to commit atrocities. Perhaps the reason why contemporary horror fiction (i.e. Barker's particular type of horror fiction) is so frightening is because it reflects the collapse of belief systems that formerly would explain or account for the unknowable. Or perhaps today's horror fiction simply mirrors our modern understanding of human psychology.

In retrospect, reading horror fiction from the nineteenth century and earlier is more of a comforting experience than a terrifying one. The reason for this is that examples of the genre from this era do not challenge our fundamental understanding of reality. They proclaim that there is a God in Heaven and a Devil in Hell, and that we should avoid the latter in favor of the former. Contemporary horror fiction is much more sophisticated in its portrayal of evil. And as Barker fully understands, the effect of horror is best generated in fiction when it challenges both the characters' (and vicariously, the reader's) sense of security with life. What denies us this sense of security is not knowing the future, not knowing fate, not knowing where and within whom evil resides, ultimately not knowing what pitfalls to avoid. Barker's protagonists are the most scared when they don't know what will happen to them. We are most scared when reading Barker's horror fiction for the same reason, and because these protagonists are an accurate reflection of our own emotions and phobias.

Barker's placement of "In the Flesh" within his *Books of Blood* is notable in that it provides an important internal support for the thematic unity of the six-volume collection. As we are told in the two framing stories in the *Books of Blood*, the tales related in this anthology are told by the dead, by the travelers on the highway of the dead in the afterlife, tales scrawled in minute detail upon the body of the unfortunate Simon McNeal. "In the Flesh" strategically reinforces Barker's "highway of the dead" imagery by directly making reference to it in the story's narrative and by also drawing attention to textual images. The text, or book, is the predominant metaphor of the *Books of Blood*, and this metaphor is utilized effectively within "In the Flesh." Cleve, an intellectual prisoner, reads books about sin and guilt. Bishop, one of the inmates of Pentonville, is a literal history text, a walking book. When Cleve seeks information from Bishop, the author depicts the character as,

> ...an expert on prisons and the penal system. Little of his [Bishop's] information came from books. He had gleaned the bulk of his knowledge from old lags and screws who wanted to talk the hours away, and by degrees he had turned himself into a walking encyclopedia on crime and punishment. He had made it his trade, and he sold his carefully accrued knowledge by the sentence....

Billy Tait is described as being like a closed book when Cleve attempts to observe in the boy some hint about the mysterious goings-on at Pentonville. Barker writes, "Such scrutiny was a lost cause...the boy became...an indecipherable book, letting no clue as to the nature of his secret world out from beneath his lids." Hence, Barker moves from text to subtext in the story. Billy possesses a secret self. Reality hides another existence. Light masks shadow. The subtext of "In the Flesh" is miracle and imagination, the miracle of an actual afterlife and the imagination wielded by dreams (Cleve's dreams) to access the miraculous. These themes—text and subtext—are all important to Clive Barker and are readily apparent throughout his *Books of Blood*.

"The Forbidden"

Clive Barker extends his prison and trap images from "In the Flesh" to the following story in the *Books of Blood, Volume Five* entitled "The Forbidden." In "The Forbidden," though, the "prison" is a run-down urban housing project appropriately named the Spector Street Estate, where people are trapped not by locks and bars, but by poverty, violence, and a lurking, secretive supernatural force that holds the residents of Spector Street in a commanding grip.

As with the Pentonville prison setting from "In the Flesh," Spector Street masks a profound Mystery (a mystery both in religious and secular terms) behind its graffiti-covered walls, a dark miracle of grand proportions. The seeker of mysteries in "The Forbidden" is Helen Buchanan, a protagonist who functions in the story as a detective (who attempts to solve the assortment of baffling, violent crimes that plague Spector Street) *and* as an academic interpreter of the urban texts of graffiti that cover the Spector Street Estate's walls. What the graffiti represents—the meaning behind its often crude and vulgar representations—is an important key to both our recognition of Barker's significant use of his text as metaphor in the story and Helen's own rite-of-passage quest for truth and understanding. Helen discovers during the course of the narrative in "The Forbidden" that the Spector Street graffiti is the religious language of a new god, a god born from folklore legend, a god who accepts sacrifices of blood and candy, a god emblematic of the contemporary urban experience. This new god, who calls himself the "Candyman," concerns himself with the process of drafting converts to his unholy sect. The Candyman's stock-in-trade is true immortality, an immortality that sacrifices the physical body in favor of notoriety, an immortality powered by the oral tradition of legend that is part of the same life force that animates the dreaded Candyman himself.

Barker's prison setting in "The Forbidden" contrasts the banal with the bizarre. The author mocks the geometrical perfection of the Spector Street Estate's design by stating that the "elegance" of its planning was "lost upon those suffering in it." In a brief aside delivered at the beginning of the story, Barker tells us that even though Spector Street may have "once been an architect's dream," it now had fallen into ruin. Despite the mathematically sound architectural perfection of the project, it had failed its purpose, tumbling into disrepute in spite of its intended geometrical cleverness. We are told that the designers of Spector Street, rather than admitting a flaw in their design, would instead place the blame for its failure upon people who lived there, that is, it was "*people* who had spoiled Spector Street." By taking several paragraphs in the beginning of the story to establish its setting, Barker is commenting on two things. The first is that geometry (and by implication, math and science in general) when it fails to recognize the human factor is a sterile, contradictory perfection—an imperfect perfection, if you will. The second is that aesthetic perfection, taken at an abstract level, is basically flawed and totally unimaginative. It is people who provide for imagination in the otherwise blasted and sterile landscape of their lives, Barker would tell us, people who provide the spark for accessing the fantastic, the miraculous. And since the Spector Street Estate in and of itself lacks the power of imagination, it falls upon the people "suffering in it" to create miracles. And yet, as the reader notes elsewhere in Barker's *Books of Blood*, miracles can just as easily be dangerous as divine. In "The Forbidden," the shape of imagination (in the guise of the Candyman) is quite dangerous indeed.

When Helen Buchanan begins her photographic investigations into the Spector Street Estate's graffiti texts (to mine "some fresh material" for her thesis entitled "Graffiti: The Semiotics of Urban Despair"), she is struck by the housing project's ugly, outward appearance. "Helen had seldom seen an inner city environment so comprehensively vandalized," Barker writes. Unfortunately, Helen Buchanan is naïve to what lurks behind the pasteboard mask of what she first sees. Early in the story, she is not yet attuned to the dark miracle that will ultimately claim her life, and her very identity, in the end. As she hones her embryonic skills as a detective, she comes to understand during the course of the story that, sometimes, one may find immense Mystery in the drabbest of surroundings, because appearances may quite often be deceiving. Her exercise in a detective-like investigation also serves as a type of emotionally transforming rite-of-passage, where she begins to understand the reality that exists behind the graffiti-lined walls. For Helen, the housing project comes to represent an ambivalent experience. She is liberated from the confines of the limitations of life when she flirts with the notion of attaining immortality at the hands (or more correctly, the hook) of Spector Street's nefarious Candyman. Unfortunately, this immortality is only achieved through violent death. She also establishes a final break in her relationship with the mentally abusive and coldly academic Trevor, but this feat is accomplished immediately before she is consumed in flames by a bonfire. Spector Street is full of momentous surprises and is a place where Helen learns much more than she could ever write about in her academic study of graffiti.

The understanding of texts (i.e. the meaning that supports texts) is an important narrative theme in "The Forbidden," as it is in the *Books of Blood* as a whole. Like a previous interpreter of texts — Mary Florescu from "The Book of Blood" framing story — Helen Buchanan in "The Forbidden" is ostensibly a seeker of truth. She is a calculating academic (like Trevor) who is described as being an interdisciplinary generalist. The reader learns that her two favorite "disciplines" are sociology and esthetics, a blend of interests that will not only serve her well in her analysis of the semiotics of graffiti, but that will also effectively support her endeavors as an amateur detective in her investigation of the violent and seemingly senseless crimes of Spector Street. Helen continually desires to dig deeper into meaning. She wants to get literally inside the graffiti that she is studying. After being challenged by one of the residents — a woman named Anne-Marie — as to what she is doing, Helen explains her function as a scholar and states that she is not from "the council" but from the university. Helen gains the confidence of Anne-Marie, and when Anne-Marie offers to take Helen into one of the vacant flats to look at graffiti there, Helen jumps at the opportunity. Barker writes, "The description [of Anne-Marie's observations] piqued Helen's curiosity. Would the graffiti on the *inside* walls be substantially different from the public displays? It was certainly worth an investigation."

The efforts of Helen's investigation of flat Number 14 provided her with a new and uniquely strange graffiti lexicon, one that was radically unlike what was displayed outside the flat. This new graffiti possessed a subtext that went far beyond Helen's mundane concepts of urban alienation. It was the language of a new urban religion; it was the holy text of the Candyman's dogma. In the bedroom of Number 14, Helen found herself being amazed by what she saw: a huge portrait of a demonic face (the face of the Candyman, the reader later understands), a face where the door looked like a massive mouth and where she appeared as if she were about to be consumed like a morsel of food. Of course, Helen is later physically consumed by fire in the loving/lethal embrace of the Candyman, but what she doesn't realize at the precise moment in the story when she first views the bedroom painting is that she, by pursuing her curiosity, in essence offers herself (albeit unknowingly) to this urban god of graffiti and death. Clive Barker later and in more detailed fashion incorporates his thematic notion of the vitality of illustration in his novel *Imajica*, where street art literally transforms into reality when this art is coupled with a strong belief in the miraculous. When Helen sees the cryptic — yet otherwise innocuous — graffiti statement "Sweets to the sweet," she doesn't realize until it is too late that *she* is the "sweet" presented for the Candyman's consumption (the two sacrificial offerings most enjoyed by the Candyman are candy, of course, and blood, best represented by the collection of wrapped candy and bloody razors Helen sees deposited at his so-called temple of worship in flat Number 14). Helen's obsessive quest for truth and meaning leads to her undoing. It brings her to the evil attention of forces beyond her control and, ironically, beyond her understanding. Helen's pursuit of knowledge becomes for her a tragic flaw. She learns too late that the Candyman's graffiti text is written in the metaphoric spilt blood of his sacrificial victims.

Clive Barker pays homage to the efficacy of contemporary folklore legends in "The Forbidden" with his use of the Candyman character as a literal representation of a walking, talking horror story, as the fact behind the adolescent's fiction, as the monster behind the monstrous tales told around the campfire. When Helen first meets the Candyman, Barker describes her observations of the monster's hook appendage and her understanding that she was confronting an actual, physical embodiment of a deadly urban legend, the notorious legend of the hook killer. In his seminal study entitled *The Study of American Folklore: An Introduction* (1968), folklore scholar Jan Harold Brunvand defines the term, "Legends, like myths, are prose narratives regarded by their tellers as true" (106). Barker incorporates Brunvand's definition of legend in "The Forbidden" within the fictional framework of the Candyman monster. This heinous, yet grotesquely beautiful, creature is apparently given a supernatural life by the persistent telling of grim tales of his mutilations and murders (the prose narrative element of what constitutes a legend), and he is regarded as being real by the residents of Spector Street (the veracity element of a legend).

Devoting an entire chapter in *Danse Macabre* to the subject of folklore, Stephen King himself spends a great deal of his critical attention in his lengthy study of the horror story on the hook killer legend, showing how folklore affects the process of writing popular horror fiction. King argues that this particular legend is "a brutal classic of horror" (33). King states that ". . . the story of The Hook exists for one reason and one reason alone: to scare the shit out of little kids after the sun goes down," and he interprets this basic impulse to provide *the scare* in the folklore legend as being a fundamental element (one that denies rational interpretation) of the horror genre itself (33-34).

Clive Barker also effectively utilizes King's *the scare* component of the hook killer legend in "The Forbidden," coloring his Candyman character more in the somber hues of nightmare than in the lighter colors of dream. The result of Barker's literary creation is undeniably frightening. The author describes the monster as being something much more than a run-of-the-mill serial killer, as possessing a deeper, more disturbing significance than mere homicidal maniac. The most terrifying aspect of the Candyman is not that he is a merciless, cruel murderer; it instead is the fact that his existence is something special, even miraculous. The Candyman is a creature who is immortal and who approaches a diabolical sort of godhood. We observe through Helen's eyes, during her climactic confrontation with the fiend near the end of the story, the shocking revelation about the Candyman, that he is not mortal. Rather, he is an animated corpse who houses a hive of bees (his buzzing icon of rank) in the rotted hollow of his torso. This image, and Helen's reaction to this image, are intended to be scary, thus reinforcing and enhancing Barker's artistic use of *the scare* element of the hook killer legend in his horror short story narrative. In addition to being the "fright" behind the frightening in "The Forbidden," Barker also interprets the hook killer legend in mythic fashion. The Candyman is more a god than a legend. He is a new god for a new urban age.

Perhaps an even more frightening thing than the Candyman's gruesome appearance is his obvious power over others. He totally dominates the residents of the Spector Street Estate, finding in these hapless people his source of sacrificial victims, his cult of devoted followers, and the force behind his very existence. His power to terrify is even greater than the power of a mother's love, as exemplified in Anne-Marie's attitude late in the story (or lack of attitude) concerning her murdered son, Kerry, who was killed as an offering to the Candyman. Anne-Marie's willingness to hide the event of her son's death is an illustration of the Candyman's overwhelming authority. Even Helen, an otherwise strong and intelligent protagonist, is first seduced by the Candyman's promise of immortality (seduced and gruesomely embraced), and then trapped in his deadly, fiery embrace. Helen learns the same bitter lesson as did Frankie in "Scape-Goats": that it is best not to tempt Fate, since one is likely also to tempt hideous supernatural retribution. Helen's final reward for her investigative curiosity—for her uncovering "the forbidden" things best left alone in Spector Street—is the Candyman's total, undivided attention, an attention that results in her death and in her probable immortality.

By finding death, Helen has learned part of the subtextual meaning of Spector Street's graffiti. As the religious language of a new god for a new, violent age, the Candyman's spray-paint text is an extended tale recounting the archetypal issues of existence—death and sex. The Candyman's promise to Helen, and no doubt to all of his victims, is a type of immortality. He tells them that this immortality may be acquired through their violent murder. Their memories will live long after their death in the hushed tales of the Spector Street residents, and this is how they will become immortal. First a story, then a legend, this is how the Candyman himself became immortal. The Candyman gives his victims a life after death, and the irony Barker implies is that a notorious death and subsequent fame are perhaps better than a commonplace existence, an existence without the paradoxical life-giving force of violent death.

Clive Barker's seeming paradox in "The Forbidden" is reflective of contemporary, urban society—a society that finds little relevance in traditional belief systems. The old ways don't work for the people of Spector Street when they are confronted by the problems of pernicious urban violence. And if the old religious traditions are incapable of giving meaning, Barker shows us that a new religion evolves to take their place. This religion—the doctrine of the Candyman—is contemporary, relevant, and it nicely mirrors the consuming violence that plagues today's citizens. In addition, it explains the origins of violence, and our seeming indifference to terribly violent acts. Barker's concept of a new god for a new age is analogous to Harlan Ellison's similar notion in his *Deathbird Stories* anthology (1975), and in particular is comparable to Ellison's award-winning "The Whimper of Whipped Dogs" short story that appears in this collection. In the *Deathbird Stories*, Ellison writes with satiric tongue-in-cheek about the more relevant—and more dangerous—deities of the twentieth century. Barker's Candyman would most likely find sympathetic company in Ellison's anthology.

When the reader is finished reading Clive Barker's "The Forbidden," he or she is struck by the story's use of ice and fire images. Throughout most of the story's narrative, because it is late October, cold dominates the various scenes—icy rain and blustery "Arctic" wind. At a metaphoric level, Helen is representative of cold, rational thought, while her relationship with the icy, academic Trevor is indicative of her passionless life. The beautiful, yet cold, design of the Spector Street Estate fails because it does not take into account the fact that living people are not coldly and calculatingly perfect. However, when the Candyman makes his appearance, the cold of rational, abstract thought is melted by the passion of religious devotion to Mystery. The Candyman is described in fiery imagery, and Helen's dire fate is determined by her heated desire for immortality. The story itself ends in the flames of Spector Street's "Bonfire Night," which serves as both a flaming trap that ends Helen's mortal life and as a beacon introducing her new existence as the stuff of legend. Helen is transformed from ice to fire in "The Forbidden," from mortal to immortal. She sacrifices her passionless life in favor of a passionate death.

"The Forbidden" was recently made into a film entitled *Candyman* (1992), which was written and directed by Bernard Rose. The film, like the story it was based upon, emphasizes the folkloric origins of the hook killer legend. Unlike "The Forbidden," however, *Candyman* is set in the United States and the Candyman serial killer is African American.

"The Madonna"

"The Madonna" is a story with profound feminist implications, one that explores several important thematic concepts seen in earlier tales from the *Books of Blood*. It, for example, investigates the notion of man as oppressor of woman, such as depicted previously in stories like "Jacqueline Ess: Her Will and Testament" and "Rawhead Rex." "The Madonna" also anticipates Barker's more extensive treatment of feminist issues that he later develops in his epic fantasy novel *Imajica*, in which he scrutinizes such things as the nature of destructive gender conflicts. Clive Barker also features the transformation tale in "The Madonna." Both of the story's two central male protagonists—Jerry Coloqhoun and Ezra Garvey—during the narrative undergo a magical physical metamorphosis from man to woman. Garvey is unable to accept his new body (his old, irrational masculine self rejects the change) and he commits suicide, while Coloqhoun does accept what has miraculously happened to him. He, unlike Garvey, is transformed mentally as well as physically. Jerry Coloqhoun not only embraces his new physical state, but he also attempts a literal and a metaphysical leap of faith at the conclusion of the story, a leap that he hopes will connect him with the celestial. As he does more thoroughly several years later in *Imajica*, Clive Barker employs in "The Madonna" fantastic visual and tactile images of the procreative power of women (of the womb specifically), images of water and the sea, of heat, and of the spiral. He combines outré and miraculous images in the form of the Madonna entity herself, an astonishing creature who, like her namesake, is capable of virgin birth. She produces life that is the literal stuff of dreams. Finally, "The Madonna" highlights Barker's continuing interest in the contrast between the mundane and the marvelous, a contrast that provides a significant thread that ties together with it the previous two stories (i.e. "In the Flesh" and "The Forbidden") in the *Books of Blood, Volume Five*.

"The Madonna" advances two basic perspectives. First, it presents the destructive nature of man, and second, in direct contrast, it shows how women are constructive, life giving, the wonderful creators of dreams. Men in the narrative are sexually driven for lust's sake alone; women are sexually driven to procreate, to give birth. Men are skilled in violence and death; women in supernatural wonder and life. Men are intellectually simple-minded, stupid, unable to see the meaning behind living, unable to solve the riddle of life; women are skilled in understanding the mystic lexicon of religious Mystery. Men are inane; women are imagination incarnate. These profound conflicts between the genders are nicely embodied in the setting of the story. Jerry Coloqhoun and Ezra Garvey are shady real estate developer and shadier real estate investor respectively. Coloqhoun attempts to sell the run-down Leopold Road Swimming Pools building to Garvey. Coloqhoun's tactics include bribery and secretiveness, while Garvey's feature base criminality. Both men attempt to deal strictly in commercial terms with the Leopold Road Pools, the hidden residence of the mystic creature called the Madonna. Men view the Pools building as simple commercial property, as something to buy and sell for a profit, when, in actuality, the Pools building is the domicile of the fantastic, the domain of the great Virgin Mother incarnate. Men stupidly think they can market the miraculous, in essence, because they cannot see miracles. Conversely, women do not dirty themselves in the crassly commercial. They do not buy and sell objects. They instead produce miracles.

The two central male characters in the story are initially portrayed as being violent, intellectually dense, and emotionally numb to the feelings of others. Ezra Garvey, for instance, harbors a criminal past. He embraces senseless as a way of life, as a way to do business. At one point late in the story, he attempts to beat a confession out of Jerry Coloqhoun, even though Coloqhoun has nothing to confess. Brutality is his foremost attribute, and Barker implies in his character a universally masculine trait. Garvey views women as mere sex objects whose sole purpose in life is to be showered with expensive gifts. As with other Barker characters who lack imagination, Garvey finds comfort with institutions. Barker writes, "Unlike many, he [Garvey] found institutions reassuring: hospitals, schools, even prisons. They smacked of social order; they soothed that part of him fearful of chaos. Better a world too organized than one not organized enough." While lustfully pursuing one (and then a second) of the Madonna's ladies-in-waiting, Garvey encounters yet another of the Madonna's female attendants, a nubile young naked woman who is nursing one of the Madonna's newly born children. He is revolted by what he sees—a baby/creature that symbolizes the life force of dreams. Garvey is unequipped to confront imagination. He instead reverts to true masculine form—Barker would tell us—and despoils it. He flings the Madonna's child of dreams from the nursing woman's grasp, killing it. Because Ezra Garvey is so mired in the banality of regimented order, when he is challenged with profound supernatural change (like the gender transformation of his body) he is unable to cope with it, and subsequently destroys what he doesn't understand, or is destroyed in turn.

Jerry Coloqhoun also initially possesses several reprehensible masculine qualities. He is insensitive to the emotional requirements of his lover, Carole, and like Helen Buchanan's icy relationship with Trevor in "The Forbidden," Coloqhoun's relationship with Carole is sterile and barren. Coloqhoun even senselessly rapes Carole at one point in the story, and though he feels some measure of remorse for his terrible act, he is unable to adequately compensate Carole for what he has put her through. However, Jerry Coloqhoun does dramatically change — both mentally and physically — in "The Madonna." When he is subjected to the same supernatural physical transformation as is Ezra Garvey (in both instances engendered by sexual intercourse with one of the Madonna's ladies-in-waiting), Coloqhoun intellectually accepts the metamorphosis that causes Garvey to take his own life. Coloqhoun not only discards his old masculine body, embracing, in turn, his new female identity, he also seeks to link up with the divine. At the conclusion of "The Madonna," Coloqhoun undertakes a literal leap of faith in pursuit of the departing Madonna by jumping into the swirling vortex of water draining away from the pool which served as the Madonna's home. The male Jerry Coloqhoun would have never made such a leap, burdened as he was by the limitations of his sex: his masculine bestiality and his inability to empathize or to imagine. The female Jerry Coloqhoun searches for a state of grace that lies beyond the realm of limited human knowledge.

The Leopold Road Pools building both houses and represents the procreative power of women. This setting allows Barker to develop a sophisticated metaphor for woman and womb. Barker describes the interior of the Leopold Street Pools building as ostensibly being in severe disrepair, and, more importantly, as being quite damp. Coloqhoun conducts Garvey on an initial tour of the site after having broken through the building's padlocked door. The electricity is turned off, and they can only see by means of a flashlight and by the paltry illumination that filters through the "mildewed panes of the skylights along the corridor." In the meager light amidst the deteriorated ceramic tiles, Garvey notes an interesting mosaic design of a "nondescript mythological scene — fish, nymphs and sea-gods at play." What neither Ezra Garvey nor Jerry Coloqhoun realize at this moment is that this particular illustration is anything but "nondescript." The picture functions as a foreshadowing of later events where the two men actually encounter mythological nymphs, and it also serves as a thematic image for the author that augments his use of water and the sea as iconic female symbols.

The several instances when Coloqhoun and Garvey wander the twisted, maze-like dark corridors of the Leopold Road Pools, the two men note that the deeper they go into the building, the warmer it gets. As they move toward the building's center, the damper it becomes. These images — heat and fluid and sea images—used in conjunction with the author's descriptions of the building's twisting, dark corridors, are intended by Barker to portray a physical approximation of a woman's womb. This womb analogy is further supported by an important scene in the story. After paying a "considerable bribe," Jerry Coloqhoun has procured from his "contact at the Architect's Department" the ground plans for the Pools. Barker writes, "On paper the complex looked like a labyrinth. And like the best labyrinths, there was [to him] no order apparent in the layout of shower rooms and bathrooms and changing rooms." While attempting to decipher some measure of meaning in the building's seemingly chaotic design—which he at first can't do—Carole proclaims that the plans depict a spiral design. If the Pools building is intended to portray the female persona, it makes sense that Coloqhoun (who is out of touch with women) does not recognize what is so alien to him. Being a woman, Carole has no problem in identifying something that is emblematic of herself. In addition, perhaps the reason why Jerry Coloqhoun and Ezra Garvey continually lose their sense of direction each time they enter the Pools building is because, as grossly insensitive men, they are quite unfamiliar with the physiognomy of the opposite gender. Each time the men explore the womb, they become confused, frightened, and ignorant in their trepidation.

Barker saves his mightiest literary punch in the story for his depiction of the Madonna creature, who is a study in shocking contrasts and hence is one of Clive Barker's favorite narrative devices. She resides in the communal shower room and in a large pool of scum-encrusted water (much like embryonic fluid) at the center of the building. When she finally reveals herself to Coloqhoun (amidst the spray of water from pipes and clothed in a "pungent smell": additional references to the womb), she gives birth (a virgin birth, of course) to what looks like a monstrous creature, but is, in actuality, a marvelous creature. She is freakish in appearance, yet beautiful in function. She seems outlandish on the surface, yet beneath the surface she is celestial. Startled at first by what he has just witnessed, Coloqhoun inquires of his female companion, who is one of the Madonna's attendants, "Are all...all the children like that?" The woman replies, "No one is like another...We feed them. Some die. Others live, and go their ways," and when Coloqhoun asks where ("for God's sake") do they go, she answers, "To the water. To the sea. Into dreams." With the Madonna, Clive Barker is parodying the traditional Christian notion of the Virgin Birth. Yet, while he is subtly—and with tongue in cheek—mocking the accepted Christian mindset, he is also paying tribute to the powerful mythology that lies behind the story of the Virgin Birth. Barker transplants his feminist agenda squarely upon one of the most revered of narratives (the birth of Christ) in the male-dominated Christian religion, at once turning upside down the accepted precepts of that religion while offering in their place a new devout Mystery where the mother of God is superior to God. The paradox of the Virgin Birth, for Barker, belongs more to woman than man. The Madonna's children in Barker's story are not profoundly masculine (and hence profoundly destructive in the author's eyes). They are not the new children of God. They are instead something better, something not condemned by the limitations of gender distinctions; they are the material of dreams, the substance of imagination.

Clive Barker extends in "The Madonna" a unifying thread from the previous two stories in the *Books of Blood, Volume Five* — his idea that the miraculous resides hand-in-hand with the mundane. In each of these three Barker stories, the fantastic is masked by the commonplace. With "In the Flesh," the Pentonville prison hides a gateway to another dimension, a place where murderers are forced to confront their crimes until they can purge their guilt. In "The Forbidden," the Spector Street Estate appears to be just another run-down housing project that can be found in any economically depressed city area, but it actually houses the temple of a new urban god known as the Candyman. The Leopold Road Swimming Pools building, rather than being the dilapidated swimming pool, and shower complex that first meets the eye, is instead the home of the mother of divinity and dreams. In each of these tales, the characters' understanding (or lack of understanding) of the presence of the wondrous in the midst of the commonplace determines whether they themselves can access that which is greater than themselves, whether they can achieve a new, reborn life through the process of using their imaginations. Barker weaves this intriguing philosophical thread — that is, the revelation of imagination *via* the contrast in setting between the miraculous and the mundane — into the fabric of the following story, "Babel's Children," as well; a nuns' convent is more than what it initially appears.

"Babel's Children"

"Babel's Children" is Clive Barker's amusing pastiche of — and homage to — the spy thriller, yet as seen previously in the *Books of Blood*, whenever Barker writes within a particular formula, he uses that formula story as a starting point from which he leaps into new fiction arenas that defy simple genre classification. In the process, Barker thus creates an interesting and unique literary hybrid, one that serves as an effective narrative vehicle for his work with allegory or satire or horror. For example, "Babel's Children" begins as a pastiche of the spy thriller, but it quickly turns from pastiche, to parody, to outright black satire. Initially, as pastiche, the story's plot reads as if it came straight from the mind of an Ian Fleming or Robert Ludlum. As parody, it seems as if Barker has further incorporated additional motifs to his hybrid mixture, like material from "high-camp" television shows such as *The Prisoner* and *The Man from U.N.C.L.E.* As black satire, Barker outright mocks the clichéd gimmicks of the spy thriller (like the technology of espionage), and even mocks the conventions of world politics, thus giving a final, outlandish shape to his idiosyncratic creation. "Babel's Children" highlights one of Barker's stronger female protagonists, a woman named Vanessa Jape, who in traditional thriller fashion has a love for adventure and a nose for trouble. It also resurrects a significant theme from earlier stories in the *Books of Blood* — the game as metaphor, an image that Barker utilizes to caustically deride the terrible global political alternative to game playing: apocalyptic world destruction. Barker debunks the myth of technology as protector and savior by portraying technology as a sarcastic apparatus that embodies the rather sophisticated idea of bureaucratic entropy.

"Babel's Children" begins as if it were a spy adventure. It co-opts a number of formulaic devices mastered by such authors of espionage fiction as Fleming, Ludlum, John le Carré, and Eric Ambler. Intrepid Vanessa Jape is exploring about the coast of Kithnos in the Aegean Sea region, searching for the so-called road less traveled. What Vanessa instead discovers is a dramatic chase scene where a man is being pursued by gun-wielding assailants; they are all "dressed from head to foot in billowing black." Rather than returning to her car and escaping, Vanessa decides to investigate the source of this deadly "hide-and-seek" chase further. Wandering about the desolate landscape, she runs across a group of buildings which, at first glance, appears to be a seemingly innocuous convent, but which in actuality houses a most baffling mystery. As pastiche of the spy thriller, Barker's story pushes all the correct formulaic buttons. The story features the correct version of a plucky heroine, as well as the correct proportions of violence, danger, and a perplexing enigma that needs to be solved. The dominant tone of the story, as in the standard spy thriller, is paranoia. And this paranoia exists both at a personal level (Vanessa is suspicious of others) and at a global level (governments are suspicious of each other). Romance, adventure, danger: Clive Barker at first propels his narrative through very familiar waters.

Yet, subtly, as the story proceeds it begins to change in form, to alter, to be recast into something that looks more like parody than pastiche. Barker informs us at one point in the narrative that Vanessa is very familiar with the subtle tactics of espionage, because her ridiculously jealous ex-husband, Ronald, had once tormented her with "spying strategies that would not have shamed the agencies of Whitehall or Washington." Barker lampoons the tale of espionage by comparing it to domestic infidelity. Early in "Babel's Children" when Vanessa slips through the opened, unattended gate into the building complex/prison, Barker depicts her subsequent capture (a legitimate expectation in the traditional spy thriller) in ludicrous fashion (an atypical expectation). In particular, Barker's utilization of a statue of the Virgin Mary that functions as a surveillance device ("Its blue eyes had followed her across the yard and now were unmistakably following her back"), is, at best, silly, and it reminds us of those terrible formulaic gimmicks that were featured in bad episodes of *The Man from U.N.C.L.E.* television show (from its later, "campy" seasons). And when Barker has Vanessa captured by the guardians of the mysterious prison complex—whom he describes as being disguised in nuns' habits, yet sporting beards and toting guns—the story transcends the ludicrous. We are told by the author that Vanessa might have laughed "at this incongruity." We, however, not being limited by any such narrative strictures, may utter a chuckle or two. Barker also makes several overt references with regards to setting and characters (like Mr. Klein) in "Babel's Children" to the *The Prisoner*, a British cult television series from the late 1960s starring Patrick McGoohan. Much of what Barker puts in "Babel's Children" is slapstick, but a slapstick that reveals an artistic motivation. Barker is debunking those things about the spy thriller that deserve debunking. He is comically parodying the outrageous fantasy that lurks in the more vulgar variety of the formula, fantasy that within the confines of the typical "gosh-awful" James Bond film (starring Roger Moore, of course) the audience is expected to swallow. It's difficult—if not impossible—to digest this fantasy in its more crass variant of the popular spy thriller movie or mass-market paperback. Barker knows this, and he allows us an unabashed laugh at the story's expense.

Further into the plot when Vanessa begins to solve the mystery of the remote prison's purpose and the reason why she is incarcerated there, Barker exchanges parody for black satire, thus disclosing the author's intent with "Babel's Children." Vanessa learns that the prison houses the remnants of a noble geo-political experiment, an experiment in which the greatest brains of the early 1960s (like Vanessa's companion in misery at the bogus convent, Harvey Gomm, professor and Nobel Prize winner) were gathered in one place to debate more rationally world events, and ultimately to shape those events. However, over time, things went wrong with the process—several of the experts died, and the others decided that it was easier to expedite global decisions by conducting games of chance in order to determine the outcome, like racing frogs! After Vanessa hears this seemingly outrageous explanation from Harvey Gomm, she initially thinks the place is a lunatic asylum. She does not accept the truth as it is offered to her because it is so far-fetched, so beyond the realm of normal experience. Mr. Klein, who is the enigmatic man in charge at the security complex, even uses Vanessa's own incredulity as a weapon against her. He reinforces her suspicion that her fellow inmates are insane, and thus hopes to keep her bound tight in her prison by her own disbelief.

Barker knows in the spy thriller that one of the more important motifs of the formula is paranoia, specifically a paranoia that highlights some aspect of political conspiracy. The spy story typically asks questions like, "Who are the good guys? Who are the bad guys? And how can the one be distinguished from the other?" In "Babel's Children," Barker takes this conspiratorial motif to its extreme. He suggests that the *ultimate* conspiracy exists in the world. He confirms our greatest paranoid fears by telling us that a very small group of power brokers solely determine world events. And then Barker deflates the whole conspiratorial motif by depicting these so-called power brokers as being doddering old fools and by having them arrive at their decisions by playing silly games. When Vanessa initially denies the truth in "Babel's Children," she confirms the truth for the reader. She tells us that what Harvey Gomm describes is insane, and it is indeed insane. We often suspect that the political process is crazy. We often suspect that special interest groups make decisions for us without our knowledge that are not in our best interest. Barker exploits our own paranoia; by exaggerating the truth, Barker enhances the truth. The plot's very insanity, its very foolishness, then, as satire serves as a dire warning. Barker whispers to us from the pages of the story that we must not be as blind to what is happening to us as Vanessa is at first. Vanessa does, by the story's conclusion, recognize the validity of what Harvey Gomm has told her, but by that time her belief in the truth cannot save her. It comes too late. Barker's satiric warning contains a bleak message.

Clive Barker confirms the story's basic pessimism (a pessimism clothed in humor) by having Vanessa Jape hopelessly trapped in a dreadful situation. Vanessa comes to this story from several sources. She represents, at one level, the intrepid "plucky gal" who may be found in a number of suspense thrillers. She is portrayed as having a love for the unusual. In fact, she never would have gotten herself into such deep trouble if she wasn't so interested in doing things differently than other people. Barker writes about her,

> Her enthusiasm for following her nose had got her into trouble often enough in the past. A near-fatal night spent lost in the Alps; that episode in Marrakech that had almost ended in rape; the adventure with the sword-swallower's apprentice in the wilds of Lower Manhattan. And yet despite what bitter experience should have taught her, when the choice lay between the marked route and the unmarked, she would always, without question, take the latter.

At first glance, Vanessa looks like one of Elizabeth Peters's resourceful female protagonists, a world traveler who either seeks out trouble or has trouble seek her out, and hence a plot is quickly hatched. On another level, though, Vanessa is still the distinct Clive Barker heroine in that she combines a profound sense of the tragic with her otherwise larger-than-life abilities. As he did with Jacqueline Ess from "Jacqueline Ess: Her Will and Testament," with Frankie from "Scape-Goats," and perhaps with Elaine Rider from "The Life of Death," Barker shows Vanessa as losing in the end despite her otherwise superior courage, intelligence, and or strength. In this sense, Barker's women are dramatically different from any popular literary tradition; his heroines are defeated. Yet even in their defeat Barker shows them as possessing a dignity, as being even more admirable for fighting the hopeless noble battle. Specifically in "Babel's Children," Vanessa is a tragic person. She will be incarcerated for the rest of her life (we suppose) in Mr. Klein's convent prison because she has inadvertently caused the deaths of all the people who raced the frogs (all but one, a man called Goldberg, and hence the games may continue). She must assume their former place and function. She must become the new player of the old game, for if the game is not played, the world ends. Her limited prospects for the future will no doubt cause her no end of torment since she is an adventure-loving person. This tragic quality in Vanessa and in other Barker heroines permits the author to explore different levels of emotional feelings in his characters, as well as to defy typical reader expectations. Clive Barker has artistically always been interested in defying convention in his work, while developing new methods of creating interesting or unusual personalities, characters who can match the wild inventiveness of his plots.

For instance, Barker contrasts the tragedy of Vanessa's imprisonment with a grand joke in "Babel's Children," one that argues that world events are determined by foolish old people who play ridiculous games of chance. The setup of his joke is the game itself, the absurdity of racing frogs to settle territorial disputes around the globe. We experience what Vanessa experiences when this joke is played upon her. We see the absurdity of things through her eyes, and as she begins to comprehend the veracity of what she sees and hears, the reader too is encouraged not only to laugh at Barker's elaborate joke, but also to understand that his intended silliness is actually more legitimate than the apocalyptic political alternative. After all, what is more absurd than total world destruction? The punch line of Barker's grand joke is his portrayal of the incompetency of all international governments to conduct rationally their problems, the inability of these governments to assume responsibility for their actions. The world in general (rather than the bogus convent) is the insane asylum in "Babel's Children."

After recapturing Vanessa, Mr. Klein gives her an official tour of the main building in the complex, the place where the results of the frog races are made known to the rest of the world. What Vanessa witnesses is total chaos. In the midst of this wall-to-wall high-tech complex, insanity actually does reign supreme because no frog races have been run for two days. In a bank of video screens in one of the rooms, Vanessa sees the interior of a variety of "war rooms and presidential suites, cabinet offices and halls of congress." In each of these locations, world leaders are losing their collective minds. She sees that governments are on the verge of collapsing because no games have been played and they have not been given information about how to conduct their affairs. When Vanessa remarks that the whole thing is "preposterous," the ubiquitous Mr. Klein replies, "I agree. But I ask you, in all honesty, is it any more terrifying than leaving power in *their* hands?" He pointed to the rows of irate faces. ... There wasn't a man or woman among them [the world government leaders] Vanessa would have trusted to guide her across the road." And the punch line of Clive Barker's joke is delivered with deceptive ease and considerable force.

Barker also ridicules the myth of technology as protector and savior in "Babel's Children." Mr. Klein's high-tech complex is a sterile symbol of power. It signifies nothing. In the scene when Vanessa attempts an escape and wanders through the complex's main building (the bell tower which is the "heart of the fortress," a place its occupants call the "Boudoir"), she enters a series of rooms "one of which was lined with dozens of clocks, all showing different times; the next of which contained upward of fifty black telephones; the third and largest was lined on every side with television screens." Vanessa notes that all the screens are "blank," except for one; a "mustachioed nun" is watching a pornographic video on it. This is the blackest of humor, ebony satire that would feel at home in the 1964 Stanley Kubrick film *Dr. Strangelove* (subtitled: *How I Learned to Stop Worrying and Love the Bomb*). Technology not only fails to serve adequately the needs of humanity in "Babel's Children," it is a source of amusement. Technology's failure in the story goes beyond mere incompetency. It is reflective of Barker's belief that too much science, too much rationalism, and too much organization are evil things. Events and people are wound overly tight in "Babel's Children." The status quo is overly regimented and systematized. The ritual of game playing is more important than the human factor (i.e. imagination), and this, in the author's view, is predictive of the type of insanity that's to be found in the story. When the bureaucracy rules supreme, it's doomed to eventual destruction. When organization dominates reality, it is destined to disintegrate into chaos, a type of bureaucratic anarchy. Observing firsthand the process of this disintegration, Vanessa tells Mr. Klein that "Systems decay," and in Barker's particular fictional universe where the bureaucrats hold sway, she's absolutely correct.

CHAPTER SEVEN

Twilight and Other Illusions: *Clive Barker's Books of Blood, Volume Six*

"The Life of Death"

A melancholy atmosphere pervades "The Life of Death." It is a sadly whimsical love story that tells of an unrequited passion between two rather different and unusual people—Elaine Rider, who is being treated for cancerous tumors, and Kavanagh, who has a fascination for crypts and other trappings of human mortality. But even though "The Life of Death" possesses this subtly melancholy tone, the tale's delicate atmosphere does not preclude the O. Henry-like wallop Clive Barker delivers to his reader at the conclusion, nor does it impede his vigorous discussion of the metaphysical complexities of death with a capital "D." He explores such issues as how people deal with the loss of things—the loss of physical integrity, the loss of health, the loss of friends—and how death itself functions as educator about the frailties of life. Indeed, funeral images abound in "The Life of Death," as does a nihilistic viewpoint about the end purpose in living. However, Barker takes this notion of nihilism and diametrically converts it, thus making "The Life of Death" a transformational story in which Elaine discovers a vitality she's never previously experienced because of her intimate contact with a virulent disease in the crypt beneath the All Saints Church. When she reawakens the ancient curse of the plague in the midst of the modern metropolis, she becomes the Mother of Death, giving death to those she comes into contact with throughout the city. Elaine's transformation is indicative of the pervasiveness of death itself, as seen in the Michael Maybury episode, and its deceptive omnipresence. People like Elaine and Kavanagh (and even places like the All Saints Church) possess clandestine secrets. They hide their true nature beneath a surface of banality, a nature that, when revealed, discloses the miraculous that flourishes within them.

"The Life of Death" is, at its most fundamental level, a love story, but a most unusual love story. The unusual participants of this love story are Elaine Rider and Kavanagh. They are brought together because of their fascination with destruction — the demolition of the All Saints Church — and they eventually attempt to consummate their romance in the midst of death, *via* death. At the beginning of the story, we learn that Elaine is recovering from a serious operation in which half of her "innards" have been removed. She is listless and exhibits a highly depressed state of mind. Once, when she attempts a return to work, she wonders why her fellow workers avoid her or look at her with grave bewilderment. Her supervisor, Mr. Chimes, finally has to tell her that she has been crying all day, a fact unknown to her. The author also implies that Elaine's peers, by avoiding her, desire to keep away from someone afflicted with a terrible illness. Elaine is not only seriously depressed emotionally, she is, in addition, unaware of the depths of her depression. She represents for Barker the traditional, emotionally vulnerable heroine who is susceptible to the potential seductions of a lover, a character akin in several respects to those heroines featured in the novels of the Brontë sisters. The single major difference, however, between Elaine and, say, Charlotte Brontë's protagonist Jane Eyre is that Elaine is courting death, rather than the lord of the manor, and her love is consummated by dying rather than by marriage.

Elaine's beau in her courtship ritual is Kavanagh, an unusual man whom she first meets at the All Saints Church; her curiosity tempts her to have a look inside the church's interior that will soon be totally demolished (a place representative of her own physical condition), where she talks to an individual who introduces himself as Kavanagh. Kavanagh is investigating inscriptions carved on the floor stones, and he reveals himself to be an easy conversationalist despite his seemingly morbid interest in church crypts and death. When Kavanagh asks to meet Elaine later for a drink, she becomes hesitant, perhaps unnerved by the prospect of romance. Barker writes,

> She looked away from his eager face. He was pleasant enough, in his uneventful way. She liked his green bow tie — surely a joke at the expense of his own drabness. She liked his seriousness too. But she couldn't face the idea of drinking with him, at least not tonight. She made her apologies, and explained that she'd been ill recently and hadn't recovered her stamina.

Elaine is misled by Kavanagh's plain appearance. Masked beneath that "drabness" is a person who is quite different from what he seems to be. Like the dutiful lover of the traditional romance, Kavanagh pursues Elaine, yet as he positions himself to become her lover and to consummate his passion for her, the reader develops a suspicion of him, the way he mysteriously stalks Elaine in the shadowy periphery of her dark world. And when Elaine is transformed by the touch of the reawakened plague — a touch that also reawakens the flow of her own life force—she decides to allow herself to be seduced by Kavanagh. Though Elaine thinks Kavanagh to be the personification of death, it is ironically *her* touch that makes him into that which she believes him to be. For Kavanagh, sexual contact with Elaine infects him with the plague. Their sexual intimacy forever changes him and what he represents to the world: death incarnate. For Elaine, sexual contact with Kavanagh leads to her immediate and swift murder. There lurks a serial killer within Kavanagh's secret self. Barker turns romantic convention rudely upon its ear in this morbidly sardonic love scene. Barker thus makes two points in this mockery of romance. The first is that having sex can be a dangerous proposition. It can even kill, and thus the author develops a cautionary tale about sex and disease that is interestingly reminiscent of the current AIDS epidemic. Yet Barker portrays sex in "The Life of Death" as a transformational act. It changes people, for better or for worse. When Kavanagh strangles Elaine after having seduced her, he is releasing her from the turmoil of her life and is granting her a type of afterlife existence (because the reader still sees events through her eyes after her death). Kavanagh is transformed from common killer to the living embodiment of death. He becomes the contemporary version of the Grim Reaper. Rather than playing at death, he metamorphosed—*via* sexual contact with Elaine—into the personification of death. Romance in "The Life of Death" does not lead to marriage. It does, however, engender fantastic transformations in mind and body, recontouring the shape of the commonplace into the figure of the startlingly unusual.

Before she became infected with the divine touch of the plague in that church crypt, Elaine acted as if she were the walking dead. She was listless, depressed, and mournful about her physical loss of integrity. Because of her operation, she felt as if she were not a whole person. She thought life had ended for her. Yet when she squeezes through the breached door (bypassing the broken seal) of the All Saints' tomb and trespasses within, she miraculously re-awakens from her state of walking death in life to an entirely different and vibrant condition, a new-found life in death. Elaine discovers grim wonderment in this tomb, depicted by Barker as a grotesque "charnel house" ("Bodies had been thrown in heaps on every side"), a place of dark magic residing underneath the plain surface of the commonplace church. The crypt is indicative of Kavanagh's secret-self. Both defy simple analysis, and both mask a profound (and profane) meaning for Elaine beneath the surface. Elaine moves a body in the tomb that is covering the corpse of a woman—again, reinforcing the author's thematic notion of discovering something consequential beneath something else. The dead woman possesses "long chestnut-colored hair" (the hair was what drew Elaine's attention in the first place). Beauty is contrasted with ugliness as Barker describes the woman's corpse,

> The flesh of the corpse was greasy to the touch and left her [Elaine's]

fingers stained, but she was not distressed. The uncovered corpse lay with her legs wide, but the constant weight of her companion [the other body on top] had bent them into an impossible configuration. The wound that had killed her had bloodied her thighs, and glued her skirt to her abdomen and groin. Had she miscarried, Elaine wondered, or had some disease devoured her there?

This gruesome scene is emblematic of Elaine's metamorphic rebirth from death to life *via* death. Because she touches the dead, plague-ridden bodies, she becomes a carrier of the plague. When she becomes a carrier of the plague, she discovers a new, ravenous vitality, a new energy, a new perspective on life. The female corpse with the beautiful hair is depicted by the author as appearing as if she has just given birth. Her body remains in the birthing position and shows the physical evidence of her labor around her groin and upon her thighs. The metaphoric infant she gives birth to is Elaine, a transformed Elaine who discards her old non-life and enters the world like a newborn child seeing the world for the first time. And when Elaine infects Kavanagh with the plague, she evolves from infant to mother, becoming the new Mother of Death, giving birth to the next stage of the plague with her symbolic husband, Kavanagh.

Both people and places harbor a reality that is hidden behind their otherwise common appearance. Elaine Rider seems like a woman on the mend after undergoing surgery. In actuality, she is walking death incarnate, granting her dubious favors upon all those she comes into contact with. Kavanagh seems like a lonely, eccentric man. In actuality, he is a serial killer constantly on the prowl for his next victim. All Saints seems like a typical run-down church in dire need of demolition. In actuality, it guards the apocalypse, a devastating virulent disease that is patiently awaiting its release upon an unsuspecting world. People and places that appear innocuous are not in "The Life of Death." Revelations of secrets in the story are a deadly affair.

Despair and joy are artfully contrasted with each other in "The Life of Death." The eventual joy experienced by the principal characters, because of their transformations, is tempered by melancholy sorrow and by a sense of loss. As the story opens, Elaine Rider is told by her physician, Dr. Sennett, that she is "healing well, both inside and out." Of course, her doctor is oblivious to her true mental state when he tells her this; she is *not* healing well. Elaine is profoundly affected by her physical loss. She views this physical loss as a partial disintegration of her self-identity, and thus she believes that she is not whole either in body or mind. In "The Life of Death," Elaine is emblematic of loss itself. She has lost her health, her physical identity as a whole woman when we first see her, and after she becomes the carrier of the new, deadly plague, she loses her friends and associates. The focus of Elaine's sense of emptiness is death (as the catalyst of loss) or, more precisely, the threat of death. Barker uses death, then, as a reminder for both Elaine and his reader of the fragility of life. Death functions as an educational device. When Elaine and Kavanagh meet again at one point midway in the story, Kavanagh reminds Elaine that when one cries over a loved one's death, it's a selfish response, and when she concurs with his observations, Kavanagh proclaims, "You see how much the dead can teach, just by lying there, twiddling their thumb bones?"

What the dead teach us in "The Life of Death" is a type of nihilism, that there is no final purpose in the end except the end. There is no point to life but the eternal perpetuation of death. Barker's point in the story is that death is more than a process. It is the termination of all things. Those ancient people may have temporarily trapped the metaphoric beast in the All Saints Church, but the beast cannot die and it will eventually escape its bonds to reassert its dominance in the affairs of humanity. For example, the Michael Maybury story-within-a-story episode (where death—as anthropomorphic entity—eventually claims a yachtsman who has temporarily eluded his fate) is a microcosm of Elaine's demise (even though she temporarily escapes death while she is a carrier of the plague) and the inevitable apocalyptic demise of humanity as a whole when the plague is released. Regarding Elaine's opening of the Pandora's Box, the phrase "Redeem the time," is used in an ironic fashion in the story. Elaine initially views the words etched in stone ("an all but eroded relief of crossed shinbones, like drumsticks") near where Kavanagh is standing when she first meets him in All Saints. The motto was inscribed in the distant past and functions as a symbolic warning to others not to open the charnel house tomb beneath the church, the crypt that houses the still virulent plague. We understand that the motto also serves as advice to Elaine to begin living her life again after she reads it. In addition to its general cryptic warning and to its specific implied advice, the phrase is a bold statement about the inevitability of death. Death cannot be defeated, even by time and the best laid plans; it is greater than man, greater than woman, greater than religion (after all, the Church was only able to forestall the inevitable, not thwart it), greater than time itself. Indeed, the plague's redemption in "The Life of Death" is a foregone conclusion.

"How Spoilers Bleed"

From "The Life of Death" to "How Spoilers Bleed," Clive Barker moves from one story about virulent, contagious diseases to another. In "How Spoilers Bleed," however, disease functions as a type of magical hex through which evil is visited upon evil. It is a revenge story, pure and simple, in which the greed of European imperialists is rewarded by the tropical native Indians whose land is being stolen with the enactment of a terrible curse that causes the recipients of the curse to rot away like old fruit. Indeed, images of rot, sickness, and the sensually oppressive jungle permeate the story's setting. It is an environment the non-native white man is totally unequipped physically or emotionally to deal with. The Europeans are portrayed by Barker as being imperialistic intruders—as being terrified strangers in a strange land—who are unable to communicate at any level with the unflappable native Indians. Barker depicts the invading Europeans' perception of the Indians as that of a stupid, barbarous people. Conversely, the Indians' society is quite sophisticated and entirely able to deal with the European intruders in an appropriately nasty fashion. The European protagonists—principally three men named Locke, Cherrick, and Stumpf—ironically are the ones shown to be ignorant, barbaric and stupid. "How Spoilers Bleed" details the severe consequences of obsessive greed; specifically, Barker contrasts the white man's notion of law with the larger notion of moral right. Moral right pronounces its dire judgment upon legal right in the story. The Europeans have their legal paperwork in proper order, and they believe this gives them the right to exploit the natives, but from a moral standpoint beyond the confines of "the law" they are villains who deserve their terrible fate.

"How Spoilers Bleed" begins in the midst of death. Locke and the German named Stumpf are burying their partner, Cherrick. After the Indian servants finish filling in Cherrick's grave, Locke observes them ("probably the worse for bad whisky") stamping the dirt down over the grave site, an act that appears as if they are dancing. Barker's deliberate foreshadowing of later events in this scene underscores the narrative's point, that "How Spoilers Bleed" is a tale of revenge. The Indian grave diggers, Barker implies, are indeed dancing upon the European's grave, and for a justified reason. The story commences in the middle of things, and following Cherrick's burial, the author supplies the events that lead up to his mysterious demise. Cherrick is, the reader learns, condemned to death in an Indian village when he and his companions, Locke and Stumpf, are attempting to evict the Indians from their land. A tribal elder of the village places the hex (as an indictment of murder) upon Cherrick (which later also affects Stumpf and Locke) after the enraged Cherrick attempts to shoot with his rifle the tribal elder, but instead inadvertently kills a young Indian boy.

The three Europeans thus must pay for their crimes—crimes brutally motivated by greed—with their lives, and they must pay in a horrible fashion because they see no wrong in what they did. Barker portrays the three Europeans as being immoral, yet they do not view themselves as being anything other than vindicated in their actions. However, the Europeans *are* evil; they are attempting to steal land and Cherrick murders a helpless child. Their lack of remorse for what they are doing (with the possible exception of Stumpf, though he is punished in the same hideous fashion as are his companions) is an evil that cannot be ignored. Fate, summoned by the old Indian's curse, then takes a hand in the story in order to facilitate a morally warranted retribution.

What Clive Barker has created in "How Spoilers Bleed" is a Developing World version of the American vigilante story — as best illustrated by popular movies like *Death Wish* (1974) and *Dirty Harry* (1971) — where justice is served by violent acts that purge criminals from society. The tribal elder's killing of Locke, Stumpf, and Cherrick is legitimized within the context of the Europeans' violation or a larger sense of justice, a justice that goes beyond ethnicity or national boundaries.

Though Barker does mirror several significant elements of the vigilante story in "How Spoilers Bleed," his use of the jungle as a symbol of moral decay differs radically from the vigilante story's urban setting. The jungle is an alien environment that causes great bodily anguish for the trespassing Europeans. Barker depicts the three white men as experiencing great physical discomfort in the jungle. The author implies that Stumpf is constantly sick because of his inability to adapt to his new, hostile environment. The jungle in "How Spoilers Bleed" is a place run amuck with growth, where life is out of control. The author suggests to us that where there is too much life, then death is not far away. And as seen in the previous story, life and death are intimately intertwined. At times, it is impossible to distinguish one from the other. The jungle — teeming with vibrant, lush tropical life — is also the setting for horrible death.

Barker illustrates how deadly the jungle is to the alien Europeans in a scene that appears midway through the story. While at a "tiny trading post to the south of Aveiro," Locke, Cherrick, and the diseased Stumpf (who is being tended to by an Englishman named Dancy) are visiting with the trading post's manager, a man called Tetelman. Tetelman tells his visitors that he came to the vile jungle for the same reason they did: greed. Tetelman says he wanted to take two years to make his fortune, and ended up staying for two decades. With a bitter look in his eyes, Tetelman states, "The jungle eats you up and spits you out, sooner or later." While noting Stumpf's illness, Tetelman's remarks outline the underlying image of the story. Barker writes,

> Next door, Stumpf had begun to howl. Dancy's consoling voice could be heard, attempting to talk down the panic. He was plainly failing.
> "Your friend's gone bad," said Tetelman.
> "No friend," Cherrick replied.
> "It rots," Tetelman murmured, half to himself.
> "What does?"
> "The soul." The word was utterly out of place from Tetelman's whisky-glossed lips. "It's like fruit, you see. It rots."

Tetelman's words are revealing. Stumpf has "gone bad," both in a physical and a moral sense. Stumpf's actions are evil, though he is not as evil as his two partners. His soul is ill. It does, as Tetelman suggests, rot. Moral decay engenders physical decay. All three men literally rot by the end of the story. As a result of the tribal elder's curse, like overdone fruit the Europeans' bodies explode upon contact with the slightest physical disturbance, even with motes of dust in the air. They are emblematic of a vile fruit that is rotten to the core. And because they lack moral integrity, they forfeit their physical integrity. Early in the story following Cherrick's bizarre death, Stumpf informs Locke that he wants out of the deal, that he wants no further part of what has happened, that he wants to sell off his share of the land. He says to Locke, "I feel dirty. We're spoilers, Locke." Stumpf's comment contains a double meaning. His notion of "spoilers" refers to the unethical, imperialistic pillaging of the Indian's native homeland. Ironically, though, the word also describes Stumpf's (and his partners') impending physical corruption. They attempt to despoil the land and become, as a consequence of their actions, despoiled.

Barker debunks two racist assumptions in "How Spoilers Bleed." The first is the belief that the white man is somehow better than people of color. The white race has typically been stereotyped in the popular mass media (that is, a mass media controlled by the same white society that it elevates) as being the most intelligent, the most cultured, the most civilized group of people, and superior to the world's other races. This explains, if one follows the line of perverted logic to its conclusion, why the European was so successful in conquering and colonizing the rest of the world. Historically speaking, such an outrageous stereotype has been reinforced, in part, through popular fiction, in works written by H. Rider Haggard and Edgar Rice Burroughs for example. Barker lampoons the Haggard/Burroughs great white hunter image in "How Spoilers Bleed" by portraying his three white protagonists—characters he intends to be analogous to Haggard's Allan Quatermain or Burroughs's Lord Greystoke (i.e. the white bwana)—as the uncivilized ones, the animal-like brutes who lack human compassion. Locke, Cherrick, and Stumpf lack intelligence, as is demonstrated by their inability to understand the native Indian mentality and by their underestimating the native Indian resolve to defend their home. In essence, the three white Europeans enact their own destruction because of their blind greed, which is the final, ultimate stupidity. Metaphorically speaking, Barker shows Quatermain to be a land-mongering fool and Lord Greystoke to be a homicidal maniac, and in the process contends that the white man can be as ignorant and barbaric as anyone.

The second racist assumption that Clive Barker debunks in "How Spoilers Bleed" is the belief that the Indian native is inherently inferior, both in technological and moral terms. The scene in which Locke, Stumpf, and Cherrick confront the Indians and order them to leave the land is most revealing not only of the white protagonists' foolish greed, but of the Indians' quietly defiant attitude as well. Barker suggests—*via* Tetelman's observations—in the story that what the European imperialists take for native Indian apathy is, in actuality, a sophisticated method of dealing with hostility and gross ignorance. And when, in anger, Cherrick unthinkingly shoots and kills one of the Indian children, Barker is showing us which culture is the most tolerant. But tolerance can be tested only so far, and when the three white men exceed the bounds of moral decency, they are condemned by the tribal elder to a terrible death. The curse is as clever as anything that European technology could come up with and is more powerful than modern medicine, one of the traditional super icons in popular fiction of the white imperialist.

The Europeans' great weakness in the story is their greed. Their desire for that which does not rightfully belong to them is the cause of both the Indians' destruction and, ironically, their own. Greed is sanctioned in "How Spoilers Bleed" by the law, but it is condemned in the higher court of morality. When Locke tells Tetelman that he and his partners have paid for the Indians' land, Tetelman answers, "Paid?...No. You just paid for a blind eye so you could take it by force. You paid for the right to fuck up the Indians in any way you could." Barker intends his story to be a cautionary tale that relates the severe repercussions when people allow themselves to be ruled by greed. We agree with the author that rampant greed most certainly corrupts the soul; Barker literalizes this metaphoric truth, making it a physical truth. The rotting, decrepit soul of the white imperialists in "How Spoilers Bleed" permeates their physical bodies and results in their rotting, decrepit appearance. Barker's moral is that those who are "spoilers," those who are corrupting in their pursuit of money and power, themselves are corrupt in the most disgusting of fashions. Greed demands payment of a terrible price in the story, a price not confined by the strictures of humanity's laws.

In "How Spoilers Bleed," humanity's law is overruled by a higher court, one that makes its judgments in moral, rather than legal, terms. Indeed, Barker distinguishes between the one perception of justice, which, the way it is portrayed in the story, makes it an oxymoron, and the other, which is valid. The Indians' moral rights preempt the European imperialists' legal rights. Physically unable to adapt to the jungle environment that they so desire to pillage, the white protagonists are morally unable to comprehend the evil of their deeds. In their blind arrogance, they are incapable of knowing when they transgress moral taboo, such as both their stealing land that does not belong to them and their killing of innocent people. Clive Barker views law and the legal system as being concepts antithetical to justice. Law is a shield behind which people with less than honorable intentions can hide while exploiting those who do not possess the resources to protect themselves. Locke, Cherrick, and Stumpf have legal right on their side — and they probably paid well for it — but they in no way are morally right in what they do. Barker sees law in "How Spoilers Bleed" as fostering evil, rather than defending against it. The judicial system is the henchman for bureaucracy, and bureaucracy for Barker is a four letter word. Moral right, the author suggests to his reader, is determined and interpreted beyond the sphere of humanity's all too flawed notion of order that is determined by self-interest.

Yet Fate — as an aspect of moral right — is a fickle thing in Barker's fiction. Though the Indians enact an effective and appropriate retribution against those who attack them with a disease endemic to their jungle society, they themselves are ironically destroyed by the white man's diseases. Blankets given to the Indians by the Europeans are laced with a pox against which the Indians have no natural immunity. The Indians destroy the white man with their jungle rot illness, and the white man, in turn, destroys the Indians with smallpox and measles, diseases conquered by our so-called civilization. Barker leaves his reader in "How Spoilers Bleed" with a final, grim joke. His jest suggests that violence is the end product of violence. When used as a weapon, death sometimes has a way of turning with impunity upon those who wield it.

"Twilight at the Towers"

Along with "Babel's Children," Clive Barker's "Twilight at the Towers" is a pastiche of the spy story. But unlike "Babel's Children," which seems an outrageous mix of several different spy thriller formula types, "Twilight at the Towers" centers upon one specific type of spy narrative; it is quite similar in atmosphere and setting to John le Carré's work, in particular similar to le Carré's novel *The Spy Who Came in from the Cold* (1963). Barker's story is set in Berlin, Germany in the recent past during the Cold War era, and like le Carré, Barker explores in "Twilight at the Towers" issues such as political ambiguity (e.g. Who are the good guys and who are the bad?), the quest for truth and understanding, and the conflict between the power of the State and the integrity of the individual. Added to the above, Clive Barker brings several of his own very distinct thematic concerns. Barker discusses in the story the individual's search for faith, as well as for truth, and suggests that both faith and truth are the same thing. He also investigates the destructive and constructive power of dreams, illustrating in "Twilight at the Towers" that dreaming possesses a transformational quality. Barker effectively incorporates his game metaphor in the story, showing his reader how political game playing can exact a heavy toll upon the individual. Finally, what Barker begins as a spy story he ends as a monster story, revealing the monsters to be much more sympathetic than their human persecutors, and thus reinforcing a similar attitude that he develops more thoroughly with his Nightbreed characters in his short novel, *Cabal*.

At first glance, "Twilight at the Towers" looks like a typical, politically obtuse John le Carré spy adventure. The story takes place in Berlin, which (like Ballard's own personality) is described as being a "wasteland of dead ambition." The Cold War is at its height as the narrative opens, and agent Ballard is requested by his superiors at the British Security Service to evaluate whether a Soviet section leader in Directorate S of the KGB named Sergei Zakharovich Mironenko is sincere in his desire to defect to the West. Ballard is asked to employ his superior senses to "sniff out the least signs of betrayal" on Mironenko's part. And after Barker inaugurates this bare-bones thriller plot in standard le Carré fashion, he clouds events and characters so that the protagonist is unsure of who his friends and enemies are and is eventually even unsure of his own personal motivations. "Twilight at the Towers" is a twilight tale. Barker emphasizes the claustrophobic nature of Berlin's dangerous streets and nondescript buildings, a setting that reflects the characters' lack of identity and their sense of paranoia. While the story commences in the twilight, it quickly moves into darkness. As Ballard negotiates his way through the complex twists of the story, his otherwise superior perceptions are befuddled and bewildered. Fog becomes the dominant image in Barker's narrative. Fog swirls about Ballard, Mironenko, the good guys and the bad guys (indistinguishable from one another), the violent events, and the miraculous transformations obscuring Ballard's and our own understanding of the truth.

As a reflection of the physical ambiguity in "Twilight at the Towers," political ambiguity is an important part of the story. Initially, Ballard's assignment seems straightforward enough, but following his meeting with Mironenko, Ballard begins to question his relationship with the higher-ups at the British Security Service. As the narrative progresses, he becomes more paranoid. Things are not what they appear to be. Ballard's so-called friends in the service—people like his superior, Cripps, and the aptly named Suckling—either attempt to manipulate him for their own selfish reasons or betray him. Ballard senses that he is being double-crossed by his side, that he is being set up to take the blame for an operation that he knows nothing about. His only true friend is the defector Mironenko, a man who encourages Ballard to overcome the brainwashing imposed upon him (by the dubiously labeled good guys) in order to get in touch with his true nature, the fact that he (along with Mironenko) is a special creature—a werewolf.

During their initial meeting, Mironenko tells Ballard a message that is pregnant with hidden, significant meaning. Answering Ballard's inquiries about his disillusionment with his Communist employers, Mironenko frames his reply by a discussion into the nature of faith before proclaiming, "I think the man who does not believe he is lost, is lost." Mironenko's paradoxical statement serves as the central paradox of the story. Like Mironenko, Ballard himself has to first become disenchanted with his own side before he can discover truth, or more correctly, before he can discover faith in himself. He has to be lost before he can find himself. As Ballard approaches the truth about Mironenko's motives or the truth about his own hidden, repressed nature, he must undergo a series of trials that first strips away his previously held assumptions about political reality, and then replaces those assumptions with a new mindset, a worldview that recognizes the integrity of the individual over the authority of the State.

The truth lurking behind Ballard's quest for understanding is not attractive. Ballard comes to learn that his government and his enemy's government are virtually one and the same; they both desire to oppress people, to control people, to destroy people for their own selfish, obscure reasons. His government, their government, all governments seek power at the expense of the individual. Ballard's relationship with his two colleagues who are representative of the State—Cripps and Suckling—is indicative of how his own government attempts either to manipulate or to kill him. Cripps desires to control Ballard's latent, supernatural powers. He tortures Ballard in order to use him, and Cripps does this with the blessings of the British Security Service. Suckling simply wants to kill Ballard. As the most emblematic representative of the bureaucratic State in the story, Suckling is too stupid to comprehend Cripp's plan. Suckling is, however, quite adept at political maneuvering and backstabbing, abilities that are crucial in the secret service. To Suckling, Ballard is simply a barrier that needs removing. To resume his climb up the ladder of success, Suckling must eliminate this occupational hazard. With either Cripps or Suckling, Ballard the dreamer is a doomed individual.

The plot of "Twilight at the Towers" is mainly constructed around the protagonist's quest for the truth. Ballard first attempts to discover the truth about Mironenko's motives. He later wants to know the truth about how his employer is using him. And finally, Ballard seeks the truth about what is buried (both metaphorically and literally) within his psyche. However, what Ballard and the reader come to realize as the story progresses is that truth is better defined by the word "faith." Barker intends "Twilight at the Towers" to be an investigation of one's faith, a philosophical investigation lightly garbed in the traditional motifs (such as the search for truth) of the spy tale. If "Twilight at the Towers" is a mystery, then the mystery element is religious in nature, not formulaic. The significant conflict in Ballard's life is not with the KGB or with paranoid elements of his own agency, but rather it is with himself, his coming to grips with the fact that he is a werewolf. Mironenko attempts to alert Ballard to what Ballard really is, and to what is being done to him. The story, in fact, is about Ballard's conversion to a new faith, a faith created by Mironenko and in which Mironenko later functions as its inspirational leader. In the dramatic concluding scene, Mironenko is reading passages from the Bible, in particular the quote from Genesis 1:22 that goes "And God blessed them, and God said unto them, Be fruitful, and multiply, and replenish the earth . . . and subdue it: and have dominion over the fish of the sea, and over the fowl of the air . . . and over every living thing that moveth upon the earth." Mironenko's sermon possesses an intended double meaning, and he will most probably be a militaristic Messiah. The tormented will soon turn on their tormentors.

An important feature of Ballard's religious conversion is the dream and what it represents. Clive Barker shows the dream as being a device used for manipulation and control. Ballard's superiors had mastery over the wolf/monster side of his nature—a control that allowed them to exploit his heightened animal perceptions without having to deal with his other, violent, more unpredictable qualities—by brainwashing him while he is dreaming. At one point when he is asleep midway through the story, a "cool voice" (the voice of his superiors) tells Ballard that dreams give him pain, that dreams mean to harm him, that he must mentally visualize his dreams and then suppress them. When Ballard's masters tell him to bury his dreams, they are actually brainwashing him into subordinating his wondrous, magical self to his bureaucratic self. The people who attempt to dominate Ballard are frightened by what his dreams represent, yet interestingly they employ this very device (i.e. the dream) to combat what they fear most in him. Clive Barker makes it clear, though, that dreaming—as a process of revelation founded upon imagination—is a powerful thing indeed, a thing that cannot long be repressed. Barker shows that, ultimately, when unencumbered by any sort of destructive limitations, like the myopic bureaucratic State, dreams are healing and procreative. Ballard does finally get in touch with himself because he unfetters his imagination. His dreams free him from his psychological prison, leading him to a new faith.

Unfortunately, faith is something that Ballard's superiors do not want him to discover. His government's motives are far more self-serving than even he realizes, and consequently are more sinister. The way in which Barker utilizes game imagery in "Twilight at the Towers" nicely illustrates the evil nature of the political State. When Ballard is first given the assignment to investigate Mironenko's motives, Barker tells us that there was a time when Ballard "would have found the puzzle fascinating." However, Ballard is already tired of puzzles, of game playing, when the story opens. Ballard tells his boss Cripps early on that he is "sick of this damn game." Later, when the despicable Suckling attempts to threaten Ballard with vague generalizations, Barker tells his reader that, "The charm of hide-and-seek was rapidly wearing thin." The spy business, the author implies, is a mind-numbing business comprised of silly, meaningless games. To find himself, to find his new faith, Ballard must leave the game playing behind him. He must change his perception of things. He must cease being a pawn in the political arena.

Ballard's journey toward self-realization mirrors the story's progression from spy thriller to monster story. As Ballard evolves from being the "pragmatist," as Barker terms him early in the narrative, to being the dreamer of magic, wonder, and faith, "Twilight at the Towers," as well, moves from the pragmatic tale of espionage to the monster tale. Clive Barker often employs monsters as victimized, persecuted characters in his fiction. They are usually attacked by those who are blinded by a lack of imagination, pigheaded, foolish mortals who are suspicious of the supernatural. In *Cabal*, for example, the community of monsters called the Nightbreed secret themselves in an isolated city named Midian, hidden in the wilds of Canada, because they are afraid of persecution from people who are unwilling to accept the creatures of the night for what they are. The Nightbreeds' fears are well justified, since once their hiding place is revealed, they are viciously attacked by an ignorant, murderous humanity. Like *Cabal*, "Twilight at the Towers" is a story about prejudice and how a lack of understanding between differing groups of individuals can lead to senseless violence. Clive Barker views monsters as being symbolic of imagination, as well as being victims of banality. Barker suggests to us in his writing that monsters are not necessarily evil. Rather, they are to be admired since they are one step closer to true divinity than we are. We have to dream of magic. They, like Ballard and Mironenko, *are* magic.

"The Last Illusion"

"The Last Illusion" is one of two Barker short stories to feature his private eye detective protagonist Harry D'Amour. Harry is Clive Barker's rendition of a hard-boiled literary tradition that has produced such memorable characters as Dashiell Hammett's Sam Spade and Raymond Chandler's Philip Marlowe, but unlike the efforts of Hammett or Chandler, Barker incorporates a substantial dose of dark fantasy in his hard-boiled detective fiction. In the typical detective story, illusion has always had an important role. The detective fiction author frequently employs literary sleight-of-hand tricks in his or her work in order to divert the reader's attention, in the process thus creating an entertaining story in which the reader (along with the detective hero) attempts to piece the mystery puzzle together and thus solve the author's intended illusion. Interestingly, the stage magician works much the same way as does the writer of detective fiction, diverting the audience's attention while the illusion is being performed.

In "The Last Illusion," Clive Barker unites the detective story with dark fantasy. The detective fiction element of Barker's narrative is delineated in the personality of Harry D'Amour, a private investigator who sacrifices everything, including health and happiness, in his quest to know the truth of the mystery. The dark fantasy element of the story is represented by the professional illusionist named Swann, a character who, with his stage career and by his death, articulates a significant discussion about the nature of true Mystery. Mystery for Barker, it turns out, is not a trick or an illusion, but something that is very real and very deadly. However, despite the magical pyrotechnics employed by the evil Mr. Butterfield, the lesson that Barker leaves us with in "The Last Illusion" is that magic — despite its seeming formidable might — is not as strong as the power of simple human love and fellowship.

After a narrative preface that depicts the unusual death of the magician Swann (as well as the metaphoric death of Swann's attractive female companion, Barbara Bernstein), Clive Barker begins "The Last Illusion" as if it were a standard hard-boiled detective story. Harry D'Amour is a tough P.I. who knows how to use a gun. He also possesses a tenacious personality. He doesn't give up his mission to get at the truth, no matter what the personal cost to him might be. Harry is a down-on-his-heels gumshoe—replete with ex-wife and nagging creditors—who has a dark, tragic past, a past known as the Wyckoff Street affair that is alluded to several times in the story. With Harry D'Amour, Barker introduces elements of *roman noir* to his hard-boiled adventure. Harry is quite similar to Jake Gittes in Roman Polanski's *film noir* classic *Chinatown* (1974) with regards to his unhappy past; each character had apparently cared for women who had subsequently died tragically, and these sad events engendered in D'Amour and Gittes both a fatalistic attitude about their work as detectives and a melancholy attitude about life in general.

Establishing the familiar hard-boiled narrative parameters of "The Last Illusion," Barker quickly leads the story in a new direction, a direction that incorporates strong elements of dark fantasy. Harry is contacted by Swann's beautiful widow, an ex-prostitute named Dorothea, requesting his help. Dorothea is familiar with Harry's experience with occult matters (having read in the newspapers of his adventure in the Wyckoff Street situation). She wants Harry to "corpse-sit" with the body of her deceased husband until it is cremated. She shows Harry her husband's letter in which he makes this most unusual entreaty. From the moment Harry begins his watch over Swann's body in the magician's brownstone on East Sixty-first Street in New York City, events in "The Last Illusion" take a decidedly fantastic turn. D'Amour is attacked by the agents of Hell who want to punish the rogue magician Swann for his mockery of his magical craft and for his many insults directed against Hell itself. While Harry is guarding Swann's body, he is assaulted with horrible illusions—visions of the floor beneath his feet disappearing and Swann's corpse rising from his coffin—images that the representative of Hell, a lawyer named Butterfield, hopes to use to scare Harry. Once on the job, however, Harry D'Amour, is not so easily dissuaded from his duty to Swann, and with the help of Swann's demon-familiar, a creature called Valentin who in mortal disguise acted as Swann's servant, Harry persists in his attempts to save Swann from the eternal torments that Hell has in store.

Barker offers a solid contribution to the hard-boiled formula with Harry D'Amour, who is the quintessential private investigator. Despite the fact that he is beaten and bruised and abused during the course of his investigation, Harry nonetheless persists in his obligation to his client, often risking his life, and as demonstrated in the Swann case, risking his very soul. D'Amour decides to investigate the name and address of Barbara Bernstein written by Valentin on a piece of paper, thus ignoring the potential hazards that will confront him. At this moment, Clive Barker takes the reader inside the head of Harry D'Amour for a revealing insight,

> A wise man, Harry reminded himself, would tear this note up and throw it down the gutter. But if the events in Wyckoff Street had taught him anything, it was that once touched by such malignancy as he had seen and dreamt in the last few hours, there could be no casual disposal of it. He had to follow it to its source, however repugnant that thought was, and make with it whatever bargains the strength of his hand allowed.

Harry is a survivor type. In circumstances where the average man or woman would be killed, Harry is able to somehow climb out of nasty situations with his skin intact. Yet despite his stamina for abuse and his courage in the face of the diabolical evil that Butterfield will throw his way, Harry is still a caring, vulnerable individual. He is haunted, perhaps even trapped, by the events of his past. His actions are governed by powerful sense of obligation, an obligation forged from guilt and a need to know the truth. As Barker reveals bits and pieces of Harry's past involvement with the Wyckoff Street tragedy, the reader begins to understand something of Harry's personality and his motivation in fighting the powers of Hell. Regarding Harry's ongoing dangerous confrontations with demons, at one point in the story Harry rhetorically asks Valentin, "Are you paying me for this?...or am I doing it all for love?" Valentin perceptively answers, "You're doing it because of what happened at Wyckoff Street...Because you lost poor Mimi Lomax to the Gulfs, and you don't want to lose Swann." Valentin correctly identifies in Harry's personality that knight-in-shining-armor characteristic that is often prevalent in the hard-boiled detective hero.

Harry D'Amour is a moral individual in an immoral world. He persists in his fight against corruption and evil, even in the face of great odds. But whereas in the typical hard-boiled crime story, evil is perpetuated by people, characters like gangsters, corrupt city politicians, and corrupt cops, in Barker's "The Last Illusion" evil is religious in nature, manufactured by the Devil and distributed by Hell. This distinction between Barker's short story and the work of the Hammett/Chandler school is fundamental. Harry is better than us because he can face supernatural horror that we, as average people, cannot. His abilities are superhuman. But Harry is also inferior to us. He is a man consumed with guilt and his own profound sense of emotional weakness. He is condemned never to enjoy the companionship of women. He "lost" Mimi Lomax to the past (perhaps Harry somehow felt attracted to Mimi), and loses Dorothea Swann to the present (perhaps Harry also felt attracted to Dorothea). His need for love in his life is unfulfilled, but this only makes his continuing search for love all the more persistent. Harry's lack of sexual love creates within his character a blank medium upon which the larger love for humanity etches itself.

In addition to being a hard-boiled detective story, "The Last Illusion" is a dark fantasy adventure that offers the reader an engaging discussion of the contrast between illusion and real magic. Following Swann's death, Harry learns in his interview with Swann's widow Dorothea that Swann preferred to call himself an illusionist and not a magician, thus diminishing his feats of magic and making the performance of magic a mundane thing. The reason for Swann's trivializing his craft becomes apparent to us when Valentin explains to Harry about Swann's past. Valentin tells Harry that some thirty-two years earlier, Swann had agreed to become Hell's ambassador on earth if he were granted the ability to perform real magic. Valentin goes on to say that Swann learned that he forfeited more in the deal than he received, so to gain some measure of revenge he tormented his masters in Hell by pretending that he was a common stage illusionist. While performing actual, supernatural feats of magic, Swann degraded his powers (and Hell) by acting as if he were performing simple illusions. Hearing Valentin's explanation, Harry then understands why Hell is so anxious to acquire Swann's corpse; they can still have their retribution upon the soul of the man that so mocked them in life. Illusion in "The Last Illusion" occurs only when magic is portrayed by Swann as being illusion.

Instead, magic is very real in the story, and it is contrasted with the fakery of Swann's stage acting. Almost always, nothing is as it seems in Barker's fiction, and in "The Last Illusion" Barker has some fun toying with the deceptiveness of surface appearances by showing the fake to be real, and the real fake. Swann employs this seeming confusion over appearances as a weapon against his masters. Ironically, though, Barker tells his reader that magic has its drawbacks, its severe limitations. In the above mentioned conversation between Valentin and Harry D'Amour, Valentin makes a profound statement. Referring to Swann's contract with Hell where he sells his soul for magic, Valentin says,

> Nothing the Prince of Lies offers to humankind is of the least value... or it wouldn't be offered. Swann didn't know that when he first made his Covenant. But he soon learned. Miracles are useless. Magic is a distraction from the real concerns. It's rhetoric. Melodrama.

Valentin's remarks, if taken out of context, would seem to contradict what Barker has indicated elsewhere in his writings, that magic and miracles are rare and treasured gifts. If we were to make such a claim against Barker, we would be misreading a more important message that Barker gives us in this story, and frequently in the rest of his work. Even though magic and miracles are wondrous, even though magic and miracles are representative of imagination, even though magic and miracles deflate the evil of banality, they are still not as important to Barker as are love and fellowship.

Harry D'Amour inquires of Valentin, after the demon-familiar's discussion of Swann's disillusionment with Hell, that if magic is "rhetoric" and "melodrama," then what *are* life's "real concerns," to which Valentin replies, "You should know better than I. . . . Fellowship, maybe? Curiosity? Certainly it matters not in the least if water can be made into wine, or Lazarus to live another year." When viewed in its totality, the basic premise of Barker's work is that a fundamental love for one another (i.e. a general camaraderie held among all people) is the mightiest of powers. It's a force that not only leads to divinity, but that also confounds the combined might of Hell. Harry D'Amour's name even gives us an indication of the source of his inner strength: love. And though Harry has lacked love in his life, and has twice lost potential love, the fact that he is capable of loving at all makes him stronger in the author's eyes than the magic of Swann, Butterfield, or the assorted demons of Hell.

"The Book of Blood (A Postscript): On Jerusalem Street"

The reader becomes reacquainted with Simon McNeal in the vignette entitled "The Book of Blood (A Postscript): On Jerusalem Street," and with this short tale Clive Barker brings to a satisfying close his six-volume anthology. In this, his concluding framing story, Barker punctuates his frequent use of text metaphors in the *Books of Blood* by having McNeal killed, but even though this living book of the dead is no longer living by story's end, the tales written upon his mutilated body persist in the telling. They refuse to be ignored, overcoming in the process the physical limitations of life and death. "On Jerusalem Street," like its companion framing story that appears at the beginning of Barker's *Books of Blood*, is a narrative of the senses, both physical and spiritual. "On Jerusalem Street" is also a confessional story, wrapping up as it does six volumes of confessional stories. And a good deal of what Clive Barker writes about in the preceding twenty-nine short stories of the *Books of Blood*—such things as the grotesque, the violent, the amazing, the beautiful—is nicely summarized in the thirtieth and final tale.

Clive Barker's very first reference to McNeal, *via* Leon Wyburd's persona, identifies the young McNeal as "the book." As we have previously been told in the opening framing story of the *Books of Blood*, because of Simon McNeal's mocking violation of the dead, the dead have their revenge upon the hapless boy by writing their stories over the entire surface of his body, in essence transforming him into both freak and miracle. While engaging McNeal in conversation, Wyburd questions McNeal about why he refers to himself only in the third person, and the reader understands this to mean that McNeal has lost his identity. His function as living text has superseded his personal ego. Wyburd wonders if McNeal is playing "some damn-fool game," or if he is "simply mad." In a rare instance in Barker's fiction, one of his characters is *not* playing a game. McNeal is quite mad, yet there is nothing simple about McNeal's madness. His insanity is born out of righteous punishment. His insanity is purchased by communication with the Other Side. His insanity reveals sanity through insane stories.

The reader soon learns that Wyburd's visit to Jerusalem Street is not a mere social call. He is a paid assassin hired by "an exile ... a collector ... of skins" in Rio to kill McNeal, and then flay the young man for his unique hide. McNeal seems to know Wyburd's motives from the start. He asks Wyburd how much his skin is worth. The assassin replies that its value is "two hundred thousand." Wyburd obviously thinks this to be a princely sum, but as Wyburd soon learns, value is relative. The assassin is baffled during the brief conversation by the boy's remarks about stories that never cease in the telling, about the road the dead travel, and about McNeal's willingness to be killed. McNeal wants to die because he desires to be reunited with the miraculous. He says to the assassin, "There's a road, you know. ... A road the dead go down. He [McNeal discussing himself in the third person] saw it. Dark, strange road, full of people. Not a day gone by when he hasn't ... hasn't wanted to go back there." Wyburd is unable to perceive the subtleties in McNeal's bizarre attitude. He is a mundane creature, a pathetic man who, despite his exotic occupation, cannot cognitively plumb beneath the surface of things. Wyburd sees nothing in McNeal but the amount of a potential bounty. His lack of imagination is tragic and leads to his untimely fate. Wyburd in a sense anticipates Barker's assassin protagonist, Pie 'oh' Pah, in *Imajica*. Both are characters who deal in the coin of death, and because of their unusual profession they both engage in strange and unearthly events.

After he kills McNeal with his knife and obtains what he seeks ("It took him two hours to complete the flaying"), Wyburd returns to his small temporary apartment (with plans made to first fly to Rio to receive the remainder of his payment, and then fly to Florida) and goes to bed. He is "lulled to sleep by the imagined scent of orange groves," and is later awakened by the smell of "something savory." Wyburd's introduction to McNeal's realm of the fantastic is by way of the senses, much the same as was Mary Florescu's in "The Book of Blood." In both framing stories, the heightened sense of smell and sight and sound heralds the arrival of the supernatural. Wyburd hears a "heavy slopping sound" from across the room, and when he leaves his bed to investigate, he feels like he's "knee-deep in warm water." His sight confirms for him what his other senses conspire to confound in him, that he is actually standing in an ever deepening pool of red blood, blood that flows from the suitcase where he packed McNeal's flayed skin. He attempts to escape the room, to stem the flood from the suitcase, but to no avail. He is soon drowned by the blood of his deed, his crime.

For Wyburd, unfortunately, was unable to recognize McNeal's earlier warning until it was too late. The boy (while surveying the writing on the palm of his hand) tells the assassin before he loses his life, "The stories go on, night and day. Never stop. They tell themselves, you see. They bleed and bleed. You can never hush them; never heal them." As Wyburd dies, he reflects upon McNeal's words and begins to hear in his head the stories himself, "Dozens of voices, each telling some tragic tale." "On Jerusalem Street" is about the power of the story. It's about how the telling of the story will not be denied by any force, natural or supernatural. McNeal's story becomes Wyburd's story, and they frame a host of tale tellers. Their stories never heal and always flow in the telling with the lifeblood of the narrative. Their stories become Barker's stories. Their confessions that have to be told become his confessions.

And yet as Wyburd (and Barker's reader) comes to understand while he is traveling down one of the highways of the dead—encountering at an intersection a man who looks like he's wearing a "red suit," but who actually is not wearing a suit at all, nor his skin—the telling of stories (i.e. the making of confessions) is a therapeutic act. The flowing blood that cannot be stemmed washes away sin. Wyburd's traveling companion relates the story about how he came to lose his skin, and Leon Wyburd, in turn, tells the flayed man the account of his own story. Both are thus purified. Both are thus made whole. Barker writes, "It was a great relief to tell the story." Both travelers down the highway of the dead also have a momentum to their existence that was denied them in their mortal lives. They now have a sense of direction. Regarding this sense of direction, Clive Barker leaves his reader with the remark, "Only the living are lost."

The *Books of Blood* are hence appropriately concluded, the last tale artfully told. But the ever so important telling of stories, Barker suggests to us, must not ever end.

CHAPTER EIGHT

Embracing Imagination: Uncollected Short Fiction and Final Comments

"Lost Souls"

"Lost Souls" is the second Clive Barker short story to feature the occult private investigator Harry D'Amour. It was originally published in the magazine *Time Out* (issue number 800; December 19, 1985–January 1, 1986). Later, it was reprinted in the horror fiction anthology edited by Dennis Etchison entitled *Cutting Edge* (1986). "Lost Souls" follows the tradition of the Victorian Christmas tale, imitating the seasonal ghost story as exemplified by Charles Dickens's *A Christmas Carol* (1843). The Christmas ghost story typically celebrated the miracle of Christ's birth with stories about the supernatural. The holiday season ghost story was an annual literary event that was practiced in the popular serial publications appearing in England from Dickens's era to the early twentieth century, when such eminent authors as Henry James and M.R. James made their own respective contributions to the tradition.

Clive Barker's rendition of the Christmas ghost story, though ostensibly working within the tradition, becomes during its telling an anti–Christmas story, one that lampoons the problematic spirit of giving as made famous by Charles Dickens's Scrooge in *A Christmas Carol*, and one that also mocks the morally hypocritical institution of the modern Church. Barker portrays the Church as destroying miracles before they take root, or fanatically preserving the *status quo*, even though such fanaticism leads to murder, and more important, to the destruction of miracles. Taking Barker's argument to its logical, ironic conclusion, if the Church had its way, there would be no Christmas and no Christ. The author thus suggests to us that self-determination (as perhaps exemplified in Harry D'Amour's character), rather than religious despotism, reveals the process by which one should conduct his or her life. It's the only way that true miracles can be nourished.

Two plots co-exist in "Lost Souls." The first of these plots recounts Harry D'Amour's efforts to track down and destroy the "sublimely malignant" demon from Hell named Cha'Chat. Within this narrative, Barker inserts his parody of *A Christmas Carol*. The second plot updates and burlesques the Biblical nativity scene of Christ's birth, though in Barker's rendition, the Church prefers things as they are and through one of its assassins—Darrieux Marchetti, also known as the Cankerist—literally murders a potential modern-day Messiah.

Both plots concurrently take place in New York City immediately preceding Christmas. Barker contrasts the seemingly joyous seasonal atmosphere with the antics of the creature from Hell, Cha'Chat. Yet Barker blurs distinctions between good and evil in the story, and what would otherwise appear to be the season of goodwill also is described by the author as the season of suicide. What is good about Christmas (i.e. love, compassion, tolerance) is vulnerable and open to attack from either supernatural evil or mortal evil. In fact, both Cha'Chat and Marchetti are flip sides of the same ugly coin. They each—as supernatural agent and mortal agent of evil respectively—exploit or seek to harm the symbolic nobility of what Christmas actually means beneath the tarnished veneer of commercialism and religious exploitation. Hence, that which initially appears a profound contrast in the setting of "Lost Souls" instead acts as a narrative reinforcement of the duplicity and hypocrisy that are the cornerstones of Barker's message. Indeed, the author describes the Christmas atmosphere as paradoxically being conducive to Cha'Chat's activities. Evil preys voraciously upon naïveté and ignorance and the mundane. Barker writes, "...it was almost Christmas in New York; season of goodwill and suicide. Streets thronged; the air like salt in wounds; Mammon in glory. A more perfect playground for Cha'Chat's despite could scarcely be imagined."

Harry D'Amour is thus compelled to solve quickly the problem that Cha'Chat presents to the mortal world ("Just as long as Cha'Chat didn't see Christmas Day this side of the Schism," the author informs the reader). He is assisted by a psychic called Norma Paine, who at first directs him to a "derelict house on Ridge Street" where she believes the demon is hiding. When Harry arrives at the house expecting the worst, he instead encounters a young, "undernourished" woman of "Puerto Rican extraction," Linda, who is "heavily pregnant"—a sign he takes as proof that the demon is nowhere in the area since she would have made a "perfect victim" for the monster. Disappointed at the prospect of possibly having to search the entire Manhattan Island area, Harry returns to Norma Paine's apartment. Norma assures Harry that she is "never wrong," that she "saw power in that house on Ridge Street ... sure as shit." Harry actually encountered the same "power" that Norma had described: he simply was looking for the wrong type of power. This early brief encounter between the P.I. hero and pregnant woman later becomes a significant coincidental irony when Harry meets her one more time near the story's conclusion, though we, as readers, come to know that he might have sincerely wished he hadn't seen her again.

A bitingly sardonic episode in "Lost Souls" serves as Clive Barker's critique of the now clichéd Scrooge character, the miserly individual who, at Christmas time, undergoes a moral conversion *via* supernatural means, and because of this re-birth of the soul subsequently becomes outlandishly generous to others. Disguising its form in the body of a grossly obese woman, Cha'Chat approaches a hapless mortal named Eddie Axel as he staggers drunkenly out of his favorite bar. Eddie is the owner of a "highly lucrative" grocery store known as Axel's Superette. Barker writes, "He [Eddie] was drunk and happy; and with reason. Today he had reached the age of fifty-five. He had married three times in those years; he had sired four legitimate children and a handful of bastards." Barker's pointed remark about Eddie's sexual prowess underscores his character's limited, self-centered mentality. The things that make Eddie happy are proficient sex and a proficient business. Otherwise, he offers the world little else. Desiring to have some wicked fun, Cha'Chat confronts Eddie while floating before him in the air. The disguised demon warns Eddie that he will die soon and that his immortal soul (visibly portrayed to Eddie as a very real, pathetic-looking creature) is in jeopardy because of his "paucity of good works." When the terrified Eddie asks what he should do, Cha'Chat replies, "Tomorrow, turn Axel's Superette into a Temple of Charity, and you may yet put some meat on your soul's bones," thus setting the stage for a grisly joke. For when Eddie opens the doors to his grocery store to give away food, he causes a riot in which thirty people are killed and sixty people injured.

Cha'Chat fulfills its nature and achieves what it so desires—making a grim mockery of the spirit of giving during Christmas. Yet Barker accomplishes more in this scene than the enactment of a fictional evil. He is also commenting about the hypocrisy of a faked Christmas generosity. Barker tells us that the act of giving gifts during the holiday season may be frequently motivated by selfish reasons. He implies that the Christmas spirit should not be bought and sold as if it were a commodity huckstered in Macy's Department Store. By inference, we understand Barker's argument to suggest that generosity must come from the soul rather than from the wallet. Giving, if done for the wrong reasons, can be quite destructive, as demonstrated in "Lost Souls" with the Axel's Superette disaster. No doubt Barker would tell us that the same thing might have happened when Scrooge opened his coffers at the conclusion of *A Christmas Carol*. His contrived generosity would have probably caused a similar riot in Victorian London. Clive Barker understands that magnanimity cannot be superficial. One should not give something while expecting something in return.

Harry senses Cha'Chat's vile hand in the calamity when he sees it reported on television, and he goes to the location to continue his hunt for the demon. Arriving at Axel's Superette on Third Avenue, Harry spots Cha'Chat (he overhears two young boys discussing the terrible smell of a woman, and he knows he has discovered the demon because all the "infernal brethren" possess this same odoriferous attribute) and pursues the creature. Barker develops a scene that wonderfully deflates our trite, horror fiction expectations when Cha'Chat defies Harry D'Amour's verbal incantations, at which point Harry draws his gun and shoots the demon. Though not fatally wounded, Cha'Chat is embarrassed at having received so ignoble a scar. Before Harry shoots the creature from Hell a second time ("It was almost impossible to slay a demon of Cha'Chat's elevation with bullets; but a scar was shame enough amongst their clan. Two, almost unbearable"), Cha'Chat offers Harry what it considers important information in order to be spared further humiliation. It tells Harry, "There's something going to get loose tonight, D'Amour . . . something wilder than me," and when Harry demands more information, the demon replies, "Who knows? . . . It's a strange season, isn't it? Long nights. Clear skies. Things get born on nights like this, don't you find?" Harry presses Cha'Chat for the location of this miracle, and after telling the occult P.I. what it knows, it tricks Harry with an ingenious disguise ("suddenly it was Norma who was bleeding on the sidewalk at Harry's feet"), thus facilitating its escape ("The trick lasted seconds only, but Harry's hesitation was all that Cha'Chat needed to fold itself between one plane and the next, and flit. He'd lost the creature, for the second time in a month"). Barker is deliberately vague when he has Cha'Chat tell Harry that "something wilder" than itself is about to "get loose." Does the demon's remark mean that this entity will be a harbinger of good or evil? Barker probably would say to us at this point that questions of good and evil are irrelevant, that the more correct issue might be the intrusion of the wondrous into the world of banality, and banality's fatal reply as an answer, *via* the actions of the insipid Church.

Unfortunately, Harry's failure was not the only loss of the evening; Christmas was to lose a potential miracle as well. Harry locates the "small hotel" that Cha'Chat had told him about ("The place was empty. It had been elected, Harry began to comprehend, for some purpose other than hostelry"). After overpowering a young man who attempts to stop him in the hotel's lobby, he climbs the stairs and hears a woman's cry and then sees a "man in a gray suit [who] was standing on the threshold [of a door at the end of the corridor], skinning off a pair of bloodied surgical gloves." Harry "vaguely" recognizes the man as Darrieux Marchetti, who is "one of that whispered order of theological assassins whose directives came from Rome, or Hell, or both." Barker's use of paradox in suggesting that Marchetti's orders come from Rome or Hell is fitting in that Marchetti, as a symbol of the Church, is a profoundly evil individual. Earlier in the story, when Marchetti is tracking the pregnant Linda, he is listening to a woman singing "some tragic aria" in Italian. Barker writes,

> Marchetti regretted having to forsake the show. The singing much amused him. Her voice, long ago drowned in alcohol, was repeatedly that vital semitone shy of its intended target—a perfect testament to imperfectibility—rendering Verdi's high art laughable even as it came within sight of transcendence. He would have to come back here when the beast had been dispatched. Listening to that spoiled ecstasy brought him closer to tears than he'd been for months; and he liked to weep.

As illustrated in the above scene, Marchetti (and, by implication, the Church) revels in fallibility. He is a vicious sadist in that, for him, life (read: art) is best appreciated when perfection is within sight, yet still tragically unattainable. Marchetti is proficient at spoiling ecstasies. He is moved to tears—a most appropriate emotion for him since it signifies more in the way of humor than of grief—when he recognizes in others some glimpse of high talent that is ignobly wasted. True art terrifies Marchetti and his masters since it grants us a glimpse at perfection, at the divine, at the miraculous. Ironically, Marchetti's job is to destroy miracles, to make perfection imperfect, to encourage art to be laughable.

Marchetti also recognizes Harry D'Amour in turn by name. When Harry demands to know what has just happened, Marchetti replies "Private business," and warns Harry to come no closer. However, Harry sees two bodies "laid out on the bare bed": one is the pregnant woman named Linda he met earlier in the house on Ridge Street, the other her aborted child. Marchetti informs Harry that the woman fatally protested, that all he wanted was the child, but that he had to kill both. Harry demands to know if the child was a demon, to which Marchetti replies, "We'll never know. . . . But at this time of year there's usually something that tries to get in under the wire. We like to be safe rather than sorry. Besides, there are those—I number myself amongst them—that believe there is such a thing as a surfeit of Messiahs." Marchetti then tells his assistant, Patrice (the youth who had grappled with Harry in the hotel lobby), to fetch the car, because he is late for Mass. Appalled, Harry says to Marchetti that he is not above the law, but Marchetti simply walks away when his assistant places a knife at the base of Harry's skull as a warning not to interfere.

To Harry's chagrin, Marchetti and the Church are indeed above the law. They are, in fact, a law unto themselves, a law that enforces senseless ritual and that prosecutes the unusual, judging and condemning to death without a fair trial that which might threaten the *status quo*. Barker leaves us in doubt as to whether Linda's murdered child will be a power for good or for evil, but because this supernatural power exists at all is a dire threat to an institution that preaches the belief in supernatural miracles, yet doesn't practice what it preaches. We are left after reading "Lost Souls" with the understanding that there are two monsters in the story. The one monster is recognizable. We expect it to do what it does because of its nature. The other monster, the mortal monster, is less comprehensible, and hence more frightening. Both creatures utilize duplicity in what they do, in the evil that they perpetuate, but Marchetti's brand of deceit is infinitely more terrifying than Cha'Chat's because what Marchetti does is so antithetical to the sacred ideology that he is supposed to represent. Marchetti's actions are unnatural because the firm he represents is supposedly in the business of miracle births. If one is looking for answers to the important questions in life, if one is attempting not to be one of the "lost souls," if one is looking for the true meaning of Christmas, if one is even looking for Christ, then the place *not* to look is the Church.

Instead, Clive Barker argues a type of self-determinism in "Lost Souls." After showing his reader the despotic attitude of the Church, Clive Barker gives us a viable alternative, one that denies political and or religious ideology and that encourages optimism in the very process of living life from moment to moment. Barker has Harry D'Amour provide a sanguine philosophical contrast to Cha'Chat and Marchetti. "Lost Souls" concludes with D'Amour presumably resuming his hunt for Cha'Chat (the demon was "Still out there somewhere. In a foul temper . . ."). Harry contemplates how no two snowflakes are alike, and this image allows Barker, through his protagonist, an opportunity to outline a hopeful future, despite the grim events that have previously taken place in the story. Barker writes,

> Each moment was its own master, he [Harry] mused, as he put his head between the blizzard's teeth, and he would have to take whatever comfort he could find in the knowledge that between this chilly hour and dawn there were innumerable such moments—blind maybe, and wild and hungry—but all at least eager to be born.

Barker's birth metaphor in the above passage is an appropriate one. The future and all that the future has to offer are like the child that Marchetti murdered. Each metaphoric child, each new instance in time, suggests great potential and new hope for a better tomorrow, and though the Church butcher Marchetti may have destroyed one such hope, many more will rise to take its place. The Church attempts to protect a past that is dead, while Harry prepares for the future. Barker breaks with the *roman noir* formula by having his detective hero face the future as master of his fate instead of the reverse. Not defeated by living, Harry adapts to life, being reborn himself like the snowflake into each subsequent fresh minute. Barker has thus transformed what is otherwise a traditionally pessimistic narrative form into an existential vehicle that denies Fate and Fate's control over human actions. In "Lost Souls," Clive Barker takes the *noir* out of the *roman noir*. Harry may be battered and beaten, but he faces the next moment as a father would his new child, with equal measures of trepidation and intense joy.

"Coming to Grief"

Barker had originally intended to include "Coming to Grief" in the *Books of Blood*, but the story instead found its way to publication in the October 1988 issue of the British edition of *Good Housekeeping* magazine. It appeared in book form in Douglas E. Winter's anthology of horror fiction entitled *Prime Evil* (1988). Looking in retrospect at Clive Barker's corpus of short fiction, "Coming to Grief" is perhaps the most difficult tale to approach critically because of its subtle tone. It is also one of the most rewarding.

"Coming to Grief" is a story about how a thirty-something-year-old woman named Miriam comes to personal terms with the death of her mother, Veronica Blessed. During the course of Barker's narrative, Miriam is not only learning how to approach an understanding of the death of a loved one — and concurrently an understanding of guilt and the dilemma of facing one's own mortality — she is also coming to terms with her past childhood memories. Barker explores the irrational nature of memories and the way they serve to define adult emotions. Miriam's adult confrontation with a dreaded, nameless monster lurking in the dark Liverpool quarry framed by the "Bogey-Walk" articulates her conquest of death and her fear of death. Miriam's monster is representative of her id, but it also, as the reader notes in the story's marvelous twist ending, is an actual, physical creature that lures the unwary to their death using the victim's emotion of grief as bait. Equally as important, Miriam, during her rite of social reintegration, deals with peripheral issues such as the terror we feel at the prospect of being alone in the world, and also the joy we should feel with living itself.

When Miriam returns to the Liverpool of her childhood, eighteen years have elapsed. She was nineteen years old when she left, the author tells us, "to taste the world: to grow; to prosper; to learn and to live." She arrives from her new home in Hong Kong a successful, fulfilled woman, having both a husband who "idolized" her and a daughter who "grew more like her with every year." Since leaving Liverpool, she has achieved her life's ambition. She has become "a wholly sophisticated woman of the world." She has become "universally adored." However, despite Miriam's many successes in life, she still harbors within her soul several tenebrous weaknesses, such as a fear of death and of the unwanted prospect of facing the death of her recently deceased mother.

Early in the story when Miriam enters her mother's house, the thought occurs to her that her mother isn't dead, that she is "camouflaged in the house somewhere, pressed against the wall or at the mantelpiece; unseen but seeing." Interestingly, this is a similar image that Barker uses to describe Miriam's camouflaged monster of the dreaded Bogey-Walk. Both monster and mother represent for Miriam the same fear, the same dread: the inevitable reality that death cannot be avoided or conquered. Yet, as Miriam discovers within herself during the course of the narrative, death may be an unbeatable foe, but the fear of death can — and must — be subdued if one is to proceed with the day-to-day reality of living. Miriam begins this process simply enough with the trivial business of organizing her mother's things. Barker writes, "The task of dividing, discarding, and packing the remnants of her mother's life was slow and repetitive. The rest — the loss, the remorse, the bitterness — were so many thoughts for another day." As noted elsewhere in Clive Barker's fiction, banality is viewed negatively; it is the antithesis of imagination, of divinity, of the things in life that are worthwhile. However, in "Coming to Grief," Barker recognizes the value of using mindless ritual to arrive at mindful contemplation. The author shows us in Miriam's early actions in the story that inane activities, though otherwise reprehensible, can temporarily soothe strained, wounded emotions.

One of the causes of Miriam's emotional wounds is her sense of guilt regarding her difficulty in learning how to come to grief. As her mother's death is an alien thing for her to deal with, so, too, is her willingness to tap the depths of her feelings about what has happened. Miriam experiences guilt when she anticipates returning to Hong Kong, wishing her mother's funeral was "soon done." Barker writes, "Ah, there was a guilt there: the ticking off of the days until the funeral, the pacing out of her mother's ritual removal from the world. Another seventy-two hours and the whole business would be done with, and she would be flying back to life." In this passage, Barker has perceptively tagged our repressed, ambivalent sentiments concerning the death of a family member or other significant loved ones. When someone we deeply care for dies, frequently we all experience a galaxy of conflicting emotions ranging from anger to remorse to guilt to fear. We are uncomfortable with death because of its finality. We are equally uncomfortable with the social rituals of death — like funerals — because they seek to organize our emotions into socially acceptable patterns of action that endeavor to lead us away from grief rather than allowing us to confront it, to deal with it, and subsequently to conquer it. Clive Barker features in "Coming to Grief" a subtle, but nonetheless effective, criticism of the funeral business — in the loathsome guise of Mr. Beckett, the funeral home director — and how this business uses empty ritual and masked professional indifference to exploit people who are having a difficult time with the difficult process of coming to grief.

Interestingly, Miriam is not as impassive about her mother's death as she would like to believe. At one point early in the narrative Clive Barker tells his reader that, "Grief ... had battened upon her and sapped her will to fight," thus explaining in some measure Miriam's outward appearing emotional lethargy. Inwardly, however, Miriam's emotions are anything but lethargic. For example, while she is "Organizing the disposal of [her mother's] personal items," she comes across some photographs of her father and herself when she was a child. The author writes that, "She could hardly bear to look at some of them. She burned first the ones that hurt the most." Miriam's seeming indifference, the reader notes, as she proceeds with the business of burying her mother is an act, a sham, a mask that covers the seething emotions deep within her. It is a contrivance that nearly succeeds in protecting her from the terrible hurt, nearly, but not quite. Several times, as illustrated by her burning of the photographs (and later in the story by her nearly suicidal leap from the Bogey-Walk), the act falls apart when closely scrutinized. The sham is revealed for what it is; the mask cracks.

What is revealed by the author as lurking beneath Miriam's actions is her reluctance to confront her own mortality. Miriam creates a cognitive dichotomy for herself in "Coming to Grief." At the one end of this dichotomy is her subconscious perception of Liverpool as being emblematic of death. It is the setting of her childhood fears of dying, the infamous locale of the Bogey-Walk. It is also the scene of her mother's funeral, which serves as a reminder of the prospect of her own impending and irreversible loneliness in life (i.e. over the loss of that part of her that needs her mother) without having the benefit of her mother's presence to comfort her. Finally, Liverpool is the place where, because of death, Miriam has to face the prospect of dying. She contrasts Liverpool (as the place of death and dying) with Hong Kong. While working in her mother's house, she thinks of Hong Kong, and of her husband and her life there. Barker writes,

> In Hong Kong, she thought, Boyd would be on duty, and the sun would be blazing hot, the streets thronged with people. Though she hated to go out at midday, when the city was so crowded, today she would have welcomed the discomfort. It was tiresome sitting in the dusty bedroom, carefully sorting and folding the scented linen from the chest of drawers. She wanted life, even if it was insistent and oppressive.

Miriam indeed prefers life, with all its limitations and irritations, to the "tiresome" business of death. Death may be an absolute state, but it is a state lacking vitality, lacking motion. The "discomfort" of living is preferred by Miriam; the simplicity of death is not.

A narrative conflict in "Coming to Grief" centers on Miriam's battles with her own personal weaknesses. The weaknesses of the present, such as her inability to face death and her unwillingness to express her true feelings about her mother's funeral, are linked to the weaknesses of her childhood. Miriam's general fear of death and dying as a child are rolled up into one specific fear: the Bogey-Walk monster. The rational side of Miriam's nature attempts to explain the Bogey-Walk in rational terms. The quarry is nothing more than a quarry her adult mind tells her; there is no monster lurking there to trap the unwary. But her adolescent mind, framed in the stark, powerful hues of a child's vivid nightmares, is more attuned to the real actuality. Miriam becomes aware of the Bogey-Walk monster's existence in her dreams, which is entirely consistent with Clive Barker's belief that dreams and dreaming are noble, wonderful things, and that they allow us to enter worlds of imagination that nurture and strengthen us. In her dreams, Miriam visualized the monster as climbing the walls of the quarry to capture her. The author writes, "But in those dreams she always woke up before the nameless beast caught hold of her dancing feet, and the exhilaration of her escape would heal the fear; at least until the next time she dreamed." By escaping the Bogey-Walk monster in her dreams, she symbolically escapes death, thus conquering it for the time being and "heal[ing] the fear" of dying. This triumph of life over death in the dream is the adolescent Miriam's temporary victory over her fears.

Of course, Miriam enacts in real life an escape from the Bogey-Walk monster. Near the conclusion of the story, as she is walking past the newly formed break in the red brick wall, she confronts — and is almost destroyed by — the monster of her childhood nightmares. It tempts her toward the edge with the image of her dead mother's face ("Horribly bloated to twice or three times its true size, her jaundiced eyelids flickering to reveal whites without irises, as though she were hanging in the last moment between life and death") and nearly succeeds in drawing her over the cliff's edge. She is saved from death by an old, childhood friend, Judy, who is an admitted lesbian and who is also a nurturing person. By not succumbing to the Bogey-Walk monster, the adult Miriam finally triumphs over her fear of death and her even greater fear of her mother's absence. Her personal, epic confrontation with the image of her deceased mother, an image very much like a putrefying corpse, parallels Miriam's ultimate confrontation and acceptance of the physical reality of her mother's death. Miriam is able to come to grips with mortality and is saved from a fate worse than death (in the truest sense of the cliché) with her friend's much-needed help ("Miriam felt Judy's arms around her, tight; more possessive of her life than she had been"). Clive Barker thus implies in this concluding act of grace that one of those things stronger than death, stronger than fear, is friendship. We need the support of our parents while we are children, Barker might suggest to us; however, when we become adults and our parents pass away, emotional support may be (and must be) found in our circle of friends.

In the frightening scene that concludes the story — where the Bogey-Walk monster lures the "husband of the late Marjorie Elliot" to his death by enticing him with the image of his dead wife to leap into the quarry, in essence, encouraging him to destroy himself because of his grief — the reader finally learns that Miriam's monster exists, that it is not a figment of her childish imagination. Death is a fact of life waiting for its proper cue. And like the monster of Miriam's Bogey-Walk, it may hide for a time lurking in the recess of life's shadows, but eventually it will make itself known and exact its due.

In the story's other major confrontation, Miriam faces for the first time the body of her dead mother in the funeral home. The moment is a moving one. It is quietly emotional without being mawkishly sentimental. It is gentle without being affected and false, powerful without being stifling. Miriam represses the desire to "reach into the coffin and shake her mother awake." She mentally wills her mother to wake up. She says "Mama" but once. Barker writes,

> She took hold of the side of the coffin to steady herself, while the tears dripped off her cheeks and fell into the folds of her mother's dress.
> So this was death's house; this was its shape and nature. Its etiquette was perfect. At its visitation there had been no violence; only a profound and changeless calm that denied the need for further show of affection.
> Her mother, she realized, didn't require her any longer; it was as simple as that. Her first and final rejection. *Thank you*, said that cold, discrete body, *but I have no further need of you. Thank you for your concern, but you may go.*

Miriam's apparent indifference to her mother's death simply conceals a powerful apprehension: that her mother no longer needs her. As do we all, Miriam possesses that very real desire for a parents' affections, and when death forever robs us of their attention, we feel cheated, hostile, angry, or in Miriam's case, we pretend indifference. What really bothers Miriam in "Coming to Grief" is the anticipation of being alone in the world. She loves life (in part, out of a fear for the alternative), but a life where others — her children, her husband, her mother — need her. Being dead is the same as being alone, from Miriam's perspective, and she likes neither. She counters this unwanted apprehension of being alone during the course of the story with thoughts of Hong Kong and her family awaiting her return. She also learns to fight the feeling of loneliness with the help of her friend, Judy. Following her nightmarish confrontation with the Bogey-Walk monster, Miriam is comforted by her companionship with her friend. The author writes,

> They stayed together through the night at the house, and they shared the big bed in Miriam's room innocently, as they had as children. Miriam told the story from beginning to end: the whole history of the Bogey-Walk. Judy took it all in, nodded, smiled, and let it be. At last, in the hour before dawn, the confessions over, they slept.

Miriam's "confessions," her telling of tales, is a cleansing experience for her soul in the truest of religious acts. The process of storytelling purges sin and evil (as Clive Barker also shows in his *Books of Blood*). It mends and makes whole what has otherwise been damaged or destroyed. And thus we see that even though "Coming to Grief" is a sad tale, though the story's atmosphere is melancholy in nature (a funeral dirge of sorts), it nonetheless offers a profound message of hope. Fear, death, loneliness: we are able to conquer all of these mortal ills, just as Miriam has conquered them, with the gentle guidance of a friend's hand or with the assistance of a loving spouse's support. For Miriam, her "coming to grief" opens the way for her "coming to joy," with the anticipation of living life to its fullest extent.

Clive Barker's Short Stories of Dark Imagination

The remainder of this chapter, as a summary of what has been discussed previously, will examine a number of important topics concerning Clive Barker's short fiction. First, Barker's own remarks about several of his short stories appearing in his *Books of Blood* will be explored, as well as Barker's generalizations about what his *Books of Blood* are intended to accomplish within the parameters of the horror genre. Second, an outline that summarizes the significant themes that appear in Clive Barker's short fiction will be developed, an outline that clarifies the artistic sophistication of his writing. Third, additional significant themes evident in Barker's writings will be compared to the work of three British literary giants of the past who wrote tales of dark imagination, including Christopher Marlowe (1564-1593), Mary Shelley (1797-1851), and Saki (pseudonym of Hector Hugh Munro, 1870-1916). Finally, Barker's literary corpus as a whole will be evaluated both inside and outside the formulaic confines of the horror genre, with the judgment being advanced that Clive Barker transforms and transcends the horror genre. He incorporates horror not as the end result of his craft, but as instead one of many narrative elements. I will suggest that Barker is not so much a horror fiction writer as he is a modern-day allegorist, a contemporary teller of morality plays (very much in the tradition of the fifteenth-century European allegorical plays in which human action is personified). Barker envisions good (i.e. wellcrafted) horror fiction as being confessional in nature (the entire *Books of Blood* are a collection of confessions). His artistic roots are, in fact, quite European and quite apart from the heavily genrefied American publishing tradition, a tradition that fostered the overcategorization of fiction in dime novels and pulp magazines (the later being the medium of H.P. Lovecraft's weird fiction) of the past century in order to sell more conveniently fiction as a commodity. And finally, as I began this book's discussion of Clive Barker's short fiction with a comparison between Barker and Stephen King, so, too, will I conclude my analysis with another comparison between Barker and King, a comparison that argues the relative difference between Barker's inventional approach to writing and King's conventional approach and that highlights the flexible durability of the literature of the *fantastique* (since it equally allows both Barker and King into its fold).

While describing his affection for his story entitled "The Age of Desire," Barker claims in his interview for the Winter 1987 issue of *American Fantasy* magazine that he tries not to duplicate other authors' efforts. He says that he "reads in the genre" a great deal, since by doing this he can avoid wasting his time "doing stuff which other people have already done better" ("British Invasion" 47). The reason why Clive Barker's short stories, novels, illustrations, and films seem so wildly inventive is because they *are* wildly inventive. He simply is not interested in traveling the well-worn path. He seeks instead to forage in new areas, to blaze his own, highly individual trail. We as his readers may become confused for a moment at the direction he takes us, but eventually we marvel at the new sights we see, the new landscape we travel, sights and landscapes that we've rarely, if ever, encountered before in the creative efforts of others. Those readers who cannot come to Barker's short fiction with an open mind, and those who come with rigid expectations to a slavish formula, will probably be disappointed with what they read. Barker does not want to indulge his reader by offering "convenient answers." He says in his *American Fantasy* interview, "I don't want to get to the end of the [horror] story and get readers all charged up and then say, by the way, the solution to this really complex and difficult problem is a silver bullet or garlic. To me that's bad storytelling, unless you're doing a pastiche" ("British Invasion" 47).

In his short fiction, Clive Barker occasionally toys with pastiche. Referring to his tale "New Murders in the Rue Morgue," Barker suggests his efforts at pastiche pay tribute to the original. His rendition of Poe (and of Poe's invention, the detective story) pays "homage to Poe," and to Poe's imagination. Elsewhere in his *Books of Blood*, Barker recognizes the talents of other authors. He states, "there's a story called "The Forbidden" . . . which has a nod and a wink to Ramsey Campbell. And there's a few Lovecraftian monsters that lurk around the corners in some of my stories, and certainly some stuff towards Arthur Machen. I mean I'm aware that I am in the company of brilliant writers" ("British Invasion" 47). In addition, Clive Barker imitates the spy thriller in "Babel's Children" and "Twilight at the Towers," and *roman noir* in "The Last Illusion" and "Lost Souls." "Lost Souls" also resounds with images of the Victorian Christmas ghost story, while "Confessions of a (Pornographer's) Shroud" and "Revelations" both flirt with the traditional ghost tale. Yet when Barker mimics another story or another writer, his interpretation soon disembarks from the confines of simple imitation, in the process redefining the pastiche into complex parody or satire. If Clive Barker tinkers with the ideas of others, he does this either to challenge those ideas or to transform them into new ones, into new visions that express Barker's own unique voice. By the conclusion of his pastiche, he has often flipped it on its head, reversing conventions, formulas and expectations.

Barker identifies "Revelations" as being one of these flipped stories in which the heroes are monsters and the monsters are heroes. Barker says,

> [In "Revelations,"] the evangelist is the monster and the ghosts, well Buck is sort of an unintentional hero and Sadie . . . I'm very fond of

Sadie. I'm very fond of that story. Partly because it's got a sort of delicate humor to it, and also because it's got a very up ending. The evangelist is dead, the ghosts have found their place in the system, and Virginia is on her way to jail with a smile on her face. Which is great ["British Invasion" 48].

The problematic question of what type of fiction Clive Barker writes thus becomes an interesting debate when he injects healthy doses of humor and optimism into the horror formula. We see that Barker not only flips pastiche upon its head, but he also flips the entire horror genre, writing stories that are neither wholly horror nor wholly anything else. Barker himself fuels this debate when he claims that, "There are a lot of stories in the *Books of Blood* which simply aren't horror in any conventional sense. They're imaginative stories but not horror stories, and my commitment is to imaginative fiction; to worlds of the imagination" ("British Invasion" 45). Barker goes on to suggest that writing horror fiction, in part, fulfills his obligation to the "worlds of imagination," but that horror is only one of many ways for him to access his imagination. He says, "I just want to write fantastic literature of various kinds, and some of it will be called horror" ("British Invasion" 45).

As noted, Clive Barker's desire to write fantastic literature is not limited to one medium. His work crosses media boundaries as easily as it does formulaic boundaries. For example, Barker incorporates material from his theatrical experience in his story "Sex, Death and Starshine." He also envisions a close relationship between movies and his short fiction. In his interview conducted with Tim Caldwell for *Film Threat* magazine, Barker links the cinematic metaphor he creates in "Son of Celluloid" with the act of viewing films. He identifies this cinematic metaphor in "Son of Celluloid" as being a walking, talking cancer that performs movie star imitations; Barker reminds us that the chameleon-like cancer calls itself a "dreaming disease" in the story, and he argues that viewing movies is like having this dreaming disease (17). Barker's wild contrast between dreaming, a concept denoting marvelous things, and disease, a word generating negative images like corruption and death, is entirely consistent with how he frequently incorporates in his writing the similar contrast between the grotesque and the beautiful. Indeed, the entirety of Clive Barker's fiction is a "dreaming disease." His writing establishes a medium of imagination that blends the unusual with the recognizable and that thus encourages the reader to join with the author in envisioning new worlds and new people, but worlds and people that seem familiar, and because of that familiarity allow us in our imagining to pierce the heart of our own reality with a powerful scrutiny.

Reality for Clive Barker, however, does not necessarily mean a physical truth. He is more concerned with psychological truth. In the Lupoff and Wolinsky interview published in the August 1988 issue of *Science Fiction Eye*,

Barker relates the story about being "invited to address a science fiction class" in London, in which a student challenged him about the logical veracity of "In the Hills, the Cities." This student identified himself as being a science fiction fan, and said that even though he liked "In the Hills, the Cities," the story, he said, didn't "make sense." He claimed that constructing a walking giant by tying together ten thousand people just, in the fan's words, "wouldn't work, they'd ... fall over." Barker learned that the science fiction fan would have been happier with the story if Barker had included a "spurious explanation," like a force field that holds the giant together. Barker answered the fan by arguing a difference between the science fiction fan and himself. Unlike the fan, he is not interested in dealing with "artificial explanations" in his writing. Barker states in the interview,

> What's important to me is to get it psychologically true, is to get it right on a dream level, is to get it right on a subconscious level, is to get it right on a Jungian level. If you get it right on that level, the inventing of the names of machines that will make this all plausible becomes academic. In fact, it almost begins to condescend to the reader. Because what it implies, to me anyway, is that the reader doesn't have the imagination or the breadth to actually say, "This idea makes sense to me, I embrace this idea. I do not need you to invent something from Doctor Who to make this work" [15].

Clive Barker's point is an intriguing one because it reveals his expectations of his audience. Barker wants his reader to meet him half way, so to speak; he wants him or her to employ imagination in order to appreciate better highly inventional stories of imagination. Imagination may be stifled, Barker suggests to us, by an overdependence upon narrative particulars. In other words, Barker doesn't want us to lose sight of the major issues he's discussing in his fiction because we are searching for other irrelevant trivia. He is an "idea" author, not a "device" author. In fact, Barker sees his work as being anti-mechanistic, which locates him outside the formulaic limitations of science fiction (a genre defined by its reliance upon gadgets and scientific plausibility) and thus places him securely within the much larger parameters of fantasy. His literary sensibility is much more attuned to Mary Shelley's novel of dark Gothic imagination, *Frankenstein* (often incorrectly cited as the first modern example of science fiction), than to the efforts of Jules Verne or Hugo Gernsback, the former identified as being the most significant person to popularize science fiction in both Europe and America before the turn of the twentieth century, and the later credited with successfully bringing science fiction to the American pulp magazines during the 1910s and 1920s. Verne, Gernsback, and their following articulate in their writings a powerful adherence to realism. Though they would undeniably also argue that their fiction is highly imaginative, nonetheless the school of Verne and Gernsback upon close scrutiny looks something like the school of Realism (that also initially flourished approximately the same time as did early modern science fiction), where characters and setting must demonstrate some sort of primary association to an empirical reality. Clive Barker's writing, conversely, looks more like the fiction of the English Romantic Movement (circa 1770–1848) with its sense of social progressivism and the transcendental; specifically, Barker's writing resembles the Gothic novels of Mary Shelley and William Beckford—after all, the Gothic novel as practiced by Shelley and Beckford found its roots in the Romantic Movement, and, in fact, is little more than an exaggerated branch of Romanticism. As were the Romantics and their Gothic descendants, Barker is concerned in his fiction of the dark *fantastique* with an investigation into the function of evil (read: close-mindedness, mean-spiritedness) that impacts the individual or the individual's society at one level, and at another level he is interested in exploring the dynamic range of the forces of our imagination, people and places that are paradoxically beautiful and grotesque concurrently. These twin areas of artistic interest, though manageable within the Romantic's worldview, differ sharply with the concerns of the literary realists, the hard-core science fiction enthusiasts, which hence explains why Barker's young critic experienced difficulty with "In the Hills, the Cities." He was looking for the type of litter wedged between the city/giant's toes, while Clive Barker was instead relating to the rest of us the city/giant's dreams (or the dream of the city/giant).

A Survey of Major Themes in Clive Barker's Short Fiction

Many authors writing within the horror genre today are producing works that lack a larger artistic unity. For the most part, these authors are primarily concerned with simple entertainment, with providing their readers with a moment's diversion, and by inference, concerned with writing commercially successful fiction. They display no true inner voice, no message that speaks something important and something essential to us. They simply are offering a commodity that they hope delivers some measure of financial return for their investment of time. They are in the business of selling *the scare*, pure and simple.

This may sound like a "put-down" of ninety percent of the horror genre's writers, or like the reductionist observations of a critic gone wild, but neither is the case, really. The paperback horror novel is actually no worse than the paperback western or the paperback romance or the paperback mystery. All popular fiction possesses a rather uncomplicated commercial purpose (as perhaps does the entirety of fiction, both high and low), and the authors of this fiction should not be condemned out-of-hand because what they do has so singular a commercial motive. After all, a number of so-called canonical authors we revere today as being foremost among the artistic elite—such erstwhile literary giants as Sir Walter Scott (1771-1832), Charles Dickens (1812-1870), Edgar Allan Poe (1809-1849), and Mark Twain (pseudonym of Samuel Clemens, 1835-1910), to name just four prominent examples—were motivated in large part to write to make money. And yet artistic integrity and commercial success need not be mutually exclusive concepts. They don't necessarily need to work in opposite directions and are frequently most rewarding when they work together in unison. The marriage of art and money in contemporary literature does not seem to pose a problem when one is discussing Joyce Carol Oates or Kurt Vonnegut. But bring up the names of Dean R. Koontz or John Saul or Anne Rice or (that most horrid of best-selling heretics) Stephen King, and the reception within the community of critics is quite frigid indeed. Perhaps this sad state of affairs should not be surprising. Historically, the horror genre has been one of the most suspect in the literary critic's mind because it seeks foremost to entertain its audience, and if that's not bad enough, to accomplish this entertainment *via* the reader's gut, rather than his or her mind. It's tough for the horror writer to break out of the "genre ghetto."

Clive Barker is one of the few to have escaped the horror "ghetto." Contrary to the attacks leveled against the horror tale, and contrary to the majority of authors who write horror fiction, Clive Barker in his work endeavors to establish a sound artistic voice and cohesive thematic unity. And the fact that he has achieved a certain degree of critical respect for his literary endeavors, while also experiencing a great measure of commercial reward, is a testament to his ability to defy both the falsely perceived aesthetic limitations of the genre and the deep-rooted prejudices of the critic. Barker goes for his reader's viscerals *and* mind with equal dexterity.

The following outline, then, as illustration of Clive Barker's complex yet wholly integrated story-telling skills, offers a brief summary of the major narrative themes in Barker's short fiction. The titles of the nine themes are: 1) "Text as Metaphor"; 2) "The Game and Game Playing"; 3) "The Deceptiveness of Appearances"; 4) "The Beautiful and the Grotesque"; 5) "Heightened Senses"; 6) "The Messiah Figure"; 7) "The Critique of Institutional Authority: The State"; 8) "The Prison (or Trap) Setting"; and 9) "The Feminist Critique." This list is neither inclusive nor comprehensive, but it does reveal the author's ability of communicating to his audience, through the entire corpus of his writing, a number of coherent and fully integrated philosophical views about life and death and imagination and the evils of banality.

Text as Metaphor

For Barker, text has significant meaning as a complex metaphor in his writing. It expresses for him the power of creative thought and is a physical representation of his own love for books and all that books embody, such things as magic and imagination. One of Clive Barker's messages to his readers in his fiction is that the telling of stories — as a specific narrative element of the text — is both a cleansing act, where old sins are purged (much like confession, in a religious sense), and an act of creation, where miracles are engendered. Barker also equates text images with how his characters survive their respective confrontations with good and evil. If, on the one hand, the Barker protagonist is literally able to read correctly the writing upon the wall, then he or she may expect not only to triumph, but also to benefit from the acquired knowledge. In "The Book of Blood," Mary Florescu, for example, by interpreting the writing carved upon Simon McNeal's body is able to decipher images of wonder and amazement that lie beyond and behind our otherwise mundane everyday experiences. McNeal himself, who was once a reprehensible individual, becomes a walking miracle after the dead use his tortured body as the medium for the telling of their stories. Barker suggests to his reader as well that the object or the person who bears a textual reference also most likely possesses some type of subtextual design that is equally significant when deciphered. If, on the other hand, the Barker protagonist is unable or unwilling to interpret the meaning of texts, then he or she is damned, destroyed. Because Helen Buchanan in "The Forbidden" is not able to identify in time the deadly meaning lurking behind the Spector Street Estate graffiti, she becomes victim to the Candyman's nasty, fatal embrace. Clive Barker, then, with his writing and in his writing has become a spokesperson for writing, and for the importance of literary empowerment. The relationship between texts and the reading of those texts generates power, and magic. All his characters (and we as his audience) can touch magic by tapping into the power of reading.

The Game and Game Playing

Several tales in the *Books of Blood* feature the game or game playing as an integral part of the story. Because of his duplicitous game playing, Simon McNeal in "The Book of Blood" is punished by those dead spirits that he pretends to have contact with for his arrogance and for his disrespect. Jack Polo in "The Yattering and Jack" plays an elaborate game with a demon from Hell. The stakes are high — life and death (and perhaps even more importantly, the integrity of Polo's family). On the surface, the contest of wills between Jack Polo and the Yattering may seem humorous, but underlying the humor is a grim, ugly battle. The type of game played in "Hell's Event" seems simple enough, a foot race, but as in "The Yattering and Jack" the context behind the game reveals Hell as being the contestant opposing the continued well-being of humanity. The stakes of the game are about as high as they can get —

the end of the world. Thankfully, humanity wins this particular race and thus postpones the apocalypse for the time being. In "The Inhuman Condition," Karney's game, the unraveling of a simple puzzle in the form of a knot, is seemingly less grand than that in "Hell's Event," but it is by no measure less significant. By untying the knotted cord, Karney unknits and reknits the age-old conflict between science and religion, in which each is fighting for total dominion over possession of humanity's knowledge. The wealthy, insane Gregorius plays a game of hide-and-seek with Satan in his Xanadu-like New Hell, discovering at the conclusion of "Down, Satan!" that he has become a great deal like that which he so desperately sought, that he himself has become the Devil incarnate. Both "Babel's Children" and "Twilight at the Towers" establish a specific relationship between game playing and politics. Barker portrays political games in these stories as being, at times, respectively obtuse or silly; however, they are equally deadly and far-reaching in their impact on others. Ultimately, the game, Barker suggests to us in his short fiction, is a useful narrative device by which he can critique the actions of individuals or institutions. The process of playing games discloses both the strengths and weaknesses of human character, and of inhuman character. It highlights during the process of play an ideal conflict where dramatic action is enhanced, and where the personalities of characters are more fully delineated.

The Deceptiveness of Appearances

Frequently in Barker's work, people or places are not what they appear on the surface. False appearances mask the good and evil (most often evil) that lie beneath that surface. Clive Barker's love of metaphor manifests itself in this thematic device. His interest in masking and then unmasking the surface appearance of things allows him the opportunity of creating a wide range of metaphoric images that comment upon the nature of reality and of our often flawed perception of it. A number of Barker's tales feature settings that conceal either bright magic or black mystery. With "The Forbidden," "The Madonna," and "In the Flesh," commonplace settings — respectively, a housing project, a dilapidated pool and bath house, and a prison — are, in reality, the residences of demons or angels. Barker's short fiction is populated throughout as well by people harboring secret selves. Mary Florescu is unaware in the beginning of "The Book of Blood" of Simon McNeal's actual duplicitous nature. Karney is initially unaware in "The Inhuman Condition" of the tremendous power that the derelict Pope hides beneath his unwashed exterior, while in "The Life of Death," an otherwise seemingly ordinary woman is the carrier of the new black plague and is the walking embodiment of death itself in the modern world. Those characters who are deceived by false appearances in Barker's stories at least experience great terror, and, at worst, experience death. Yet those who are able to penetrate false appearances are more likely not only to survive, but to become stronger individuals in the process. Miriam, for example, in "Coming to Grief" does not submit to the monster falsely bearing her mother's face (though she is helped by her childhood friend), and consequently does not submit to death. She is strengthened by her ordeal at the Bogey-Walk. She regains control of her life because of her confrontation with the chameleon-like monster. Mr. Elliot is not as fortunate as Miriam. He is deceived by the Bogey-Walk monster into thinking he is seeing his departed wife, Marjorie, and soon joins her in death.

The Beautiful and the Grotesque

One of the wildly inventive aspects of Clive Barker's short fiction is the paradoxical contrast he develops between the beautiful and the grotesque. In several of his tales, ugliness is good and beauty is evil; or the wondrous is made wondrous by images of the grotesque; or inner moral strength and virtue are housed in the body of a monster. Barker enjoys incorporating opposing physical, spiritual, or visual characteristics because he continually desires to challenge his reader's conventional expectations. Thus, after startling us with portrayals of good and evil (or more important, of some unique blending of good and evil), he directs us away from the boundaries of convention into a new direction, a direction where he encourages us to re-examine those important things in life that we otherwise ignore or take for granted. In "Sex, Death and Starshine," Barker counterpoises the hideousness of death with the beauty of artistic perfection. Lichfield and his troupe of actors are the walking dead, yet these actor/zombies are more committed to theatrical art and the correct performance of that art than are their human counterparts. Barker blends the humorous with the grotesque in the story "Dread" when he portrays the transformed Stephen Grace as an axe-wielding murderer done up in a clown's costume. Lurking behind the beautiful face in "Human Remains" is either the intellectually vacuous, narcissistic, male prostitute Gavin, or his vampire-like doppelgänger. In each instance, Barker shows us with this character and with this creature how beauty without substance is both an empty beauty and an evil beauty. Near the conclusion of "The Body Politic," Barker interjects a scene into the story that is quite bizarre—the rain of amputated hands following Charlie George as he leaps from the hospital roof—and is seen by the nurses and hospital patients who witness the event and perceive it as being wondrous, miraculous. Magic and terror are not mutually exclusive concepts, Barker implies with this moment; they might be the flip sides of the same coin. Evil done to mankind is what the amputated army of hands promise in "The Body Politic." Good done to womankind is what is promised in "The Madonna." The Madonna creature is described as being visually freakish, shockingly incongruous. In direct contrast to this grotesque appearance, the Madonna is the physical symbol of female procreative power. To the chagrin of the male characters in the story, the Madonna is not only able to birth the children of dreams (who are also grotesque looking), but she is able to produce gender transformations.

She changes Jerry Coloqhoun and Ezra Garvey from men into women, turning them from silly, pathetic, victimizing males into women who are, after the metamorphosis, not too unlike the Madonna.

Heightened Senses

The senses play an important role in Barker's writing. His fiction resounds with a love of sensory images. He is very skilled at providing detailed descriptions of scenes and characters that are easily visualized in the mind's eye. We see and smell terror when he wants us to. We hear beauty. We touch magic.

In several of his short stories, the physical senses have an even more important role as a thematic motif. Mary Florescu in "The Book of Blood," for example, because of her unexpected contact with the supernatural, develops otherworldly senses. Barker utilizes meta-sensual images in "Confessions of a (Pornographer's) Shroud" in discussing Ronnie Glass's interesting transformation (from man into ghost), intending them to act as a means to access the sublime (or the tragic, or the comic). Barker's somewhat humorous, somewhat hideous depiction of what happens when the ultimate aphrodisiac drug escapes the confines of the laboratory setting in "The Age of Desire" relies in large measure upon the detailing of the hapless Jerome's abnormally exaggerated senses (which inflame his lust), senses that make him a dangerous sexual freak. Images of shadow and darkness frame the narrative action within and without the confines of the Pentonville prison setting from "In the Flesh." What inmate Cleve Smith witnesses or can't witness—because it is obscured by thick, mysterious, frightening shadows—enhances the stark, dramatic tension of the plot.

Tactile impressions of heat, water, and humidity, as well as fantastic visions of beautifully grotesque women and their children, are symbolic of women and the procreative power of women; their use reinforces Barker's intention in "The Madonna" to create a profound feminist allegory. Indeed, perception (both visual and intellectual) is crucial for Barker. In order to see the subtext of life, in order to see the reality beneath the surface appearance, in order to see the miraculous, in order to see the romance in life that is obscured by the debris of everyday banality, one must have a perceptively acute eye that can observe clearly in Heaven and in Hell, and in the world that lies in between.

The Messiah Figure

There exists in much of Barker's writing a healthy dose of social satire. He frequently criticizes various secular and religious institutions that in his view negatively affect the way we live our lives. In particular, Barker is fascinated with the workings of religious fanaticism and how fanaticism manifests itself in the Messiah figure. Interestingly, Barker's scrutiny of the Messiah figure in his short fiction appears to be somewhat ambivalent. He writes about good and evil Messiahs, but the unsavory variety seems to crop up more often in his work than the other, and this might suggest that fanaticism, though it may be something that enriches our existence or something that may destroy us, more often than not is something we should avoid. The Messianic Quaid from the story "Dread" preaches a new religion of terror, and definitely is a distasteful character. The insane Dr. Welles in "The Age of Desire" (like Quaid) represents the evil side of our nature in that he wants to propagate a new age not of simple perverted sexual desire, not of a manic scientific mindset, but a new age of havoc and ruin, an age of the black plague's reappearance in the world. In "The Skins of the Fathers" and "Lost Souls," Barker caustically suggests that the modern world does not act charitably toward prospective young Messiahs, since the Messianic children in each tale are either destroyed by a narrow-minded and intolerant secular society (as seen in "The Skins of the Fathers"), or by a narrow-minded and intolerant Church (as seen in "Lost Souls"). When the State and the Church assassinate these aspiring prophets, Clive Barker is suggesting that when the offspring of the truly divine are murdered by institutional society, then institutional society is effectively maintaining its mind-numbing control over people by stifling their ability to touch the miraculous, to experience imagination in its most wondrous form, to worship the divine.

The Critique of Institutional Authority: The State

Elsewhere in his short fiction, Barker attacks secular institutional order. "Hell's Event" provides a biting satire of politics, claiming that politicians are in league with the powers of Hell (which explains a great deal, Barker would tell us). "The Body Politic," as its title might imply, is a parody of political terminology. It also critiques political social movements and the senseless ideological rhetoric that accompanies violent revolution. Barker moves from criticizing politics to lampooning the police state in "Rawhead Rex" and "The Age of Desire." Both stories feature policemen who are something less than heroic, who are, in fact, ignorance-loving incompetents acting to impede justice rather than working to protect it. Barker negatively portrays the related areas of world politics and political espionage in "Babel's Children" and "Twilight at the Towers." He sees both as subverting the personal freedoms of the individual. Governments, Barker suggests, are only interested in gaining power and in the maintenance of power, abandoning all sense of ethical decency in their blind, greedy pursuit of that power. In addition to a serious question about the morality (or lack of morality) in how governments govern in several of Barker's tales, the corrupt legal system is placed under close scrutiny in "How Spoilers Bleed," with Barker coming to the conclusion that the law is manipulated by those in authority in order to subvert social justice and that the phrase "legal rights" is an oxymoron. Barker contends in "How Spoilers Bleed" that legal rights and moral rights are mutually exclusive terms. Business as an unethical institution also attracts Barker's attention. In "Coming to Grief," he examines the hypocrisy of the funeral business and how this business exploits the grief of others (by trivializing emotion and by ritualizing how we confront — or fail to confront — death in our culture). All in all, Clive Barker regards secular institutional authority as being antithetical to the interests of the individual. It also tends to stifle imagination in our lives by attempting to enforce silly rules and senseless regulations. If left unchecked, if left unexamined, the State in Barker's short fiction is a vicious brute, dogged in the extreme, and extreme in its attack upon individual liberties. The organized mind — the cop, the bureaucrat, the spy, the businessman — as agent of institutional authority, according to Barker, is uncomprehending of magic, is destructive of wonder, and is flagrantly insensitive to our basic intellectual and emotional needs.

The Prison (or Trap) Setting

One institution in particular which seems to manifest itself often in Clive Barker's short fiction is the prison. Barker uses images of prisons or traps to dictate the tone and setting of several tales and to underscore dramatic tension. Prisons are emblematic of persecution. They embody the physical (and sometimes the mental) tyranny of banality, the persecution of the socially disenfranchised. An individual's triumph over the trap, the escape from the prison, when rarely (if ever) enacted suggests to us an escape from cruelty and despair. The domestic prison setting of "The Yattering and Jack" encourages us to sympathize with the plight of the Yattering, a demon trapped by his mission to torment Jack Polo, and who is thus tormented in return, being nearly driven insane by the horrors of the suburban lifestyle and by Polo's pretended indifference. In "Pig Blood Blues," Tetherdowne, or the Remand Center for Adolescent Offenders, is little more than a prison for children. The young boys are entrapped at Tetherdowne by a system indifferent to reform, and more importantly, by a looming supernatural evil (a new, wicked religious cult, in fact) powerful enough to possess even the adult authorities of the system. The fear of returning to prison ironically traps the monstrous Barberio, the escaped convict from "Son of Celluloid," into metamorphosing into a vicious monster of cinematic images. "In the Flesh" features an actual prison for its setting in which Barker scrutinizes how inmates cope with day to day life. He features an afterlife prison in the story as well, in which he shows us the punishment (and the redemption) awaiting those who murder others. The activities of the one prison are framed by the generally unperceived existence of the other. Together, they allow Barker to demonstrate how characters react with the prospect of entrapment by an uncaring, antagonistic legal bureaucracy or of an otherworldly entrapment where sins committed in life serve to chain people to those sins in death. Helen Buchanan experiences another type of prison in "The Forbidden," a prison hypocritically intended to be a humanitarian social welfare housing project called the Spector Street Estate (a housing project that is anything but humanitarian or social), where the inmates are poor families and where the jailers are ignorance and violence. Helen herself is eventually trapped by the supernatural warden of this welfare prison, a serial killer known as the Candyman. Her punishment, decreed by the Candyman at the conclusion of the story, is death.

The Feminist Critique

A great deal of what's to be found in the horror genre tends to be sexist in nature. For the most part, women are rarely granted an equal footing with men in regards to intelligence or courage, and often they serve no better purpose in the horror story than being the damsel in distress. As evidence, note the cinematic parade of "slasher" films where sexually promiscuous women are violently murdered by a male slasher figure; intriguingly, however, Carol J. Clover in her book, *Men, Women, and Chain Saws: Gender in the Modern Horror Film* (1992), suggests a feminist interpretation of the slasher film that is more sympathetic to the roles women assume in these movies. Nevertheless, for the most part, the tradition of horror has not been kind to women through the years. As the genre evolved from its distant Gothic origins, two general types of female characters have emerged. The first type comes to us from Horace Walpole (1717–1797) and his short novel *The Castle of Otranto* (1764/1765), which is commonly thought to be the first modern example of the Gothic story. In this novel (and the many others that imitated it), women are passive, domestic creatures, who are in need of men's protection and moral reverence, as nicely illustrated in Walpole's narrative of Hippolita and Isabella. These women are subservient to men, victimized by men, then perhaps rescued by men. The second type of Gothic — the romantic (or woman's) Gothic — was first popularized by Ann Radcliffe (1764–1823), and the literary tradition as it descends from Radcliffe does show a greater, more active involvement in the genre by women authors, who write about women for women. Radcliffe's most famous novel is *The Mysteries of Udolpho* (1794), in which she features, instead of the male protagonist common to the Walpole model, a female protagonist named Emily St. Aubert. However, Emily is little better than Walpole's Hippolita or Isabella. Regrettably, Radcliffe's heroines in many ways are just as encumbered by the restrictions of social conventions as are Walpole's female victims. And the disciples of Radcliffe — popular women authors such as Daphne du Maurier (1907-1989) with her romantic Gothic novel, *Rebecca* (1938) — have done little to change the situation.

Clive Barker, on the other hand, has adopted a strong feminist stance in much of his writing. Several of his short stories document the victimization of women by men; they also depict the strong feminist response to this victimization. In "Jacqueline Ess: Her Will and Testament," the female protagonist of the story is tormented by the men in her life, until she discovers a tremendous supernatural power within herself that she then uses to antagonize her antagonists. As in "Jacqueline Ess: Her Will and Testament," "The Madonna" also portrays a conflict between men and women where women triumph (physically and symbolically) over their male oppressors. The gender battle lines are even more clearly drawn in "Rawhead Rex" — where men are representative of destruction, chaos, and death, while women are representative of order and of life. In the epic conflict which ensues, the power of woman triumphs, and the evil harvest king is defeated by the earth mother queen. Closely related to Barker's feminist stance is his use of strong female protagonists. "Scape-Goats," "Revelations," "Babel's Children," "The Life of Death," and "Coming to Grief" all emphasize female protagonists who are intelligent, compelling, and realistically courageous in their actions. In fact, Clive Barker seems to create some of his best ideas while working within the woman's point-of-view. Indeed, more than any of his contemporary male peers writing in the genre, Barker — as one of the major authors today of the *fantastique* — is profoundly sensitive to women's issues.

Clive Barker and the British Tradition of the Fantastique

Our discussion of the major themes readily evident in Clive Barker's short fiction continues in this section as we examine Barker's use of: 1) "The Faustian Pact Tale"; 2) "The Tale of Transformation"; and 3) "The Joke as Narrative Motif." In the W.C. Stroby interview published in the March 1991 issue of *Writer's Digest*, Clive Barker, by implication, places himself within the British tradition of fantasy that includes as some of its authors Bram Stoker, C.S. Lewis, J.M. Barrie, J.R.R. Tolkien, H.G. Wells, and Mary Shelley. Referring to the large number of British writers who have also written tales of dark imagination over the years, Barker adds that "the list goes on" (27). He tells Stroby,

> I read those books [of science fiction, horror fiction, and fantasy fiction] as forbidden pleasures, never was taught them in school, never heard them celebrated from the mouths of educators whom I admired. So it took me three or four years after I started writing to get past the fact that this was a forbidden form—not even forbidden, that gives it too much mystique, but just a disparaged fiction—to realize that this was where my strength lay and that these forms of fiction could be extraordinarily vital and rich. And I wish to God someone had said that to me [27].

In part, Barker is discussing in the above passage how the literature of the *fantastique* in England is the literature of protest, and the literature of intellectual rebellion. And as such, because of its profound anti-establishment flavor, historically it has failed to achieve a comparable artistic recognition with the school of literary Realism: as invented in the novel and practiced by the likes of Samuel Richardson or Henry Fielding.

Though the Romantic movement in England and Europe enjoyed a substantial measure of critical success in the genre of poetry—such as that received by William Wordsworth, Samuel Taylor Coleridge, Lord Byron, Percy Bysshe Shelley, and John Keats—for some reason, the Gothic novels which were an offshoot of this same Romantic movement engendered considerably more scorn from the critics, despite their popularity with the mass readership. John Langhorne's review of Walpole's *Castle of Otranto* published in the February 1765 issue of the *Monthly Review*, though fairly complimentary of Walpole's novel, is nonetheless generally indicative of the literary critic's disregard of the artistic merits of the Gothic imagination. Langhorne wrote, "Those who can digest the absurdities of Gothic fiction, and bear with the machinery of ghosts and goblins, may hope, at least, for considerable entertainment from the performance before us: for it is written with no common pen" (Sabor 71). Exotic invention was then perhaps more palatable in the guise of poetry, or maybe the Gothic novels of the time were too deeply rooted in folklore and in a culture indigenous to the lower classes. Perhaps Langhorne's "ghosts and goblins" suggested a repulsively common entertainment that was more emotional in its appeal than intellectual, and thus more suspect to the educated elitist. Whatever the reasons, for the European literary critics the fantastic imagination worked throughout the nineteenth century in poetry, but not in prose. And this is the artistic, historical context that fostered the prejudice against fantasy that Barker identifies in his *Writer's Digest* interview.

Ironically, the embryonic Gothic imagination in America was better tolerated than in Europe. It was, in fact, the impetus that inspired much of what was published throughout the literary era known as the American Renaissance. During the relatively same period in the nineteenth century, while the Gothic in Britain was little more than a guilty pleasure of the English middle-class reader, in America the psychological Gothic tale was the narrative form of choice of such talents as Charles Brockden Brown, Edgar Allan Poe, Nathaniel Hawthorne, and Herman Melville. It, unlike the European Gothic, was the fiction of the culturally elite, written by the New England elite for the New England elite. It was rarely challenged as being sub-standard or sub-literate, as was its European cousin. Though Americans appeared more comfortable with stories of dark imagination than did their British counterparts, this is not to say that horror and dark fantasy were beaten into total oblivion in Europe. Instead, the authors of the *fantastique* disguised what they wrote. Some of the finest British horror, for example, was not written by horror writers. Instead, it was written by authors— like Barker himself—who were not limited by the strict confines of genre expectations, and who, in fact, were more mainstream (and thus more acceptable in the eyes of the *London Times* literary critic) in their overall approach to their craft. Rather than being the focus of their stories, horror was only one narrative element from among many that they selected to construct their tales.

There's no denying Clive Barker's use of the horror genre as a form of artistic and ideological protest against the school of Realism (or more correctly, against the mainstream), but I would also argue Barker's connection to the legitimate British literary heritage, a heritage of fantasy equally as important as the American. This section, then, intends to trace three additional major themes in Barker short stories to specific works of literature written by three significant British authors—Christopher Marlowe, Mary Shelley, and Saki—works that are difficult to pigeonhole as genre fiction, yet nevertheless house a core of dark imagination beneath their otherwise respectable appearance. The time frame involved in this brief survey ranges from the Elizabethan through the Edwardian periods.

Christopher Marlowe's Doctor Faustus, and the Faustian Pact Tale

In a book entitled *Horror: 100 Best Books*, edited by Stephen Jones and Kim Newman, Christopher Marlowe's play *Doctor Faustus* (first performed in 1594, and first published in 1604) is ranked as the top entry, though technically speaking, *Doctor Faustus* is not a "book" in the sense that a novel is a book. Clive Barker wrote the entry entitled "The Tragical History of Dr. Faustus" (which was later reprinted in *Clive Barker's Shadows in Eden*), in which he discusses the appeal of Marlowe's play, and in which he defines *Doctor Faustus* as an *essential* story. In Barker's own words, he describes the essential story, "It is not that the old stories are necessarily the *best* stories; rather that the old stories are the *only* stories. There are no new tales, only new ways to tell" ("Tragical History" 11).

The specific essential story that interests Barker in *Doctor Faustus* is the Faustian pact tale. Sylvan Barnet recognizes a religiously conservative theme in Marlowe's play, a didactic conservatism that "teaches us to adhere to traditional Christian behavior rather than to practice the unlawful things that exceptional minds give themselves to" (viii). Barker identifies this Christian conservatism in his analysis of *Doctor Faustus* as the fall of an "ambitious man, brought down through an excess of pride, or curiosity, or half a dozen other sweetly human qualities" ("Tragical History" 12). Barker's attraction to the Faust legend is thus understandable because much of what Clive Barker writes celebrates emotional passion and intellectual excess, which are to what Faust's ambitions ultimately lead him. For Barker, Faust is a type of tragic hero who envisions himself as a rebel, much as Barker envisions his own writing as an act of rebellion against and challenge to the *status quo*. Barker is also fascinated by Faust's quest for forbidden knowledge, the vulnerable mortal seeking to know and control divine (or demonic) forces, and who, conversely, despite his magnificent efforts is the one controlled by those forces, the one destroyed by his aspirations and his flawed pride. Again, Clive Barker's artistic interest in this particular aspect of *Doctor Faustus* is understandable, since many of Barker's characters search for forbidden knowledge of some type. Often, Barker's characters possess sinister ambitions or mask shadowy recesses within their psyche. They frequently thirst for that which is just beyond their reach and are damned for having the thirst in the first place. Noble evil (or ignoble goodness) is a paradox that Barker is most interested in writing about. He fashions moral paradox to motivate better his characters' actions in their quest for knowledge. Barker further identifies the relationship of the Faustian pact story, the horror story, and the essential story in the following passage,

> [The pact] story [as an essential story] will survive any and all reworkings, however radical, because its roots are so strong. That far-sighted backward glance I spoke of earlier [in the essay] — the one that leads back to the rocky place — shows us in the Faust tale one of the most important roads in all fantastic fiction. At its center is a notion essential to the horror genre and its relations: that of a trip taken into forbidden territory at the risk of insanity and death ["Tragical History" 13].

Clive Barker incorporates the Faustian pact story in several of his *Books of Blood* stories, as well as in his novella *The Hellbound Heart*, and in his first novel, *The Damnation Game*. "The Yattering and Jack" highlights the consequences of making a bargain with Hell and the attempt to renege on that bargain. Jack Polo must suffer for the sins of his mother, for it was she who made the infernal pact. Like Daniel Webster from the Stephen Vincent Benét tale, Polo successfully beats Hell at its own game. The Faustian pact story also appears in "Hell's Event." Gregory Burgess, a distinguished Member of Parliament, is in actuality an agent for Hell, having sold his soul for political power. With Burgess, Barker is satirically illustrating the evil self-interest that underlies the motives of a number of politicians, and the evil of politics in general. Burgess is punished for his perverted ambitions, and he is damned as well as dead at the story's conclusion—a just fate, Barker implies in the story, for the duplicitous politician. Young Billy Tait from "In the Flesh" makes a pact with his dead grandfather, Edgar Tait (who is the story's equivalent of Lucifer), for the promise of supernatural power. What the naïve Billy doesn't know about the nefarious Edgar is the maleficent reason that compels his grandfather to share his secrets. Billy is ultimately doomed in his bargain and must pay a terrible price for his foolishness. The lure of forbidden knowledge, as it tempted Billy Tait, tempts the magician Swann in "The Last Illusion" as well into selling his immortal soul in exchange for the ability to perform real magic. Then, disappointed with the bargain, Swann spends the remainder of his life showing the power of magic to be trivial, thus antagonizing his fiendish masters into retributive action. Swann is similar to Jack Polo from "The Yattering and Jack" in that each character endeavors to trick Hell into terminating the conditions of the pact instead of terminating them. However, Swann's physical body is already dead as "The Last Illusion" opens (murdered by the demonic Mr. Butterfield; score one for Hell), though his soul may still be saved from the diabolical tortures planned for it. To enact this salvation, the private investigator Harry D'Amour is recruited, the designs of Hell are thwarted, and Swann escapes his punishment.

Mary Shelley's Frankenstein, *and the Tale of Transformation*

The atmosphere of Marlowe's *Doctor Faustus* is undeniably bleak; it even has moments of genuine terror. As the editors of *Horror: 100 Best Books* have correctly identified, *Doctor Faustus* is a first-rate horror tale. And yet, why did Elizabethan audiences—who, though more broad minded and tolerant than their distant medieval relatives, were still profoundly superstitious in a religious sense—not reject such a fantastic story? Why did they not outright condemn the play as blasphemy? Part of the reason why Marlowe got away with the horror story of *Doctor Faustus* is that he effectively disguised it by making it look like something other than a horror story. Marlowe—as expert storyteller—knew that his audience was fascinated with magic and evil and demons from Hell (as were the readers of Dante's and John Milton's epic poetry, and as are horror film audiences today), and that's exactly what Marlowe gave them. But he packaged his horror story as moral allegory. He flirted with scary, blasphemous things in his play, yet he also presented a conclusion that judiciously punished the people who sought these scary, blasphemous things. His audience entered the realm of cultural taboo in *Doctor Faustus*, looked at it, thought about it, and then was led back to the social norm in the end, seeing sinners properly punished (lest it look too inviting) and God glorified over Satan. The threat of damnation made nice, frightened, cooperative men and women of his play's viewers. Indeed, *Doctor Faustus* is fundamentally dressed up as a cautionary tale. Mary Shelley successfully follows this same tradition in her most famous novel. However, unlike *Doctor Faustus*, *Frankenstein* is not an effective horror story; it's not even mildly frightening. It is undeniably a Gothic novel in its use of setting, and it obviously originates from Walpole's model. But Shelley's effort is much less terrifying than, say, Matthew Gregory Lewis's *The Monk* (1796), or even the Walpole original. Rather than generating horror for the sake of horror (or shock for the sake of shock, as did Lewis and Walpole), *Frankenstein* is Shelley's rather tame, sometimes slow-moving debate about revolutionary knowledge, specifically about what constitutes forbidden wisdom. As in Marlowe's *Doctor Faustus*, Mary Shelley's *Frankenstein* is a story about the sin of human pride gone wrong, and of mortal humanity tragically seeking that which is (and must remain) God's divine province. Marlowe is simply more frightening in the way he discusses sin than is Shelley.

The subtitle of Mary Shelley's novel *Frankenstein* is *The Modern Prometheus*, thus suggesting to her readers that the novel's narrative focus should be on the creator rather than the monster. We know from our Classical sources that Prometheus stole fire from the gods to give to humanity and was punished for his theft. Shelley intends there to be a thematic connection between the scientist Frankenstein and Prometheus, the metaphoric "fire" in question being the secret of giving life to lifelessness. Unfortunately for Shelley, history has shown her audience through the years to be decidedly more attracted to fire than the bringer of fire. The monster, and not the creator, has sparked and inflamed our imaginations. Regrettably, however, those readers of *Frankenstein* drawn to the novel expecting Boris Karloff will be disappointed; Shelley's monster is certainly less horrifying than the Universal Studios' version, yet infinitely more interesting in that he is such an atypical character, such an inventive combination of Adamic figure, melancholy philosopher, pitiful murderer, and persecuted freak. He, rather than Frankenstein, offers the fully realized Romantic ideal, the tragic, yet noble, Byronic figure. Victor Frankenstein himself is little more than a melodramatic protagonist, an arrogant sap and a fool who gets what he deserves. His monster, on the other hand, is both tragic and sympathetic. Nothing quite like him was written before Shelley's novel, and he represents—as does no other aspect of her story—the novel's great genius.

If, then, Frankenstein's monster is the proper focus of our attention in Shelley's non-horror, horror novel, then one of the more important aspects of the monster's story is the tale of transformation, and this is specifically where Barker's own short fiction philosophically and artistically connects to Shelley. The monster basically undergoes three significant types of transformation in *Frankenstein*: 1) a physical transformation, where the monster's body is physically re-born (*via* Frankenstein's science) from lifeless clay to living tissue; 2) an intellectual transformation, where the monster's intellect evolves from being a *tabula rasa* to becoming that of a sophisticated savant; and 3) a moral transformation, where the monster's new soul, which at first is good and devoid of sin, changes into something evil—a murderer's soul—because of his persecution and because of his maniacal desire for a mate like himself. The tale of transformation is what, in part, makes Mary Shelley's *Frankenstein* one of the great works of dark imagination, and Barker, in his own fictional efforts, seems to mine the same literary fields as did Shelley.

Numerous characters in Clive Barker's short fiction, like the monster in *Frankenstein*, undergo some manner of physical, intellectual, or moral transformation. Simon McNeal and Mary Florescu from "The Book of Blood" are each radically transformed—the one physically, the other intellectually, both spiritually. In "Pig Blood Blues," boy becomes pig, in the process becoming cult leader; in "Sex, Death and Starshine," the living die, then are re-born into a more perfect, a more aesthetic state-of-being. With "In the Hills, the Cities," giants walk the earth, giants whose frames are composed of the innumerable bodies of otherwise simple townsfolk. Normal Stephen Grace in "Dread" changes into an abnormal axe-murderer; victimized Jacqueline Ess in "Jacqueline Ess: Her Will and Testament" changes into formidable victimizer; Phillipe Laborteaux's ape in "New Murders in the Rue Morgue" changes into something closely resembling a human; and the criminal named Barberio in "Son of Celluloid" changes into cinematic vampire. Ronnie Glass from "Confessions of a (Pornographer's) Shroud" physically transmutes from man to ghost, as does Frankie in "Scape-Goats." In "Human Remains," a young male prostitute named Gavin completes his metamorphosis into a soulless echo of humanity, and the echo, in turn, assumes Gavin's former role. A knotted cord in "The Inhuman Condition" transforms into the riddle of evolution; and people's hands in "The Body Politic" transform into a murderous army of revolutionaries, rebelling against their former bodies. Immaterial ghosts become material briefly in "Revelations." A religious fanatic morally evolves into the mortal equivalent of the Devil in "Down, Satan!" A human guinea pig in "The Age of Desire" becomes an inhuman sexual freak. A prison inmate from "In the Flesh" changes into a murderous smoke-like creature; killers and victims are made into the stuff of folklore and legend in "The Forbidden"; men are made into women in "The Madonna." A woman dying of disease becomes Death incarnate in "The Life of Death," inflicting upon others the unwanted gift of the plague. Imperialistic Europeans from "How Spoilers Bleed" change into the semblance of rotting fruit before they die of a supernaturally infectious jungle rot. Werewolves are made into agents of espionage in "Twilight at the Towers," while a master illusionist becomes a master magician, becomes dead, then becomes saved in "The Last Illusion." And finally, Miriam's moral transformation in "Coming to Grief" makes her a stronger person in the end, a person toughened by death enough to confront death squarely.

More than any other thematic device evident in Barker's fiction, the tale of transformation is the most prevalent, and obviously the author's favorite. Clive Barker's frequent use of transformation as a narrative motif reinforces his philosophical connection to the Mary Shelley school of Gothicism, and to the larger school of nineteenth-century Romanticism. Barker is enamored with telling stories of magical metamorphoses because these changes represent for him the defeat of the commonplace and the celebration of imagination. Imagination, for Barker, is change, is a crucially needed change if we, as humans, seek to improve our lot in life. Barker recognizes that physical, intellectual, and moral transformations are the stuff of life itself, and of death. Those characters who are better suited for change, those characters who are not disillusioned nor destroyed by change, in a Nietzschean sense become stronger in the process, more magical and more divine than what they had previously been or previously known. Even the act of Clive Barker writing his tales of the *fantastique* involves several levels of metamorphosis. At the most basic level, the author transforms words and sentences into meaningful texts. At another, more abstract level, these texts are read, and interpreted as a philosophic dialogue between the author and the reader. At a final level, this philosophical dialogue becomes a part of the reader's own imaginative process, so that, returning full circle, the product of Barker's imagining motivates us into imagining, and we are each inclusively changed by the catalyst of our imagination.

Saki's "The Unrest-Cure," and the Joke as Narrative Motif

Perhaps the British author who Clive Barker resembles the most in his short fiction is Saki. Like Barker, Saki is a true craftsman of the written word, where each sentence, each scene, and each character are carefully devised for the precise effect, and, in addition, like Barker, Saki in his exquisitely wrought short stories relies heavily upon the joke as narrative device. For both Barker and Saki, the joke serves as an effective means by which people and people's attitudes may be closely examined and satirized. A representative tale from

The Chronicles of Clovis (1911) entitled "The Unrest-Cure" nicely illustrates how Saki employs the joke as social satire, while also outlining the points of comparison between Saki's and Clive Barker's work. Basically, Saki's "The Unrest-Cure" attacks complacency and routine—in the guise of J.P. Huddle and his sister—by making fun of these traits, as do many of Barker's stories. "The Unrest-Cure" also attacks the conventions of organized religion (as well as its prejudices and its hypocrisies). A number of Barker's tales criticize organized religion, including (as a sampling) "The Midnight Meat Train," "Pig Blood Blues," "Rawhead Rex," "Confessions of a (Pornographer's) Shroud," "Revelations," "Down, Satan!," and "Lost Souls." Both Saki and Barker see the bureaucracy of organized religion as being silly, or self-serving, or just downright vicious. "The Unrest-Cure," lastly, elevates the trickster figure—a character named Clovis, who also appears elsewhere in a number of Saki's other short stories—to a heroic level. Clovis represents Saki's "voice" in the narrative, and through Clovis, Saki is more effectively able to parody that which needs parodying in the Edwardian upper-middle class. Clive Barker, though he doesn't employ a specific persona who is consistently featured in a variety of adventures, nevertheless, as does Saki, frequently assumes a character's point-of-view in the story in order to comment specifically about our modern day foibles.

Saki's so-called cruelty in his stories has often been unfortunately misunderstood. His critics, uncomfortable with his seeming delight in constructing the bitingly caustic joke in his fiction, attempt to draw biographical connections to an unhappy childhood (hence, the explanation for the unhappy child protagonist in a number of his stories) or to a repressed homosexuality. Auberon Waugh, writing in his introduction to the Penguin Modern Classics edition of *The Chronicles of Clovis*, would like us to view Saki's humor as "a lonely cry for pity and understanding," so that we, as "normally kind-hearted" readers, will not feel too guilty for enjoying his stories (xii). This remark not only condescends to Saki's immense storytelling abilities, but it also takes that frustratingly familiar critical stance that anyone who writes about the dark side of human nature must necessarily be part of that same dark side. Barker's fiction is most definitely not a "cry for pity and understanding" (nor, I suspect, is Saki's). Instead, it is an assault against that which Barker finds malevolent (or marvelous, or both) in our society, and in us. The joke, as Saki and Barker well know, is a way in which cruelty may be instructive.

Indeed, there is a serious didactic element to Barker's use of humor. "The Book of Blood" and "Dread" each have characters who play cruel practical jokes, and who, as a consequence of playing jokes, in turn become the butt of even crueler jokes. Simon McNeal from "The Book of Blood," for example, pretends that he is a psychic capable of communicating with the dead. He is making fun of something that should not be made fun of; he is mocking a powerful social taboo. Offended by McNeal's sense of humor, the dead decide to play their own joke on McNeal, transforming the pretend storyteller into a literal (and a more precise) teller of tales. The deranged Quaid in "Dread" plays an even more vicious variety of practical joke on Cheryl Fromm and Stephen Grace. Ostensibly conducting scientific research about the emotion of fear, Quaid is instead merely enacting his own sadistic fantasies at the expense of innocent others. With Stephen Grace, Quaid goes a bit too far in his joke, becomes trapped by it, and dies because of it. Two *Books of Blood* short stories that take the joke to an extreme are "The Yattering and Jack" and "Hell's Event." Barker decimates the stereotypical domestic Christmas setting in "The Yattering and Jack" with slapstick images of homicidal turkey dinners, spinning Christmas trees, and the silly antics of an intellectually slow-as-molasses demon, who humorously vents his hellish rage (a rage that should make the strong tremble in fear) upon simple house pets. "Hell's Event" is less outrageous, but no less comical; the story takes the apocalypse and turns it into a sporting event, poking fun at both religion and sports in the process. The tale also has some fun making fun of politicians. As evidenced in the above-mentioned examples, the levels of sophistication of Clive Barker's narrative jokes are great, ranging from the merely amusing to the outrageously farcical, from light to grim humor. Sometimes Barker develops his jokes throughout the course of the entire narrative, one amusing event stacked upon another until it all becomes burlesque. Other times, Barker focuses his attention upon word play. In many of his short stories, for example, he puns in order to attack clichéd expressions, to mock expectations, to lampoon conventions of communication. One of his stories in particular, "The Body Politic," takes word play to the limit, ridiculing the trite language of political movements to such an extent that the story itself becomes one huge pun. Barker's love of the word (and the symbolic context of language) is most evident in his love of puns; they provide the careful reader of Barker's fiction many entertaining moments of amusement.

Clive Barker as Allegorist

The domain of the dark *fantastique* is flexible enough to accommodate equally the likes of both Stephen King and Clive Barker. It permits each author to prosper in his own unique fashion, and it rewards each with a substantial devoted following. In fact, King and Barker frame the opposite ends of the *fantastique*. Their efforts detail radically different approaches to the writing of their craft. Both approaches work well; they both share the same basic realm of Gothic imagination, yet they also express an artistic point-of-view that is quite distinct from one another.

In his autobiographical article entitled "On Becoming a Brand Name" that discusses his rise from obscurity to the status of best-selling author,

Stephen King proclaims that he is a "brand name" writer, the "Green Giant of what is called the 'modern horror story.'" He defines a brand name author as, "one who is known for a certain genre of popular novel" (15). King's willingness to identify himself as the producer of a market-sensitive commodity does his honesty about his writing justice, yet it also reveals how securely his fiction is tied to his understanding of the commerciality of literature, and how typically part of the current American publishing scene he is.

Stephen King and Clive Barker are each preeminently successful fantasists. Each, as mentioned in the first chapter, are recognized by their peers, their audiences, and the critics as two of the foremost of today's horror fiction writers. Yet the one author is comfortable with the designation of horror fiction writer, while the other is not. King writes to fulfill his reader's and his publisher's expectations. Clive Barker does not. King follows (and frequently imitates) what has worked well within the strict confines of the horror genre as established by the recent past (and has even written a detailed analysis of the genre's immediate history, *Danse Macabre*, in which he demonstrates his formidable knowledge of what has preceded his own work). Barker defies formulaic conventions, undermines expectations, and continually tests the limits of his publisher's willingness to experiment. Both King and Barker are very skilled at what they do; they just go about it from opposite ends. For the most part, Stephen King sees genre fiction as being a good thing. Clive Barker does not. Stephen King has co-opted the commercial prerequisites of the horror genre. He has adapted — and has certainly thrived by — the dictates of the literary marketplace. He has directly or indirectly profoundly reinforced with his "brand name" reference the ability of the industry to designate for the author artistic standards of conduct. King greatly empowers his readers and his publishers with the ability to determine the direction of his work. And he has done all these things while still writing some of the very best popular fiction being published today.

Returning to an earlier notion developed in the first chapter of this study, Clive Barker is very British (read: very non-traditional and very suspicious of the horror genre tag) in his approach to writing fantasy, while Stephen King is very American (read: very traditional and very comfortable with the horror genre designation). King is more intimately part of the recently evolved American business of publishing for profit than is Barker. The American publishing scene, when it made the transition from cottage industry to mass media business during the latter half of the nineteenth century, also made what was previously not condemned as being sub-standard literature — the Gothic horror story — and turned it into something that sold immensely well and that became reviled by the American critic as artistic trash. When the Gothic narrative was packaged as genre fiction (in order to be sold for profit), it lost respect in this country as a legitimate art form. And as the American popular press became even more commercial around the turn-of-the-century, as genre became even more codified as the essential medium of the dime novel, the pulp magazine, and the paperback best-seller, then genre fiction—like the horror story—became ensconced as "lowbrow" entertainment.

In Europe and America during the nineteenth century, the tale of horror was not understood to be the sole province of the unwashed masses. It was more integrated (as was discussed in the previous section) throughout the total literary culture of the period than it is today. But as our culture itself began to organize along vertical lines rather than horizontal, the Gothic horror story—as commercial entertainment—toppled to the bottom of the artistic hierarchy. What was once highbrow in American literature became lowbrow. Lawrence W. Levine argues in his study, *Highbrow/Lowbrow: The Emergence of Cultural Hierarchy in America*, that the notions that define high, middle, and low culture in our society are primarily determined by the prevailing ideology, the definitions of which are constantly in flux rather than permanently fixed. Levine also goes on to say that during the nineteenth century, American culture was a more "shared" experience than it is today (8-9). He states,

> What I mean, in referring to a shared culture, is that in the nineteenth century, especially in the first half, Americans, in addition to whatever specific cultures they were part of, shared a public culture less hierarchically organized, less fragmented into relatively rigid adjectival boxes than their descendants were to experience a century later [9].

I would argue that American fiction was fragmented into Levine's designations of high and low culture (what I would phrase "elite" and "popular") about the same time as the entertainment print mass media began to establish its dominance over how the business of publishing was conducted in this country, a time frame encompassing the Civil War to World War II. Even the hardcover novel, once the sole domain of the cottage industry book seller/book publisher, by the end of the nineteenth century defined its success in commercial, rather than artistic, terms with the advent of concept of the "best-seller" (Tebbel 180). As each segment of the mass media handled genre fiction—the dime novel from approximately 1860 to 1910; the pulp magazine from approximately 1910 to 1950; and the paperback book from the late 1930s to the present—it was attacked more vigorously by Levine's newly evolving cultural elite. By the time Stephen King inherited the distinction of being one of the top best-selling authors of the 1970s, 1980s, and 1990s, the damage caused horror fiction by its very popularity with a mass audience was complete. King's tremendous success engendered mistrust and dislike by the literary critic. And yet, King found solace in his sales figures, comfort in his multi-million dollar contracts, protection from the stabbing barbs of the hostile *New York Times* book reviewer. The American Gothic horror novel, with King's defiant assistance, is now both successful and vilified. It has relinquished the hold it once enjoyed upon the American literary imagination of the nineteenth century (as outlined in the previous section). It has become primarily concerned with cheap thrills, with *the scare*, with shock value, because these things sell to a large audience.

If the European Gothic novel was intellectually suspect during the nineteenth century, it never added to that problem the additional problem of being commercially suspect as well. The British authors identified in the previous section did not have to combat the equivalent of the contemporary American commercial press. The British did have their "penny dreadfuls," but these never defined the standards of the entire British publishing industry. Having not been cursed (or blessed, depending upon your perspective) with a dominant commercial press where the financial bottom line reigned supreme, authors like Shelley and Saki were given a much freer hand in writing fantasy, in incorporating fantasy as part of their larger narratives, in utilizing dark fantasy for something more than mere shock-for-shock's sake entertainment. And this is where Barker again differs fundamentally from Stephen King. Barker wants to transform the horror genre, King wants to enforce it.

Clive Barker makes known his dislike of popular genres in the following statement,

> Genre makes a most reliable noose; a man could strangle himself a dozen times attempting to separate the threads of one fictional form from another. It's true that both publishers and booksellers make the process seem easy, dividing Romances from Thrillers from Science Fiction from Horror Fiction, as though these definitions were self-evident. To slicken the process still further, many authors actively strive to produce work that merely echoes previous pieces (their own, or other people's) thus offering little challenge to the generic status quo ["FT Forum" 3-4].

What is obvious, finally, in our comparison between King and Barker is that King endeavors to entertain his readers, while Barker wants to instruct them. Clive Barker's creative efforts, like Christopher Marlowe's and Mary Shelley's and Saki's and a handful of others, are didactic in nature, and the subject of their instruction is Mystery. Indeed, Barker's writings are similar to the European mystery plays where sin is examined and divine passion is revealed to an audience. Like these mystery plays, Barker balances reality with fantasy, subjectivity with objectivity. He employs fanciful concepts to explain that which desires to become fanciful. Barker is a modern-day allegorist. His fiction, as I hope I have illustrated, is replete with subtextual references. It contains extended metaphors, complex structures of socio-political references, ideas crammed with double meaning, rich symbolic narratives that reveal the world to us, while concurrently mystifying it. First and foremost, Barker strives to teach us in his writings, to show us how to approach imagination, embrace imagination, revere imagination. Barker is less the horror fiction writer, and more the instructor. If we read Barker's short fiction carefully, we may become enlightened by his instruction.

In leaving our analysis of Clive Barker's short fiction, a scene in Oscar Wilde's *The Picture of Dorian Gray* (1891) reminds me of Barker's *Books of Blood*. At the end of the tenth chapter of Wilde's novel, Lord Henry Wotton gives Dorian Gray a "yellow book" (yellow representing to the Victorian mind evil, corruption, death). This book comes to define Dorian's descent into decadence as being equally as important in Wilde's narrative as is Dorian's magical portrait that records his every wrinkle and sin, while leaving the picture's subject eternally young and beautiful. This book is but another attempt on the part of the depraved Lord Henry to corrupt further the morally declining Dorian Gray. Wilde writes,

> After a few moments [of reading] he [Dorian Gray] became absorbed. It was the strangest book that he had ever read. It seemed to him that in exquisite raiment, and to the delicate sound of flutes, the sins of the world were passing in dumb show before him. Things that he had dimly dreamed of were suddenly made real to him. Things of which he had never dreamed were gradually revealed [155].

Dorian's initial experience with Lord Henry's book of forbidden knowledge is the quintessential metaphor for the Gothic itself. Power, albeit dark power, is revealed to Dorian, a power that fundamentally and forever alters the course of his life. Dorian is eventually consumed by this power, his life forfeited in the bargain, yet power he does possess for a brief time, the power of moral transformation, of altered perceptions of life and death, of the knowledge of gods and devils. The book has force. It has vitality. It has the ability to affect reality. It sparks desire and thought, divines or obscures the truth, makes profound change.

Wilde's sinister book-within-a-book is closely analogous to Barker's texts-within-texts. For Barker, the book symbolizes magic. It represents dreams and nightmares and the entire realm of human thought existing in-between. The book for Barker is the medium of instruction. It is the medium of confession. It is the place where people, living and dead, tell their tales, and are cathartically purged during the telling (as we are perhaps cathartically purged during the listening). It is the source of redemption, the dictionary of inspiration, and the encyclopedia of ingenuity. Wilde's rendition of the efficacy of the book and of the process of reading the book, however, only shows the negative side. Barker approaches imagination from both the dark and the light, since both qualities are essential components of the human condition (and of divinity). Wilde's book is only dark, while Barker's books disclose the totality of our experience, and of our dreams. At times, Barker's message is grim, but equally it is hopeful. At times, Barker writes of horror and of death, but equally he writes of love and fellowship. At times, Barker shows us ugly demons, but equally he shows us beautiful angels.

Most certainly, Clive Barker's *Books of Blood*—as well as his other uncollected short fiction—are his generous gifts to imagination, and we are most thankful for the fine presents.

WORKS CITED

Atkins, Peter. "A Dog's Tail." *Clive Barker's Shadows in Eden*. Ed Stephen Jones. Lancaster: Underwood-Miller, 1991. 115-148, 211.
Barker, Clive. "FT Forum: Speaking from the Dark." *Fantasy Tales*. Eds. Stephen Jones and David Sutton. New York: Carroll & Graf, 1991. 3-8.
———. "An Introduction: The Bare Bones." *Clive Barker's Shadows in Eden*. Ed. Stephen Jones. Lancaster: Underwood-Miller, 1991. 389-392.
———. "The Tragical History of Dr. Faustus." *Horror: 100 Best Books*. Eds. Stephen Jones and Kim Newman. New York: Carroll & Graf, 1988. 11-14.
Barnet, Sylvan. Introduction. *Doctor Faustus*. By Christopher Marlowe. New York: Signet, 1969.
Birkhead, Edith. *The Tale of Terror: A Study of the Gothic Romance*. New York: Russell & Russell, 1963.
"The British Invasion: Clive Barker." *American Fantasy*. Win. 1987: 42-48, 50.
Brown, Michael. "So Many Monsters, So Little Time...." *Pandemonium*. Ed. Michael Brown. Staten Island: Eclipse, 1991. 17-21.
Brunvand, Jan Harold. *The Study of American Folklore: An Introduction*. New York: W. W. Norton, 1968.
Caldwell, Tim. "Clive Barker: Wherein *Film Threat* Peels Back Layers to See What Makes Him Tick." *Film Threat* 19 (1989): 16-23.
Carroll, Noël. *The Philosophy of Horror: or, Paradoxes of the Heart*. New York: Routledge, 1990.
Carter, Margaret L. *Specter or Delusion?: The Supernatural in Gothic Fiction*. Ann Arbor: UMI Research, 1987.
Cawelti, John G. *Adventure, Mystery, and Romance: Formula Stories as Art and Popular Culture*. Chicago: University of Chicago Press, 1976.
Dalby, Richard. "Stevenson, Robert Louis." *The Penguin Encyclopedia of Horror and the Supernatural*. 1986 ed.
Daniels, Les. *Living in Fear: A History of Horror in the Mass Media*. New York: Scribner's, 1975.
Grixti, Joseph. *Terrors of Uncertainty: The Cultural Contexts of Horror Fiction*. New York: Routledge, 1989.
Gross, Louis S. *Redefining the American Gothic: From* Wieland *to* Day of the Dead. Ann Arbor: UMI Research, 1989.
Hoppenstand, Gary. "From Here to Quiddity: Clive Barker's *The Great and Secret Show*." *Clive Barker's Shadows in Eden*. Ed. Stephen Jones. Lancaster: Underwood-Miller, 1991. 227-260.
Jones, Stephen. "Clive Barker: Anarchic Prince of Horror." *Clive Barker's Shadows in Eden*. Ed. Stephen Jones. Lancaster: Underwood-Miller, 1991. 9-22.
Kendrick, Walter. *The Thrill of Fear: 250 Years of Scary Entertainment*. New York: Grove Weidenfeld, 1991.
King, Stephen. *Danse Macabre*. New York: Everest House, 1981.

———. "On Becoming a Brand Name." *Fear Itself: The Horror Fiction of Stephen King*. Eds. Tim Underwood and Chuck Miller. New York: Signet, 1985. 15–42.

Lackey, Mike. "The Clive Barker Interview." *Marvel Age*. Dec. 1991: 8–14.

Levine, Lawrence W. *Highbrow/Lowbrow: The Emergence of Cultural Hierarchy in America*. Cambridge: Harvard UP, 1988.

Lovecraft, Howard Phillips. *Supernatural Horror in Literature*. New York: Ben Abramson, 1945. Introd. E. F. Bleiler. New York: Dover, 1973. (Note: A draft of this essay was published circa 1927 in W. Paul Cook's *The Recluse*.)

Lupoff, Richard, and Richard Wolinsky. "Eye to Eye: An Interview with Clive Barker." *Science Fiction Eye*. Aug. 1988: 9–20.

Maddox, Mike. "Clive Barker: On the Beauty of the Beast." *Amazing Heroes*. Dec. 1989: 24–31.

Nutman, Philip. "Bring on the Monsters! Part One." *Fangoria*. Oct. 1989: 30–33, 61.

———. "If You Knew Clive Like We Know Clive...." *Fangoria*. Oct. 1988: 27–30, 67.

Sabor, Peter. *Horace Walpole: The Critical Heritage*. London: Routledge & Kegan Paul, 1987.

Sammon, Paul M. "Outlaws." *Splatterpunks: Extreme Horror*. Ed. Paul M. Sammon. New York: St. Martin's, 1990. 272–346.

Stroby, W.C. "Clive Barker: Trust Your Vision." *Writer's Digest*. Mar. 1991: 22–27.

Tebbel, John. *Between Covers: The Rise and Transformation of American Book Publishing*. New York: Oxford University Press, 1987.

"To Hell and Back." *Speakeasy*. Sept. 1989: 25–27.

Twitchell, James B. *Dreadful Pleasures: An Anatomy of Modern Horror*. New York: Oxford University Press, 1985.

Vince, Nick. "The Luggage in the Crypt." *Pandemonium*. Ed. Michael Brown. Staten Island: Eclipse, 1991. 9–16.

Waugh, Auberon. Introduction. *The Chronicles of Clovis*. By Saki. New York: Penguin, 1986. vii–xii.

Wiater, Stanley. *Dark Dreamers: Conversations with the Masters of Horror*. New York: Avon, 1990.

———. *Dark Visions: Conversations with the Masters of the Horror Film*. New York: Avon, 1992.

Wilde, Oscar. *The Picture of Dorian Gray*. London: Ward, Lock, 1891. Ed. Peter Ackroyd. New York: Penguin, 1985.

Winter, Douglas E. *Faces of Fear: Encounters with the Creators of Modern Horror*. New York: Berkley, 1985.

SELECTED BIBLIOGRAPHY

Primary Texts

In the following highly selective chronological listing of Clive Barker's published writings, only the first book publication is noted. For a more comprehensive listing of Clive Barker's work, refer to the article entitled "Clive Barker: A Working Bibliography," published in the Underwood-Miller anthology (edited by Stephen Jones) entitled Clive Barker's Shadows in Eden.

Barker, Clive. *Clive Barker's Books of Blood, Volume One*. London: Sphere Books, 1984.
    Contents: "Introduction" by Ramsey Campbell; "The Book of Blood"; "The Midnight Meat Train"; "The Yattering and Jack"; "Pig Blood Blues"; "Sex, Death and Starshine"; "In the Hills, the Cities"
_____. *Clive Barker's Books of Blood, Volume Two*. London: Sphere Books, 1984.
    Contents: "Dread"; "Hell's Event"; "Jacqueline Ess: Her Will and Testament"; "The Skins of the Fathers"; "New Murders in the Rue Morgue"
_____. *Clive Barker's Books of Blood, Volume Three*. London: Sphere Books, 1984.
    Contents: "Son of Celluloid"; "Rawhead Rex"; "Confessions of a (Pornographer's) Shroud"; "Scape-Goats"; "Human Remains"
_____. *The Damnation Game*. London: Weidenfeld & Nicolson, 1985.
_____. *Clive Barker's Books of Blood, Volume Four*. London: Sphere Books, 1985.
    Contents: "The Inhuman Condition"; "The Body Politic"; "Revelations"; "Down, Satan!"; "The Age of Desire"
_____. *Clive Barker's Books of Blood, Volume Five*. London: Sphere Books, 1985.
    Contents: "In the Flesh"; "The Forbidden"; "The Madonna"; "Babel's Children"
_____. *Clive Barker's Books of Blood, Volume Six*. London: Sphere Books, 1985.
    Contents: "The Life of Death"; "How Spoilers Bleed"; "Twilight at the Towers"; "The Last Illusion"; "The Book of Blood (A Postscript): On Jerusalem Street"
_____. "Lost Souls." *Cutting Edge*. Garden City: Doubleday, 1986.
_____. *The Hellbound Heart*. Night Visions 3. Arlington Heights: Dark Harvest, 1986.
_____. *Weaveworld*. New York: Poseidon Press, 1987.
_____. *Cabal*. New York: Poseidon Press, 1988.
_____. "Coming to Grief." *Prime Evil*. New York: New American Library, 1988.
_____. *The Great and Secret Show*. London: Collins, 1989.
_____. *Clive Barker Illustrator*. Ed. Steve Niles. Forestville: Arcane/Eclipse Books, 1990.
_____. *Clive Barker's Nightbreed: The Making of the Film*. London: Fontana-Collins, 1990. (Note: this book publishes Clive Barker's screenplay of the film.)
_____. *Clive Barker's The Nightbreed Chronicles*. London: Titan Books, 1990.

———. *Imajica*. New York: Harper-Collins, 1991.
———. *The Thief of Always: A Fable*. New York: Harper-Collins, 1992.

Secondary Texts

The following titles are works of non-fiction not specifically quoted in this analysis, but they nonetheless provide cultural, historical, social, and literary backgrounds to the study of the horror genre in general, and to the study of Clive Barker's short stories specifically. Only book-length works are identified, and greater attention has been given to recent publications.

Aguirre, Manuel. *The Closed Space: Horror Literature and Western Symbolism*. Manchester: Manchester University Press, 1990.
Barron, Neil, ed. *Horror Literature: A Reader's Guide*. New York: Garland, 1990.
Bataille, Georges. *Literature and Evil*. Trans. Alastair Hamilton. London: Marion Boyars, 1990.
Bayer-Berenbaum, Linda. *The Gothic Imagination: Expansion in Gothic Literature and Art*. Rutherford: Fairleigh Dickinson University Press, 1982.
Briggs, Julia. *Night Visitors: The Rise and Fall of the English Ghost Story*. London: Faber, 1977.
Brooke-Rose, Christine. *A Rhetoric of the Unreal: Studies in Narrative and Structure, Especially of the Fantastic*. Cambridge: Cambridge University Press, 1981.
Burleson, Donald R. *Lovecraft: Disturbing the Universe*. Lexington: University of Kentucky Press, 1990.
Büssing, Sabine. *Aliens in the Home: The Child in Horror Fiction*. New York: Greenwood, 1987.
Carpenter, Lynette, and Wendy K. Kolmar, eds. *Haunting the House of Fiction: Feminist Perspectives on Ghost Stories by American Women*. Knoxville: University of Tennessee Press, 1991.
Clarens, Carlos. *An Illustrated History of the Horror Films*. New York: Putnam, 1967.
Clover, Carol J. *Men, Women, and Chain Saws: Gender in the Modern Horror Film*. Princeton: Princeton University Press, 1992.
Curtis, Richard. *Beyond the Bestseller: A Literary Agent Takes You Inside the Book Business*. New York: NAL, 1989.
DeLamotte, Eugenia C. *Perils of the Night: A Feminist Study of Nineteenth-Century Gothic*. New York: Oxford University Press, 1990.
Docherty, Brian, ed. *American Horror Fiction: From Brockden Brown to Stephen King*. New York: St. Martin's, 1990.
Dove, George N. *Suspense in the Formula Story*. Bowling Green: Bowling Green State University Popular Press, 1989.
Drake, Douglas. *Horror!* New York: Macmillan, 1966.
Ellis, Kate Ferguson. *The Contested Castle: Gothic Novels and the Subversion of Domestic Ideology*. Urbana: University of Illinois Press, 1989.
Fiedler, Leslie A. *Love and Death in the American Novel*. 3rd ed. Briarcliff Manor: Stein and Day, 1982.
Frank, Frederick S. *Through the Pale Door: A Guide to and Through the American Gothic*. New York: Greenwood, 1990.
Frost, Brian J. *The Monster with a Thousand Faces: Guises of the Vampire in Myth and Literature*. Bowling Green: Bowling Green State University Popular Press, 1989.
Gilbert, Sandra M., and Susan Gubar. *The Madwoman in the Attic: The Woman Writer and the Nineteenth-Century Literary Imagination*. New Haven: Yale University Press, 1984.

Glut, Donald F. *Classic Movie Monsters.* Metuchen: Scarecrow, 1978.
Golden, Christopher, ed. *Cut!: Horror Writers on Horror Films.* New York: Berkley, 1992.
Goulart, Ron. *An Informal History of the Pulp Magazine.* New York: Ace, 1972.
Haggerty, George E. *Gothic Fiction/Gothic Form.* University Park: Pennsylvania State University Press, 1989.
Haining, Peter, ed. *The Penny Dreadful: or, Strange, Horrid & Sensational Tales!* London: Victor Gollancz, 1976.
Heller, Terry. *The Delights of Terror: An Aesthetics of the Tale of Terror.* Urbana: University of Illinois Press, 1987.
Hennessy, Brendan. *The Gothic Novel.* Burnt Mill: Longman, 1978.
Hogan, David J. *Dark Romance: Sexuality in the Horror Film.* Jefferson: McFarland, 1986.
Hoppenstand, Gary, and Ray B. Browne, eds. *The Gothic World of Stephen King: Landscape of Nightmares.* Bowling Green: Bowling Green State University Popular Press, 1987.
_____. *In Search of the Paper Tiger: A Sociological Perspective of Myth, Formula and the Mystery Genre in the Entertainment Print Mass Medium.* Bowling Green: Bowling Green State University Popular Press, 1987.
Jackson, Rosemary. *Fantasy: The Literature of Subversion.* London: Methuen, 1981.
Jones, Robert Kenneth. *The Shudder Pulps: A History of the Weird Menace Magazines of the 1930's.* New York: Plume, 1978.
Jones, Stephen, ed. *Clive Barker's Shadows in Eden.* Lancaster: Underwood-Miller, 1991.
Joshi, S.T. *The Weird Tale.* Austin: University of Texas Press, 1990.
Kerr, Howard, John W. Crowley, and Charles L. Crow, eds. *The Haunted Dusk: American Supernatural Fiction, 1820-1920.* Athens: University of Georgia Press, 1983.
MacAndrew, Elizabeth. *The Gothic Tradition in Fiction.* New York: Columbia University Press, 1979.
Magistrale, Tony, ed. *The Dark Descent: Essays Defining Stephen King's Horrorscape.* New York: Greenwood, 1992.
_____. *Stephen King: The Second Decade,* Danse Macabre *to* The Dark Half. New York: Twayne, 1992.
Massé, Michelle A. *In the Name of Love: Women, Masochism, and the Gothic.* Ithaca: Cornell University Press, 1992.
Monleón, José B. *A Specter Is Haunting Europe: A Sociohistorical Approach to the Fantastic.* Princeton: Princeton University Press, 1990.
Munster, Bill, ed. *Sudden Fear: The Horror and Dark Suspense Fiction of Dean R. Koontz.* Mercer Island: Starmont House, 1988.
Newman, Kim. *Nightmare Movies: A Critical History of the Horror Film, 1968-88.* London: Bloomsbury, 1988.
Penzoldt, Peter. *The Supernatural in Fiction.* New York: Humanities Press, 1965.
Railo, Eino. *The Haunted Castle: A Study of the Elements of English Romanticism.* New York: Dutton, 1927.
Ramsland, Katherine. *Prism of the Night: A Biography of Anne Rice.* New York: Dutton, 1991.
Reilly, John M., ed. *Twentieth-Century Crime and Mystery Writers, Second Edition.* New York: St Martin's, 1985.
Reino, Joseph. *Stephen King: The First Decade,* Carrie *to* Pet Sematary. Boston: Twayne, 1988.
Reynolds, David S. *Beneath the American Renaissance: The Subversive Imagination in the Age of Emerson and Melville.* New York: Knopf, 1988.
Ringe, Donald A. *American Gothic: Imagination and Reason in Nineteenth-Century Fiction.* Lexington: University of Kentucky Press, 1982.

Roberts, Garyn G., Gary Hoppenstand, and Ray B. Browne, eds. Old Sleuth's *Freaky Female Detectives (From the Dime Novels)*. Bowling Green: Bowling Green State University Popular Press, 1990.
Sage, Victor, ed. *The Gothick Novel*. Houndmills: Macmillan, 1990.
———. *Horror Fiction in the Protestant Tradition*. Houndmills: Macmillan, 1988.
St. John Barclay, Glen. *Anatomy of Horror: The Masters of Occult Fiction*. London: Weidenfeld and Nicolson, 1978.
Schweitzer, Darrell, ed. *Discovering Modern Horror Fiction*. Mercer Island: Starmont House, 1985.
———, ed. *Discovering Modern Horror Fiction: II*. Mercer Island: Starmont House, 1988.
Spignesi, Stephen J. *The Complete Stephen King Encyclopedia: The Definitive Guide to the Works of America's Master of Horror*. Chicago: Contemporary Books, 1991.
Steinbrunner, Chris, and Otto Penzler, eds. *Encyclopedia of Mystery and Detection*. New York: McGraw-Hill, 1976.
Sullivan, Jack. *Elegant Nightmares: The English Ghost Story from Le Fanu to Blackwood*. Athens: Ohio University Press, 1978.
———, ed. *The Penguin Encyclopedia of Horror and the Supernatural*. New York: Viking, 1986.
Summers, Montague. *The Gothic Quest: A History of the Gothic Novel*. New York: Russell & Russell, 1964.
Tropp, Martin. *Images of Fear: How Horror Stories Helped Shape Modern Culture (1818–1918)*. Jefferson: McFarland, 1990.
Van Hise, James. *The Illustrated Guide to Clive Barker*. Las Vegas: Pioneer, 1989.
———. *Stephen King and Clive Barker: The Illustrated Guide to the Masters of the Macabre*. Las Vegas: Pioneer, 1990. (Note: This title reprints Van Hise's previously published study entitled *The Illustrated Guide to Clive Barker*.)
Varma, Devendra P. *The Gothic Flame*. New York: Russell & Russell, 1966.
Varnado, S.L. *Haunted Presence: The Numinous in Gothic Fiction*. Tuscaloosa: University of Alabama Press, 1987.
Veeder, William. *Mary Shelley & Frankenstein: The Fate of Androgyny*. Chicago: University of Chicago Press, 1986.
Wagenknecht, Edward. *Seven Masters of Supernatural Fiction*. New York: Greenwood, 1991.
Waller, Gregory A., ed. *American Horrors: Essays on the Modern American Horror Film*. Urbana: University of Illinois Press, 1987.
———. *The Living and the Undead: From Stoker's* Dracula *to Romero's* Dawn of the Dead. Urbana: University of Illinois Press, 1986.
Wiesenfarth, Joseph. *Gothic Manners and the Classic English Novel*. Madison: University of Wisconsin Press, 1988.
Winter, Douglas E. *Stephen King: The Art of Darkness*. New York: NAL, 1984.

"The Breed" is the name of the "authorized Clive Barker fan club." To join, write: Phantom Press, 180 Woodward Avenue, Staten Island, New York, 10314. Included with membership to "The Breed" is a one year subscription to the publication entitled *Dread: The Official Clive Barker Newsletter*.

INDEX

Ackroyd, Peter 212
Adventure, Mystery, and Romance: Formula Stories as Art and Popular Culture 22, 211
"The Age of Desire" 25, 120-126, 182, 191, 192, 201, 213
Aguirre, Manuel 214
Alger, Horatio 91, 99
Alien 37
Aliens in the Home: The Child in Horror Fiction 214
American Gothic: Imagination and Reason in Nineteenth-Century Fiction 215
American Horror Fiction: From Brockden Brown to Stephen King 214
American Horrors: Essays on the Modern American Horror Film 216
Anatomy of Horror: The Masters of Occult Fiction 215
Atkins, Peter 26, 35

"Babel's Children" 144-149, 160, 189, 195, 213
Barker, Clive: allegorist 204-209; artistic philosophy 12, 14, 26-27, 34-44; British *fantastique* 195-204; comics 28-29; early life 23-25, 28-29; Gothic tales/novels 13, 14, 18-19, 20; illustration 27-28; novels 29, 32, 33-35; screenplays 35-37; sex 19-20, 39-40, 41; Stephen King comparison and contrast 9-13, 14, 18, 19-20, 25, 182, 204-207; violence 39, 40-42
Barnet, Sylvan 198, 211
Barrie, J. M. 58, 59, 195
Barron, Neil 214
Bataille, Georges 214
Bayer-Berenbaum, Linda 214

beautiful and the grotesque (theme) 187, 190-191
Beckford, William 186
Beneath the American Renaissance: The Subversive Imagination in the Age of Emerson and Melville 215
Benét, Stephen Vincent 70, 199
Between Covers: The Rise and Transformation of American Book Publishing 212
Beyond the Bestseller: A Literary Agent Takes You Inside the Book Business 214
Birkhead, Edith 22, 211
Blake, William 12, 30
Bleiler, E. F. 212
"The Body Politic" 63, 106-111, 192, 201, 213
Bond, James 146
"The Book of Blood" 6, 8, 17, 45-47, 96, 112, 188, 189, 191, 201, 203-204, 213
"The Book of Blood (A Postscript): On Jerusalem Street" 32, 168-170, 213
Boote, Barbara 31
Boswell, James 110
Bradbury, Ray 7, 30, 45, 76
Briggs, Julia 214
"Bring on the Monsters! Part One" 35-36, 212
British Fantasy Award 31
"The British Invasion: Clive Barker" 26, 42, 43, 182-184, 211
Brooke-Rose, Christine 214
Brown, Charles Brockden 197
Brown, Michael 24, 29, 211, 212
Browne, Ray B. 215
Brunvard, Jan Harold 137, 211
Burleson, Donald R. 214
Burroughs, Edgar Rice 15, 158
Burroughs, William S. 15
Büssing, Sabine 214
Byron, Lord 196

Cabal 9, 32, 35, 76, 79, 160, 164, 213
Caldwell, Tim 41, 184, 211
Campbell, Ramsey 15, 25, 42, 183, 213
Candyman 35, 140
Capone, Al 93
Carpenter, Lynette 214
Carrie 11
Carroll, Noël 17, 211
Carter, Margaret 20, 211
Cartland, Barbara 11
The Castle of Otranto 13, 194, 196
Cawelti, John G. 22, 211
Chandler, Raymond 164, 166
Chaplin, Charlie 52
Chinatown 165
Christine 11
The Chronicles of Clovis 203, 212
Churchill, Winston 93
Citizen Kane 117, 118
Clarens, Carlos 214
Classic Movie Monsters 214
"Clive Barker: A Working Bibliography" 213
"Clive Barker: Anarchic Prince of Horror" 33, 211
"Clive Barker: On the Beauty of the Beast" 27-28, 212
"Clive Barker: Trust Your Vision" 212
"Clive Barker: Wherein *Film Threat* Peels Back Layers to See What Makes Him Tick" 211
Clive Barker Illustrator 213
"The Clive Barker Interview" 212
Clive Barker's Hellraiser 28
Clive Barker's Nightbreed 28
Clive Barker's Nightbreed: The Making of the Film 213
Clive Barker's Nightbreed vs. Rawhead Rex 28
Clive Barker's Shadows in Eden 7, 198, 211, 213, 215
Clive Barker's The Nightbreed Chronicles 213
The Closed Space: Horror Literature and Western Symbolism 214
Clover, Carol J. 194, 251
Cocteau, Jean 30
Coleridge, Samuel Taylor 196
Colossus 25
"Coming to Grief" 177-182, 190, 193, 195, 202, 213

The Complete Stephen King Encyclopedia: The Definitive Guide to the Works of America's Master of Horror 216
Conan Doyle, Sir Arthur 16
"Confessions of a (Pornographer's) Shroud" 91-93, 183, 201, 203, 213
The Contested Castle: Gothic Novels and the Subversion of Domestic Ideology 214
Cook, W. Paul 212
The Crawling Eye 85
Crazyface 25
critique of institutional authority: the state (theme) 187, 192-193
Crow, Charles L. 215
Crowley, John W. 215
Curtis, Richard 214
Cut!: Horror Writers on Horror Film 214
Cutting Edge 171, 213

Dalby, Richard 121, 211
The Damnation Game 33, 39, 50, 52, 69, 93, 127, 199, 213
Daniels, Les 21, 211
Danse Macabre 11, 12, 16, 138, 211
Dante 12, 70, 118, 200
The Dark Descent: Essays Defining Stephen King's Horrorscape 215
Dark Dreamers: Conversations with the Masters of Horror 24, 30, 34, 42, 43, 212
Dark Forces 30
Dark Romance: Sexuality in the Horror Film 215
Dark Visions: Conversations with the Masters of the Horror Film 36-37, 212
Death Wish 157
Deathbird Stories 139
deceptiveness of appearances (theme) 187, 189-190
DeLamotte, Eugenia C. 214
The Delights of Terror: An Aesthetics of the Tale of Terror 215
"The Devil and Daniel Webster" 70, 199
Dickens, Charles 171, 187
Dillinger, John 93
Dirty Harry 157
Discovering Modern Horror Fiction 216
Docherty, Brian 214

Doctor Faustus 197–200, 211
Dr. Strangelove 149
Dog Company 25
"A Dog's Tail" 211
Dove, George N. 214
"Down, Satan!" 116–120, 189, 201, 203, 213
Dracula 98
Drake, Douglas 214
"Dread" 19, 65–68, 192, 201, 203–204, 213
Dread: The Official Clive Barker Newsletter 216
Dreadful Pleasures: An Anatomy of Modern Horror 19, 212
du Maurier, Daphne 195

E.C. Comics 28
Elegant Nightmares: The English Ghost Story from Le Fanu to Blackwood 216
Ellis, Kate Ferguson 214
Ellison, Harlan 139
Encyclopedia of Mystery and Detection 216
Epic Comics 28

Faces of Fear: Encounters with the Creators of Modern Horror 43, 212
"The Fall of the House of Usher" 118
Fantastic Four 28
Fantasy: The Literature of Subversion 215
Faustian pact tale (theme) 195, 197–199
Fear Itself: The Horror Fiction of Stephen King 212
feminist critique (theme) 187, 194–195
Fiedler, Leslie A. 214
Fielding, Henry 196
Fleming, Ian 144–145
"The Forbidden" 35, 134–140, 142, 144, 183, 188, 189, 194, 201, 213
Frank, Frederick S. 214
Frankenstein, Victor 67, 200
Frankenstein 13, 66–67, 79, 120–121, 185, 199–202, 216
"From Here to Quiddity: Clive Barker's *The Great and Secret Show*" 211
Frost, Brian J. 214
"FT Forum: Speaking from the Dark" 15, 30, 207, 211

game and game playing (theme) 187, 188–189
Gerald's Game 20
Gernsback, Hugo 185–186
Gilbert, Sandra M. 214
Gilligan's Island 94
Glut, Donald F. 214
Golden, Christopher 214
Good Housekeeping 177
Gothic Fiction/Gothic Form 214
Gothic Flame 216
The Gothic Imagination: Expansion in Gothic Literature and Art 214
The Gothic Quest: A History of the Gothic Novel 216
The Gothic Tradition in Fiction 215
The Gothic World of Stephen King: Landscape of Nightmares 215
The Gothick Novel 215
Goulart, Ron 214
grand guignol 25
Grant, Charles 41
The Great and Secret Show 33–34, 39, 41, 58, 67, 73, 74, 83, 84, 90, 213
Grimm, Brothers 12
Grixti, Joseph 17–18, 211
Gross, Louis S. 18–19, 211

Haggard, H. Rider 158
Haggerty, George E. 214
Haining, Peter 215
Hammett, Dashiell 164, 166
Harris, Thomas 15
The Haunted Castle: A Study of the Elements of English Romanticism 215
The Haunted Dusk: American Supernatural Fiction 215
Haunted Presence: The Numinous in Gothic Fiction 216
Haunting the House of Fiction: Feminist Perspectives on Ghost Stories by American Women 214
Hawthorne, Nathaniel 197
heightened senses (theme) 187, 191
Hellbound: Hellraiser II 35
The Hellbound Heart 35, 67, 70, 102–103, 198, 213
Heller, Terry 215
Hellraiser 35, 36, 76

"Hell's Event" 68-71, 188-189, 199, 204, 213
Hennessy, Brendan 215
Henry, O. 151
Highbrow/Lowbrow: The Emergence of Cultural Hierarchy in America 206, 212
Hitchcock, Alfred 25
Hogan, David J. 215
Hogg, James 133
Holmes, Sherlock 16
Hopkins, Gerard Manley 12
Horace Walpole: The Critical Heritage 212
Horror! 214
Horror: 100 Best Books 197, 199, 211
Horror Fiction in the Protestant Tradition 215
Horror Literature: A Reader's Guide 214
"How Spoilers Bleed" 155-160, 202, 213
Howard, Robert E. 13
"Human Remains" 20, 42, 97-100, 201, 213
Hydra Theater Company 25

"If You Knew Clive Like We Know Clive..." 32-33, 38, 42-43, 212
The Illustrated Guide to Clive Barker 216
An Illustrated History of the Horror Films 214
The Illustrated Man 7, 30, 45
Images of Fear: How Horror Stories Helped Shape Modern Culture 216
Imagica 10, 19, 34, 38, 137, 140, 169, 213
In Search of the Paper Tiger: A Sociological Perspective of Myth, Formula and the Mystery Genre in the Entertainment Print Mass Medium 215
In the Flesh 32
"In the Flesh" 39, 127-134, 140, 144, 189, 191, 194, 199, 201, 213
"In the Hills, the Cities" 20, 31, 61-64, 185, 186, 201, 213
In the Name of Love: Women, Masochism, and the Gothic 215
Inferno 69, 118
An Informal History of the Pulp Magazine 214
The Inhuman Condition 32, 42

"The Inhuman Condition" 101-106, 189, 201, 213
"An Introduction: The Bare Bones" 40, 211
"Israfel" 118
It 11

Jackson, Rosemary 215
"Jacqueline Ess: Her Will and Testament" 71-74, 83, 140, 147, 195, 201, 213
James, Henry 171
James, M.R. 171
"Jerusalem's Lot" 13
Johnson, Samuel 110
joke as narrative motif (theme) 195, 202-204
Jones, Robert Kenneth 215
Jones, Stephen 23, 33, 38, 197, 211, 213, 215
Joshi, S.T. 215
Joyce, James 27

Kafka, Franz 12
Karloff, Boris 90, 200
Keats, John 196
Kendrick, Walter 21-22, 211
Kerr, Howard 215
King, Stephen 4, 5, 7, 9-13, 14, 16, 18, 19-20, 23, 25, 32, 42, 182, 187, 204-207, 211
Koontz, Dean R. 4, 187
Kubrick, Stanley 149

Lackey, Mike 38, 212
L'Amour, Louis 11
Langhorne, John 196
"The Last Illusion" 164-168, 183, 199, 202, 213
le Carré, John 160-161
Leroux, Gaston 60-61
Levin, Ira 23
Levine, Lawrence W. 206, 212
Lewis, C.S. 195
Lewis, Matthew 13, 14, 200

"The Life of Death" 147, 151-155, 189, 195, 202, 213
Literature and Evil 214
The Living and the Undead: From Stoker's Dracula *to Romero's* Dawn of the Dead 216
Living in Fear: A History of Horror in the Mass Media 211
London Times 197
"Lost Souls" 171-176, 183, 192, 203, 213
Love and Death in the American Novel 214
Lovecraft, H.P. 13, 16-17, 21-22, 32, 44, 182, 183, 212
Lovecraft: Disturbing the Universe 214
Ludlum, Robert 144-145
"The Luggage in the Crypt" 212
Lupoff, Richard 25-26, 31-32, 184-185, 212

MacAndrew, Elizabeth 215
MacArthur, General Douglas 6
McCammon, Robert R. 4
McCauley, Kirby 30
McGoohan, Patrick 146
Maddox, Mike 27-28, 212
"The Madonna" 74, 140-144, 189, 191, 195, 202, 213
The Madwoman in the Attic: The Woman Writer and the Nineteenth-Century Literary Imagination 214
Magistrale, Tony 215
The Man from U.N.C.L.E. 144, 145-146
Marlowe, Christopher 182, 197-200, 207, 211
Mary Shelley & Frankenstein: The Fate of Androgyny 216
"The Masque of the Red Death" 24-25, 118
Massé, Michelle A. 215
Melville, Herman 197
Men, Women, and Chain Saws: Gender in the Modern Horror Film 194, 214
Messiah figure (theme) 187, 192
Mickey Mouse 6
"The Midnight Meat Train" 18, 42, 47-49, 86, 203, 213
Miller, Chuck 212
Milton, John 87, 89, 200
"The Mist" 11

Moby-Dick 12
The Monk 13, 14, 200
Monleón, José B. 215
Monroe, Marilyn 6, 85
The Monster with a Thousand Faces: Guises of the Vampire in Myth and Literature 214
Moore, Roger 146
Munster, Bill 215
"The Murders in the Rue Morgue" 24-25, 78-79
The Mysteries of Udolpho 195

Needful Things 11
"New Murders in the Rue Morgue" 25, 60, 78-81, 83, 86, 183, 213
New York Times 206
Newman, Kim 197, 211, 215
Night Visions 3 213
Night Visitors: The Rise and Fall of the English Ghost Story 214
Nightbreed 9, 23, 35, 36
Nightmare Movies: A Critical History of the Horror Film, 1968-88 215
Niles, Steve 213
Nosferatu 6
Nutman, Philip 32-33, 35-36, 38, 42-43, 212

Oates, Joyce Carol 187
Old Sleuth's *Freaky Female Detectives (from the Dime Novels)* 215
"On Becoming a Brand Name" 204-205, 212
"Outlaws" 13-14, 41, 212
Oz 15

Pal, George 25
Pandemonium 7, 12, 24, 211, 212
Paradise Lost 87, 89
The Penguin Encyclopedia of Horror and the Supernatural 211, 216
The Penny Dreadful: Or, Strange, Horrid & Sensational Tales! 215
Penzler, Otto 216
Penzoldt, Peter 215

Perils of the Night: A Feminist Study of Nineteenth-Century Gothic 214
Peter Pan 12, 24, 53, 58, 59
Peters, Elizabeth 147
The Philosophy of Horror: or, Paradoxes of the Heart 17, 211
The Picture of Dorian Gray 208, 212
"Pig Blood Blues" 53-59, 193, 201, 203, 213
Pinewood Studios 9, 36
Poe, Edgar Allan 12, 24, 62, 63, 78, 79, 80, 118, 183, 187, 197
Popular Culture Association 3
Prime Evil 177, 213
Prism of the Night: A Biography of Anne Rice 215
prison (or trap) setting (theme) 187, 193-194
The Prisoner 144, 146
Psycho 25

Radcliffe, Ann 194-195
Railo, Eino 215
Ramsland, Katherine 215
Randel, Tony 35
"The Raven" 118
"Rawhead Rex" 18, 20, 47, 86-91, 97, 195, 203, 213
Rawhead Rex 35
Reagan, Ronald 14
Realism 186, 196, 197
Rebecca 195
The Recluse 212
Redefining the American Gothic: From Wieland to Day of the Dead 18-19, 211
Reilly, John M. 215
Reino, Joseph 215
"Revelations" 28, 111-116, 117, 183-184, 195, 201, 203, 213
Reynolds, David S. 215
A Rhetoric of the Unreal: Studies in Narrative and Structure, Especially of the Fantastic 214
Rice, Anne 4, 7, 15, 187, 215
Richardson, Samuel 196
Ringe, Donald A. 215
Roberts, Garyn G. 215
roman noir 165, 176, 183
Romantic Movement 186, 196, 202

Sabor, Peter 196, 212
Sage, Victor 215
St. John Barclay, Glen 215
Saki 182, 197, 202-204, 207, 212
'Salem's Lot 11
Sammon, Paul M. 13-14, 41, 212
Saul, John 187
"Scape-Goats" 93-97, 111, 138, 195, 201, 213
Schow, David J. 41
Schweitzer, Darrell 216
Science Fiction Eye 184-185, 212
Scotland Yard 92
Scott, Sir Walter 88, 187
The Secret Life of Cartoons 25-26
Seven Masters of Supernatural Fiction 216
"Sex, Death and Starshine" 26, 59-61, 83, 184, 201, 213
Shakespeare, William 60
Shelley, Mary 12, 13, 67, 120-121, 182, 185-186, 196, 197, 199-202, 207, 216
Shelley, Percy Bysshe 196
The Shining 11
The Shudder Pulps: A History of the Weird Menace Magazines of the 1930's 215
The Silence of the Lambs 15
"The Skins of the Fathers" 75-78, 192, 213
Skipp, John 41
Sleepwalkers 20
Smith, Clark Ashton 13
"So Many Monsters, So Little Time..." 211
"Son of Celluloid" 28, 42, 77, 83-86, 184, 201, 213
A Specter Is Haunting Europe: A Sociohistorical Approach to the Fantastic 215
Specter or Delusion?: The Supernatural in Gothic Fiction 20, 211
Spector, Craig 41
Spignesi, Stephen J. 216
splatterpunk 13-14, 32, 41-42
Splatterpunks: Extreme Horror 13-14, 212
The Stand 11
Star Wars 36
Steel, Danielle 11
Steinbrunner, Chris 216
Stephen King: The Art of Darkness 216
Stephen King: The First Decade, Carrie to Pet Sematary 215
Stephen King: The Second Decade, Danse

Macabre *to* The Dark Half 215
Stephen King and Clive Barker: The Illustrated Guide to the Masters of the Macabre 216
Stevenson, Robert Louis 13, 120, 121–122, 123, 133, 211
"Stevenson, Robert Louis" 211
Stoker, Bram 98, 195
The Strange Case of Dr. Jekyll and Mr. Hyde 14, 120, 121–122, 123, 133
Straub, Peter 4, 5, 42
Stroby, W.C. 25, 29–30, 38–39, 195–196, 212
The Study of American Folklore: An Introduction 137, 211
Sudden Fear: The Horror and Dark Suspense Fiction of Dean R. Koontz 215
Sullivan, Jack 216
Summers, Montague 216
Supernatural Horror in Literature 16, 17, 212
The Supernatural in Fiction 215
Suspense in the Formula Story 214
Sutton, David 211

The Tale of Terror: A Study of the Gothic Romance 22, 211
tale of transformation (theme) 195, 199–202
Tales from the Crypt 28
Tapping the Vein 28
Tebbel, John 206, 212
"The Tell-Tale Heart" 118
Terrors of Uncertainty: The Cultural Contexts of Horror Fiction 18, 211
text as metaphor (theme) 187–188
Thatcher, Margaret 14
Theater of the Imagination 25
The Thief of Always: A Fable 34, 213
The Thrill of Fear: 250 Years of Scary Entertainment 21, 211
Through the Pale Door: A Guide to and Through the American Gothic 214
"To Hell and Back" 28–29, 212
Tolkien, J.R.R. 195
"The Tragical History of Dr. Faustus" 15, 197–198, 211
Tropp, Martin 216

Twain, Mark 187
Twentieth-Century Crime and Mystery Writers, Second Edition 215
"Twilight at the Towers" 160–164, 183, 189, 202, 213
Twitchell, James B. 19–20, 212

Underwood, Tim 212
Underworld 35
Universal Studios 84, 90, 121, 200
"The Unrest Cure" 202–203

Van Hise, James 216
Varma, Devendra P. 216
Varnado, S.L. 216
Veeder, William 216
Verne, Jules 185
Vince, Nick 12, 212
Vonnegut, Kurt 187

Wagenknecht, Edward 216
Waller, Gregory A. 216
Walpole, Horace 13, 194–195, 200
War of the Worlds 25
Waugh, Auberon 203, 212
Wayne, John 84–85
Weaveworld 12, 24, 28, 33, 39, 47, 58, 213
The Weird Tale 215
Weird Tales 13
Wells, H.G. 196
"The Whimper of Whipped Dogs" 139
Wiater, Stanley 24, 30, 34, 36–37, 42, 43, 212
Wiesenfarth, Joseph 216
Wilde, Oscar 208, 212
The Wind in the Willows 24
Winter, Douglas E. 23, 24–25, 30–31, 40–41, 43, 177, 212, 216
Wolinsky, Richard 25–26, 31–32, 184–185, 212
Wordsworth, William 196

"The Yattering and Jack" 42, 49–53, 68, 69, 127, 188, 193, 199, 204, 213

www.ingramcontent.com/pod-product-compliance
Lightning Source LLC
Chambersburg PA
CBHW030107170426
43198CB00009B/523